CAMBRIDGE LIBRARY COL

Books of enduring scholarly value

Philosophy

This series contains both philosophical texts and critical essays about philosophy, concentrating especially on works originally published in the eighteenth and nineteenth centuries. It covers a broad range of topics including ethics, logic, metaphysics, aesthetics, utilitarianism, positivism, scientific method and political thought. It also includes biographies and accounts of the history of philosophy, as well as collections of papers by leading figures. In addition to this series, primary texts by ancient philosophers, and works with particular relevance to philosophy of science, politics or theology, may be found elsewhere in the Cambridge Library Collection.

A System of Moral Philosophy

Often described as the father of the Scottish Enlightenment, Francis Hutcheson (1694–1746) was born in the north of Ireland to an Ulster-Scottish Presbyterian family. Organised into three 'books' that were divided between two volumes, *A System of Moral Philosophy* was his most comprehensive work. It synthesised ideas that he had formulated as a minister and as the Chair of Moral Philosophy at the University of Glasgow (1729–46). Published posthumously by his son in 1755, prefaced by an account of his life, it is the only treatise by Hutcheson for which a manuscript is known to have survived. Asserting that individual natural rights derive from an innate understanding of moral behaviour, Hutcheson offers a model that mediates between individual interests and communal ideals. Containing Book 1 and part of Book 2, Volume 1 describes the role and perception of 'perfect' and 'imperfect' natural rights.

Cambridge University Press has long been a pioneer in the reissuing of out-of-print titles from its own backlist, producing digital reprints of books that are still sought after by scholars and students but could not be reprinted economically using traditional technology. The Cambridge Library Collection extends this activity to a wider range of books which are still of importance to researchers and professionals, either for the source material they contain, or as landmarks in the history of their academic discipline.

Drawing from the world-renowned collections in the Cambridge University Library and other partner libraries, and guided by the advice of experts in each subject area, Cambridge University Press is using state-of-the-art scanning machines in its own Printing House to capture the content of each book selected for inclusion. The files are processed to give a consistently clear, crisp image, and the books finished to the high quality standard for which the Press is recognised around the world. The latest print-on-demand technology ensures that the books will remain available indefinitely, and that orders for single or multiple copies can quickly be supplied.

The Cambridge Library Collection brings back to life books of enduring scholarly value (including out-of-copyright works originally issued by other publishers) across a wide range of disciplines in the humanities and social sciences and in science and technology.

A System of
Moral Philosophy

In Three Books

VOLUME 1

FRANCIS HUTCHESON

CAMBRIDGE
UNIVERSITY PRESS

CAMBRIDGE
UNIVERSITY PRESS

University Printing House, Cambridge, CB2 8BS, United Kingdom

Published in the United States of America by Cambridge University Press, New York

Cambridge University Press is part of the University of Cambridge.
It furthers the University's mission by disseminating knowledge in the pursuit of
education, learning and research at the highest international levels of excellence.

www.cambridge.org
Information on this title: www.cambridge.org/9781108060288

© in this compilation Cambridge University Press 2014

This edition first published 1755
This digitally printed version 2014

ISBN 978-1-108-06028-8 Paperback

A SYSTEM

OF

MORAL

PHILOSOPHY,

IN THREE BOOKS;

WRITTEN BY THE LATE

FRANCIS HUTCHESON, L.L.D.

PROFESSOR OF PHILOSOPHY

IN THE UNIVERSITY OF GLASGOW.

PUBLISHED FROM THE ORIGINAL MANUSCRIPT,

BY HIS SON FRANCIS HUTCHESON, M.D.

To which is prefixed

SOME ACCOUNT OF THE LIFE, WRITINGS, AND CHARACTER OF THE AUTHOR,

BY THE REVEREND WILLIAM LEECHMAN, D.D.

PROFESSOR OF DIVINITY IN THE SAME UNIVERSITY.

VOLUME I.

GLASGOW: PRINTED AND SOLD BY R. AND A. FOULIS PRINTERS TO THE UNIVERSITY.

LONDON,

SOLD BY A. MILLAR OVER-AGAINST KATHARINE-STREET IN THE STRAND,
AND BY T. LONGMAN IN PATER-NOSTER ROW.
M.DCC.LV.

TO THE RIGHT REVEREND

FATHER IN GOD,

EDWARD,

LORD BISHOP OF ELPHIN.

MY LORD,

YOUR Lordſhip's known regard for the ſacred in-tereſts of Virtue and true Religion, is ſufficient to enſure your favourable reception of any work which tends to promote thoſe great and important ends. The following has yet a farther claim to your Lordſhip's favour. The Author, my excellent Father, (your Lord-ſhip knows I exceed not the truth in calling him ſo) was formerly honoured with a place in your friendſhip. As this was a ſource of the higheſt pleaſure to him while he lived, ſo it muſt reflect particular honour upon his memory. It is with pleaſure I embrace this public opportunity of declaring myſelf, with the higheſt re-ſpect and gratitude,

MY LORD,

Your LORDSHIP's *moſt obedient,*

and moſt humble Servant,

DUBLIN,
Jan. 25, 1755.

FRANCIS HUTCHESON.

THE

SUBSCRIBERS.

A.

HIS Grace the Lord Archbifhop of Armagh, Primate of all Ireland.

The Rt. Hon. Richard Earl of Anglefea.

The Hon. Baron Arefkine.

Mr. John Abernethy.

Mr. Patrick Adair, Merchant in London.

William Adair, Efq;

James Adair, Efq;

Mr. John Adams.

Thomas Adderley, Efq;

William Agnew, Efq;

John Alcock, D.D. Dean of Ferns.

The Rev. Andrew Alexander, A.M.

Mr. William Alexander.

Mr. John Anderfon, Profeffor of Oriental Languages in the Univerfity of Glafgow.

John Armour, A.M.

The Rev. John Averell, A.M.

B.

The Rt. Hon. Henry Boyle, Efq; Speaker of the Houfe of Commons of Ireland.

The Hon. Patrick Boyle.

Nathaniel Barry, M. D. King's Profeffor of Surgery, Dublin.

Conftantine Barber, M. D. King's Profeffor of Materia Medica, Dublin.

John Bagwell, Efq;

James Balfour of Pilrig, Efq;

The Rev. Mr. Balguy of St. John's College, Cambridge.

Richard Brown-Bamber, Efq;

Mr. ——Banantyne, Merchant in Air.

Thomas Batefon, Efq;

Richard Barry, Efq;

The Rev. Benjamin Barrington, D.D.

Mr. George Bell.

Henry Bellingham, Efq;

William Henry Bernard, Efq;

Mr. Matthew Biggar, Minifter at Kirkof-wall.

The Rev. Alexander Biffet, D.D.

John Blackwood, Efq;

The Rev. Adam Blair, A.M.

George Bogle of Dildowie, Efq;

Cornelius Bolton, Efq;

The Rev. Mr. Boult.

Mr. John Bowden, A.B. F.T.C.D.

Mr. John Bowman, Merchant in Glafgow.

John Bond of Granjo, Efq;

Charles Boyd, Efq;

Mr. Jofeph Boyd.

John Boyd, Efq;

The Rev. Mr. John Bradfute.

Edward Brice, Efq;

The Rev. Clotworthy Brown, A.M.

Mr. Francis Browne.

The Rev. Mr. Bruce.

Mr. William Bruce.

Mr. James Bruce.

Mr. Michael Bruce.

Archibald Buchanan of Silverbanks, Efq;

Andrew Buchanan of Drumpeller, Efq;

The Rev. Mr. Bulkly.

The Rev. John Bumford, A.M.

Benjamin Burton, Efq;

C.

The Rt. Hon. Lord Cathcart.

The Rt. Hon. Thomas Carter, Efq;

The Hon. Francis Caulfield, Efq;

Sir James Colquhoun of Luffe, Bart.

Andrew Caldwell of Dublin, Efq;

William Campbell, Efq;

THE SUBSCRIBERS.

Samuel Campbell, Efq;
Capt. Duncan Campbell.
Mr. Charles Campbell.
Mr. George Chalmers, Merchant in Edinburgh.
The Rev. Mr. Samuel Chandler.
Mr. Robert Chriftie, Merchant in Glafgow.
George Clavell of Smedmore, Efq;
William Clements, M. D. fen. F. T. C. D.
The Rev. James Clewlow, A. M.
Mr. James Clow, Profeffor of Philofophy in the Univerfity of Glafgow.
The Rev. Robert Clive, Rector of Atherly.
Mr. James Clugfton.
Mr. William Coats, Minifter at Kilmaurs.
John Cooper, Efq;
The Rev. Mr. John Colquhoun, Minifter of Badernock.
The Rev. Mr. James Connel, Minifter at Sorn.
The Rev. Walter Cope, A. M.
Maurice Copinger, Efq;
Gabriel Cornwall, A. M.
Richard Cox, Efq;
John Craig, Efq; Advocate.
The Rev. Mr. William Craig, one of the Minifters of Glafgow.
The Rev. George Crump, D. D.
Dr. William Cullen, Profeffor of Phyfic in the Univerfity of Glafgow.
Charles Cunningham, Efq;
George Cuningham, Efq;
Mr. John Cunninghame, Preacher, at Kilmarnock.
John Curtis, Efq;
The Rev. Ephraim Cuthbert, A. M.

D.

His Grace the Lord Archbifhop of Dublin.
The Rt. Hon. Lord Dalmeny.
Sir David Dalrymple of Newhales, Bart.
David Dalrymple, Efq; Advocate.
Mr. William Dalrymple, Minifter at Air.
John Dalrymple, Efq;
John Damer of Came, Efq;
John Damer, Efq;
Jofeph Damer, Efq; of Molton Abbey.
Mr. John Davidfon, junior, Writer to the Signet.

William Henry Dawfon, Efq;
Jonathan Darby, Efq;
Jofhua Davis, Efq;
William Dean, Efq;
Mr. Robert Deans, Preacher, at Irvine.
Theophilus Debrifay, Efq;
Mr. Robert Dick, Advocate, and Profeffor of Civil Law in the Univerfity of Edinburgh.
Dr. Robert Dick, Profeffor of Philofophy in the Univerfity of Glafgow.
The Rev. Brabaron Difney, fenior, D. D. F. T. C. D.
Conway Richard Dobbs, Efq;
Hugh Donaldfon, Efq;
William Doudefwell, Efq;
George Doudefwell, Efq;
The Rev. Charles Doyne, A. M.
Allan Dreghorn, of Roughhill, Efq;
The Rev. Thomas Drenan, A. M.
The Rev. James Duchal, D. D.
Capt. Patrick Dunbar.
Mr. James Dunbar, Student of Philofophy.
The Rev. William Dunn, A. M.
Mr. Samuel Dyer.
Jeremiah Dyfon, Efq;

E.

The Right Rev. Lord Bifhop of Elphin, ten Sets:
Archibald Edmonftone, Efq;
Campbell Edmonftone, Efq;
Gilbert Elliot, Efq; Member of Parliament.
Patrick Ewing, Efq;

F.

The Hon. Henry Fagel, Principal Secretary to their High Mightineffes the States General of the United Provinces.
Mr. Adam Fairholm, Merchant in Edinburgh.
John Farrel, M. D.
Robert Fergufon of Reath, Efq;
The Rev. Adam Fergufon, A. M.
The Rev. Andrew Fergufon, A. M.
The Rev. Victor Fergufon, A. M.
Mr. Robert Finlay, one of the Minifters of Paifley.
Samuel Fleming, M. D.

THE SUBSCRIBERS.

The Rev. John Foster, D. D.
Mr. Joseph Fowke.
Mr. David Fullerton, Student of Philosophy.

G.
The Rt. Hon. the Earl of Glasgow.
The Rt. Hon. Lord Garlies.
The Hon. Lockhart Gordon, Esq;
The Rev. Hugh Gaston, A. M.
Mr. Robert Getty.
Bartholomew William Gilbert, Esq;
James Gladstanes of Dublin, Esq; Counsellor at Law.
Thomas Gladsterns, Esq;
John Gordon, Esq;
Mr. George Gordon.
John Graham of Dougalston, Esq;
John Graham, Esq;
Richard Graham. Esq;
John Grant, Esq; Advocate.
Joseph Green, Esq;
John Green, Esq;

H.
The Rt. Hon. the Earl of Hillsborough.
The Hon. Frederick Hamilton.
Alexander Haliday, M. D.
William Hall of Whitehall, Esq;
Mr. Hall.
Mr. Thomas Hall.
The Rev. Mr. Robert Hall, one of the Ministers of Kilmarnock.
Roger Hall, Esq;
John Haly Hutchinson, Esq;
Alexander Hamilton, Esq;
Mr. Francis Hamilton.
William Hamilton, Esq; of Dunnemanagh.
William Hamilton, Esq; of Londonderry.
The Rev. John Hamilton, A. M.
Henry Hamilton, Esq;
The Rev. Mr. James Hamilton, one of the Ministers of Paisley.
Dr. Robert Hamilton of Ardrie, Esq; Professor of Anatomy in the University of Glasgow.
Gabriel Hamilton of Westburn, Esq;
William Hamilton, M. D.
The Rev. Hugh Hamilton, A. M. F. T. C. D.
Ambrose Harding, Esq;

John Hardman, Esq; Member of Parliament for Liverpool.
The Rev. John Harlet, A. M.
Thomas Harris, Esq;
Myles Harrison, Esq;
Mr. Travers Hartley.
Cheney Hart of Salop, M. D.
The Rev. John Hastings, A. M. F. T. C. D.
The Rev. David Harvey, A. M.
The Rev. Adam Harvey.
John Hatch, Esq;
Mr. John Hawkins.
Mrs. Hays.
Mr. Arthur Hemphill.
The Rev. John Henderson of Liverpool, A. M.
The Rev. Michael Henry, A. M.
Peter Heron, Esq;
Mr. Arthur Heywood, Merchant in Liverpool.
Mr. William Holmes.
The Rev. John Hood, A. M.
Mr. Thomas Hopekirk, Merchant in Glasgow.
Mr. John Hornby.
Vansittart Hudson, Esq;
The Rev. Mr. Hurd, Fellow of Emanuel College, Cambridge.
Hans Hutcheson, Esq;
Mr. Alexander Hutcheson.
Francis Hutchinson, Esq;
Mr. Robert Hyde, Merchant in Manchester.

I.
The Rt. Hon. the Lord High Chancellor of Ireland.
Simon Isaac, Esq; two Sets.
Matthew Jacob, Esq;
Mr. David Johnston.
Arthur Johnston, Esq;
Joseph Johnston, Esq;
The Rev. James Johnston, A. M.
James Johnston, Esq;
Joseph Johnston, M. D.
John Jones, Esq;

K.
The Rt. Rev. Lord Bishop of Killaloe and Kilfenora.

THE SUBSCRIBERS.

The Rt. Rev. Lord Bishop of Killalla and Achonry.
The Rt. Hon. the Lord Kaims.
The Rev. Ebenezer Kellburn, A. M.
George Kelley, M. D.
The Rev. Gilbert Kennedy, A. M.
Hugh Kennedy, Esq;
Hugh Ker, Esq;
Andrew Knox, Esq;
Mr. George Knox, Bookseller in Air.

L.

The Rt. Rev. the Lord Bishop of Leighlin and Ferns.
The Hon. Sir George Littleton, Baronet.
Hercules Langford-Rowley, Esq;
Mr. James Lang.
Samuel Lard, Esq;
The Rev. Joseph Lard, A. M.
The Rev. John Lawson, senior, D. D.
The Rev. William Leechman, D. D. Professor of Divinity in the University of Glasgow.
The Rev. Thomas Leland, B. D. F. T. C. D.
William Lenox, Esq;
The Rev. Mr. James Lesly, one of the Ministers of Kilmarnock.
The Rev. Henry Leslie, A. M.
Dr. Hercules Lindsay, Professor of Law in the University of Glasgow, three Sets.
Theophilus Lindsay, A. M.
William Littleton, Esq;
The Rev. Dr. Littleton, Dean of Exeter.
William Lloyd, Esq;
John Lodge, Esq;
The Rev. Mr. Smyth Loftus.
The Rev. Mr. Lord.
The Library of the University of Glasgow.
The Library of the Greek Class in that University.

M.

The Rt. Hon. Lord Viscount Molesworth.
The Rt. Hon. the Lord Milton.
Sir John Maxwell of Pollok.
Alexander M'Aulay, L. L. D.
Oliver MacCasland of Strabane, Esq;
The Rev. James Mackay, A. M.
The Rev. Arthur Mahon, A. M.
George Maconchy, M. D.

Mr. George Macquay.
Dr. Munckley, Physician in London.
The Rev. Isaac Mann, D. D.
The Rev. William Martin, B. D. F. T. C. D.
Mr. Samuel Mattcare.
John Mattcare, M. D.
The Rev. Henry Matthew, A. M.
George Maxwell, Esq; Advocate.
The Rev. John Maxwell, D. D.
The Rev. John Maxwell, A. M.
Dalton M'Carthy, Esq;
Mr. Robert M'Clintock.
Mr. Henry M'Culloch.
Mr. John M'Dormit, Minister at Stratton.
John M'Gill, Esq;
The Rev. Archibald M'Lean, Minister of the English Church at the Hague.
The Rev. William M'Neely, A. M.
Daniel M'Neil of Liverpool, Esq;
Donald M'Neil, Esq;
The Rev. Mr. James M'Night, Minister at Maybole.
Robert M'Queen, Esq; Advocate.
The Rev. Mr. Andrew M'Vey, Minister of Dreghorn.
The Rev. John Mears, A. M.
The Rev. John Menagh, A. M.
Mr. Thomas Millar, Advocate.
The Rev. Mr. James Millar, one of the Ministers of Hamilton.
The Rev. Andrew Millar, A. M.
Mr. Andrew Mitchell, Minister at Muirkirk.
The Rev. James Moody, A. M.
Mr. Richard Moore.
Mr. Robert Montgomery.
Mr. John Morris.
William Muir of Caldwall, Esq; Member of Parliament.
Major James Muir-Campbell, Member of Parliament.
Mr. James Moor, Professor of Greek in the University of Glasgow, two Sets.
Mr. George Muirhead, Professor of Humanity in the University of Glasgow.
William Mussenden, Esq;

N.

The Rt. Hon. the Earl of Northumberland.

THE SUBSCRIBERS.

The Rt. Hon. the Countefs of Northumberland.
Alexander Nefbit, Efq;
Ezekiel Nefbit, M.D.
The Rev. Mr. Nevil, Fellow of Emanuel College, Cambridge.
Thomas Neville, A. M. Fellow of Jefus College, Cambridge.
The Rev. William Nevin, A.M.
Mr. John Nicholfon, Merchant in Liverpool.

O.
John Olpherts, Efq; .
The Rev. John Orr, A. M. Rector of Maryborough.
Dr. Ould.
The Rev. John Owen, D. D. Dean of Clonmacnoife.

P.
Robert Parkinfon, Efq;
Mr. James Park.
John Parnell, Efq;
The Rev. Mr. Walter Paterfon, Chaplain to the North Britifh Dragoons.
William Paul, Efq;
Mr. John Payne.
The Rev. James Pitcairn, D. D.
Mr. Robert Pettigrew.
Mr. John Potts.
Andrew Pringle, Efq; Advocate.

Q.
Henry Quin, M. D. King's Profeffor of Medicine in Dublin.

R.
The Rt. Hon. Lord Rawdon.
The Rt. Hon. Lord Rofs.
The Hon. William Rofs.
The Rev. Mr. John Rae, one of the Minifters of Paifley.
Arthur Rainey-Maxwell, Efq;
Francis Rainey, M. D.
Thomas Reid, Efq;
William Richards, Efq;
Mrs. Richardfon.
Archibald Roberton, Efq; of Bedlay,
Lewis Roberts, Efq;
Chriftopher Robinfon, Efq;

Mr. David Rofs.
David Rofs, Efq; Advocate,
Mr. George Rofs, late Profeffor of Humanity in the Univerfity of Glafgow.
The Rev. Mr. Andrew Rofs, Minifter at Newmills.
Mr. William Ruat, Profeffor of Church Hiftory in the Univerfity of Glafgow.
Mr. James Ruddock.

S.
The Rt. Hon. the Earl of Selkirk, twelve Sets.
Matthew Sankey, Efq;
John Sargent, Efq;
William Scott, M. D.
Walter Scott of Harding, Efq; Member of Parliament.
William Scott, Efq;
William Scot, Efq; Recorder of Londonderry.
Mr. Abraham Seawright of Drumore, in the County of Down.
The Rev. Mr. John Seddon of Warrington.
The Rev. Patrick Simpfon, A. M.
Mr. Adam Smith, Profeffor of Moral Philofophy in the Univerfity of Glafgow, two Sets.
The Rev. Robert Smyth, A. M.
George Smyth, Efq;
The Rev. Benjamin Span, A. M.
Mr. Stephens of Exeter.
Dr. Stevenfon, two Sets.
James Stevenfon, Efq;
The Rev. Guy Stone, A. M.
Peter Storer, Efq;
The Rev. John Strong, A. M.
The Rev. James Strong, A. M.
Andrew Thomas Stuart, Efq;
James Stuart, Efq;
Alexander Stuart, Efq;
William Stuart, Efq;
William Stuart, Efq; of Londonderry.
Walter Stewart, Efq; Advocate.
George Swinton, Efq; Advocate.

T.
The Rev. Mr. William Thom, Minifter of Gova n.

THE SUBSCRIBERS.

Mr. Edwin Thomas.
Mr. William Thurlburn, Bookſeller in Cambridge.
John Tickell, Eſq;
The Rev. John Torrence, A. M.
Mr. Peter Touchett, Merchant in Mancheſter.
Mr. James Trail.
Mrs. Mary Trevor.
The Rev. Mr. Turner.

U.
Clotworthy Upton, Eſq;

V.
James Veitch, Eſq; Advocate.

W.
The Hon. Mr. Juſtice Ward.
James Waddel, Eſq;
Capt. James Wallace of Liverpool.
James Wallace, Eſq;
Mrs. Sarah Wallace.
Mr. Robert Wallace.
James Wallace, Eſq;

The Rev. Bernard Ward, A. M.
Bernard Ward, Eſq;
Alexander Wedderburn, Eſq; Advocate.
The Rev. Peter Weſteura, A. M.
Richard Weld, M. D.
The Rev. Iſaac Weld.
Mark White, Eſq;
Mr. Abraham Wilkinſon.
Godfrey Wills, Eſq;
Mr. Thomas Williams.
Joſeph Williamſon, Eſq; Advocate.
The Rev. John Williamſon, A. M.
William Wilſon, Eſq;
Mr. Robert Wilſon.
Mr. William Wilſon.
Rcbert Wood, Eſq;
Hans Wood, Eſq;
The Rev. Mr. Patrick Woodrow, Miniſter of Tarbolton.
William Wray, Eſq;

Y.
Benjamin Yates, Eſq;
Mr. John Young, Profeſſor of Philoſophy in the Univerſity of St. Andrews.

OMITTED;
The Rev. Ebenezer Keay, A. M.

CONTENTS of the FIRST VOLUME.

CONTENTS.

B O O K   II.

Containing a Deduction of the more ſpecial Laws of Nature, and Duties of Life, previous to Civil Government, and other adventitious States.

THE

PREFACE,

Giving some ACCOUNT of the LIFE, WRITINGS, and CHARACTER of the AUTHOR.

DR. FRANCIS HUTCHESON was born on the 8th of Auguſt, A. D. 1694. His father, Mr. John Hutcheſon, was miniſter of a diſſenting congregation in the North of Ireland; a perſon of good underſtanding, conſiderable learning, and reputation for piety, probity, and all virtue. His ſon Francis, when about eight years of age, was ſent to be educated along with his elder brother, under the eye and direction of their grandfather Mr. Alexander Hutcheſon, who was alſo a worthy diſſenting clergyman in the ſame part of the country, but had come from Scotland. He was ſecond ſon of an ancient and reputable family in the ſhire of Ayr in that kingdom.

A ſuperior capacity, an ardent thirſt for knowledge, and the ſeeds of the fineſt diſpoſitions ſoon began to

a

shew themselves in Francis: particularly a singular
warmth of affection and disinterestedness of temper,
for which he was distinguished thro' his whole life, appeared in many instances in this early period of it.
The innocence and sweetness of his temper, his great
capacity and application to his learning soon procured
him a distinguishing place in his grandfather's affections. But such was his love for his brother, that his
grandfather's fondness gave him no joy while his brother did not equally share it: nay the preference that
was shewn him gave him real concern, and put him
upon employing all means and innocent artifices in his
power to make his brother appear equally deserving of
his grandfather's regard. And when his grandfather
in his last will had made an alteration of a prior settlement of his family-affairs in his favour, tho' many
arguments were used by his relations to prevail with
him to accept of it, he peremptorily refused, and
insisted to the last that the first settlement should
take place. These, and many other instances of the
like kind which might be related, were promising pre-
sages of remarkable disinterestedness in more advanced years.

When he had gone thro' the common courfe of fchool education he was fent to an Academy at fome diftance from his parents to begin his courfe of Philofophy: he was taught there the ordinary Scholaftic Philofophy which was in vogue in thofe days, and to which he applied himfelf with uncommon affiduity and diligence.

In the year 1710 he removed from the Academy, and entered a ftudent in the Natural Philofophy clafs in the Univerfity of Glafgow, and at the fame time renewed his ftudy of the Latin and Greek languages: and in all parts of literature, to which he applied himfelf, he made fuch proficiency as might be expected from a genius like his cultivated with great care and diligence.

After he had finifhed the ufual courfe of philofophical ftudies, his thoughts were turned toward Divinity, which he propofed to make the peculiar ftudy and profeffion of his. life. For profecution of which defign he continued feveral years more at the Univerfity of Glafgow ftudying Theology under the direction of the reverend and learned Profeffor John Simfon.

Among the manifold theological enquiries which occurred to him as deserving his moſt ſerious examination; he chuſed to begin with the grand fundamental one concerning the being, perfections, and providence of God. The reverend Dr. Clark's learned and ingenious book on this ſubject, publiſhed a ſhort time before, fell into his hands. Tho' he moſt heartily approved of all the Doctor's concluſions, and had the higheſt ſenſe of his ſingular abilities and virtues, yet after the moſt ſerious and attentive conſideration of his arguments, he did not find that conviction from them which he wiſhed and expected. In order to procure more ſatisfaction on this ſubject, and particularly with regard to the force and ſolidity of the arguments *a priori* (as they are commonly called) he wrote a letter to him, about the year 1717, urging his objections, and deſiring a further explication. Whether the Doctor returned any anſwer to this letter does not appear from Dr. Hutcheſon's papers. After all the enquiry he could make, he ſtill continued extremely doubtful of the juſtneſs and force of all the metaphyſical arguments, by which many have endeavoured to demonſtrate the exiſtence, unity, and perfections of the Deity. He not only thought that thefe kind of arguments were not adapted to the capacity of the bulk of mankind, but even that they could afford no folid and permanent conviction to the learned themfelves. It was his opinion in this early part of his life; and he never faw caufe to alter it, that as fome fubjects from their nature are capable of a demonftrative evidence, fo others admit only of a probable one; and that to feek demonftration where probability can only be obtained is almoft as unreafonable as to demand to fee founds or hear colours. Befides he was perfuaded that attempts to demonftration on fuch fubjects as are incapable of it were of very dangerous confequence to the interefts of truth and religion: becaufe fuch attempts inftead of conducting us to the abfolute certainty propofed, leave the mind in fuch a ftate of doubt and uncertainty as leads to abfolute fcepticifm: for if once we refufe to reft in that kind of evidence, which the nature of the fubject only admits of, and go on in purfuit of the higheft kind, ftrict demonftration, we immediately conclude there is no evidence, becaufe we do not meet with that kind of it which we expected: and thus the mind remains in a ftate of abſolute uncertainty, imagining there is no evidence, when all that the nature of the caſe admits of is laid before it, and enough to ſatisfy every one whoſe underſtanding is not diſordered with an unnatural thirſt for ſcientifical knowledge on all ſubjects alike. This opinion of the various degrees of evidence adapted to various ſubjects firſt led Dr. Hutcheſon to treat morals as a matter of fact, and not as founded on the abſtract relations of things. But of this more particularly hereafter.

After he had ſpent ſix years at the Univerſity of Glaſgow, he returned to Ireland, and ſubmitted to trials, in order to enter into the miniſtry, and was licenſed to preach among the Diſſenters. He was juſt about to be ſettled a miniſter in a ſmall diſſenting congregation in the North of Ireland, when ſome gentlemen about Dublin, who knew that his abilities and virtues qualified him to be more extenſively uſeful than he could poſſibly be in that remote congregation, invited him to take up a private academy there. He complyed with the invitation, and acquitted himſelf in that ſtation with ſuch dignity and ſucceſs as gave entire ſatisfaction to all thoſe who committed their children to his care; and foon drew the attention of the public upon him. He had been fixed but a fhort time in Dublin when his fingular merit and accomplifhments made him generally known: men of all ranks, who had any tafte for literature, or efteem for learned men, fought his acquaintance and friendfhip. Among others he was honoured with a place in the efteem and friendfhip of the late Lord Vifcount Molefworth, who took pleafure in his converfation, and affifted him with his criticifms and obfervations to improve and polifh the Inquiry into the Ideas of Beauty and Virtue, before it came abroad. The reverend Dr. Synge, now Lord Bifhop of Elphin, whofe friendfhip Dr. Hutchefon always regarded as one of the greateft pleafures and advantages of his life, likewife revifed his papers, and affifted him in the general fcheme of the work.

The firft edition came abroad without the author's name, but the merit of the performance would not fuffer him to be long conceal'd: fuch was the reputation of the work, and the ideas it had raifed of the author, that Lord Granville, who was then Lord Lieutenant of Ireland, whofe difcernment and tafte as to

works of genius and literature is univerfally acknowledged, fent his private fecretary to enquire at the
bookfellers for the author, and when he could not
learn his name, he left a letter to be conveyed to him,
in confequence of which he foon became acquainted
with his Excellency, and was treated by him all the
time he continued in his government with the moft
diftinguifhing marks of familiarity and efteem.

From this time his acquaintance began to be ftill
more courted by moft men of diftinction either for
ftation or literature in Ireland. Archbifhop King, the
author of the book *De Origine Mali*, held Dr. Hutchefon in great efteem, and his friendfhip was of great ufe
to him in an affair which might otherwife have been
very troublefome to him, and perhaps ended in putting an entire ftop to his ufefulnefs in that place.
There were two feveral attempts made to profecute
Mr. Hutchefon, in the Archbifhop's court, for daring
to take upon him the education of youth, without
having qualified himfelf by fubfcribing the ecclefiaftical canons, and obtaining a licence from the Bifhop.
Both thefe attempts were effectually difcouraged by
his Grace, with expreffions of hearty difpleafure againft

the perfons who were fo forward as to commence them. And at the fame time he affured him that he needed be under no apprehenfion of difturbance from that quarter, as long as it continued in his power to prevent it.

He had alfo a large fhare in the efteem of the late Primate Bolter, who, thro' his influence, made a donation to the Univerfity of Glafgow, of an yearly fund for an exhibitioner, to be bred to any of the learned profeffions. This is only one inftance among many of that prelate's munificent temper. Mr. Weft, a gentleman of great abilities, and of known zeal for the interefts of civil and religious liberty, was particularly fond of Dr. Hutchefon, and lived in great intimacy with him, while he continued in Ireland.

A few years after the Enquiry the Treatife on the Paffions was publifhed: as both thefe books have been long abroad in the world and undergone feveral impreffions, a fufficient proof of the reception they have met with from the public, it would be needlefs to fay any thing concerning them. About this time he wrote fome philofophical papers accounting for Laughter, in a different way from Mr. Hobbs, and more honourable to human nature: thefe papers were publifhed in the collection called Hibernicus Letters. Some letters in the London Journal 1728 fubfcribed Philaretus, containing objections to fome parts of the doctrine in *the Enquiry*, occafioned Mr. Hutchefon's giving anfwers to them in thofe public papers: both the letters and anfwers were afterwards publifhed in a feparate pamphlet. The debate was left unfinifhed, Philaretus's death having put an end to the correfpondence, which was propofed to have been afterward carried on in a more private manner.

After he had taught the private Academy in Dublin for feven or eight years with great reputation and fuccefs; in the year 1729 he was called to Scotland to be a Profeffor of Philofophy in the Univerfity of Glafgow. His eftablifhed reputation for literature and worth was the only confideration that induced the Univerfity to elect him into the place vacant by the death of the learned and worthy Mr. Gerfhom Carmichael. The public approved of their choice, and the event abundantly juftified the wifdom of it. The Profeffors were foon fenfible, that his admiffion into their body had good effects both upon the reputation and interests of the society.   Several young gentlemen came along with him from the Academy, and his just fame drew many more both from England and Ireland. But it will probably be rather matter of surprize to the reader, that he accepted of the place, than that the University unsolicited made him the offer of it.   If any one should ask, as it is natural to do, how it came to pass that a man of Dr. Hutcheson's accomplishments and virtues, and who could count such lists of honourable persons, and many of them of great authority and influence, in the number of his friends, should continue to teach a private Academy for seven or eight years in the heart of a country where there were so many beneficial places proper to be bestowed on men of genius and merit.   Or if any one should ask, how it came to pass that he was permitted, to leave his country, break off all connections with his relations and friends, and in the midst of life remove to another kingdom to accept a place in an University far from being lucrative and very laborious?   It is sufficient to answer to these questions: that it was not the want either of inclination or power in his friends to serve him that was the stop to his preferment.   He

had private reafons which determined him neither to
feek promotion, nor to encourage the moft probable
fchemes propofed to him for obtaining it. It is but
juftice to his character to fay, that he was ufeful and
contented in that ftation in which it had pleafed Divine Providence to fix him, and that neither the love
of riches, nor of the elegance or grandeur of human
life prevailed fo far in his breaft as to make him offer
the leaft violence to his inward fentiments. To which
it may be added, that the filent and unfeen hand of
an all-wife Providence which over-rules all the events
of human life, and all the refolutions of the human
will, conducted him to that ftation in life, which tho'
far from being the higheft in external diftinction, yet
was perhaps of all others the moft fuited to the fingular talents with which he was endowed, and gave him
the opportunity of being more eminently and exten
fively ufeful than he could have been in any other.

    After his fettlement in the College he was not obli-
ged (as when he kept the Academy) to teach the languages and all the different parts of Philofophy, but
had leifure to turn his chief attention to his favourite
ftudy Human Nature: he had high thoughts of its

original dignity, and was perfuaded, that even in this corrupt ftate, it was capable of great improvements by proper inftruction and affiduous culture. The profeffion of Moral Philofophy was the province affigned him in the College. In cultivating this fcience he purfued the fame method in which he began, fetting afide all refearches into the abftract relations and eternal fitnefs and unfitnefs of things, and directing his enquiries into what is more obvious and immediately known from obfervation and experience, viz. What is in fact the prefent conftitution of human nature; what is that ftate of heart, and courfe of life which is moft correfpondent to the whole frame.

He had obferved, that it was the happinefs and glory of the prefent age, that they had thrown off the method of forming hypothefes and fuppofitions in natural philofophy, and had fet themfelves to make obfervations and experiments on the conftitution of the material world itfelf, and to mark the powers and principles which are difcerned operating in it: he faw plainly that it was by adhering ftrictly to this method that natural philofophy had been carried to a greater degree of perfection than ever it was before, and that

it is only by purfuing the fame method that we can
hope to reach higher improvements in that fcience. He was convinced that in like manner a true
fcheme of morals could not be the product of genius
and invention, or of the greateft precifion of thought
in metaphyfical reafonings, but muft be drawn from
proper obfervations upon the feveral powers and principles which we are confcious of in our own bofoms,
and which muft be acknowledged to operate in fome
degree in the whole human fpecies. And that therefore, one proper method at leaft to be followed in
the moral fcience, is to inquire into our internal ftructure as a conftitution or fyftem compofed of various
parts, to obferve the office and end of each part, with
the natural fubordination of thofe parts to one another, and from thence to conclude what is the defign
of the whole, and what is the courfe of action for
which it appears to be intended by its great Author.
He thought there was ground to hope, that from a
more ftrict philofophical enquiry into the various natural principles or natural difpofitions of mankind, in the
fame way that we enquire into the ftructure of an animal body, of a plant, or of the folar fyftem, a more

exact theory of morals may be formed, than has yet appeared: and a theory too built upon such an obvious and firm foundation as would be satisfactory to every candid enquirer. For we can be as certain of the several parts of our internal frame from inward perception and feeling, as we are of the several parts of an animal structure from ocular inspection: and we can as little doubt of the ends for which the principal parts at least of our internal constitution are intended, as we can doubt of the ends for which the members of our body, or our external senses were framed: and whatever evidence we have for the existence and perfections of the Supreme Being, we have the same evidence that the moral constitution of our nature is his work, and thence we conclude, that it is most certainly his will, that we should cultivate that temper of mind, and pursue that course of life, which is most correspondent to the evident ends and purposes of his divine workmanship; and that such a state of heart and plan of life, as answers most effectually the end and design of all the parts of it, must be its most perfect manner of operation, and must constitute the duty, the happiness, and perfection of the order of beings to whom it belongs.

Our author has attempted in the following work, firft to unfold the feveral principles of the human mind as united in a moral conftitution, and from thence to point out the origin of our ideas of moral good and evil, and of our fenfe of duty, or moral obligation; and then to enquire what muft be the fupreme happinefs to a fpecies conftituted as mankind are; and then he proceeds to deduce the particular laws of nature, or rules neceffary to be obferved for promoting the general good in our common intercourfes with one another as members of fociety. How far he has fucceeded, muft be left to the judgment of the attentive and candid reader.

Whatever corrections or improvements his fcheme may be fuppofed to admit of, after longer obfervation and further examination into the frame and operations of our minds, one thing is certain that the refult of his obfervations and reafonings muft meet with entire approbation, as it places the higheft virtue and excellence of a human character, where all found Philofophy and Divine Revelation has placed it, viz. *In fuch habitual and prevailing exercife of all thefe good affections to God and man, as will reftrain all other appetites, paffions, and affections within juft bounds, and*

*carry us out uniformly to pursue that course of action,
which will promote the happiness of mankind in the most
extensive manner to which our power can reach**. And
it must also be acknowledged, that our Author's doctrine, which asserts that we are laid under a real internal obligation, of a most sacred kind, from the very
constitution of our nature †, to promote the good of
mankind, tho' at the expence of sacrificing life itself
and all its enjoyments, coincides, or at least is no way
inconsistent with these precepts of Christianity, by
which we are enjoined to lay down our lives for the

---

* Some seem to have mistaken our Author's doctrine so widely, as to imagine
that he placed virtue in the mere sentiment
or perception of moral beauty and deformity in affections and actions, which it is
owned the worst of mankind may retain in
a very considerable degree. Whereas he
always places it in the exercise of these affections and actions flowing from them
which the moral faculty recommends and
enjoins. Or in other words, virtue does
not lye in the mere sentiment of approbation of certain affections and actions, but
in acting agreeably to it.

† Some seem to have mistaken Dr.
Hutcheson so far on this subject, as to imagine, that when he says we are laid under
a most real and intimate obligation by the
moral sense to act virtuously, he meant to
assert that all other obligations from the
consideration of the will of God, and the
effects of his favour or displeasure in this

and in another world were superseded. Nothing could be farther from his thoughts;
nor is it a consequence of his scheme. He
was fully sensible of the importance and
necessity of inforcing the practice of virtue
upon mankind from all possible considerations, and especially from these awful
ones of future rewards and punishments.
If any one should say, that there is a natural sense of equity implanted in the human
mind, which will operate in some degree
even on those who know not that there is
a God or a future state: it could not justly
be concluded from thence, that such a person also maintained, that this natural sense
of equity alone, was sufficient to ensure
the uniform practice of justice, in all mankind, even when meeting with number-
less strong temptations to depart from it.
The application is so obvious, that it is
needless to insist upon it.

c

bretheren; while at the fame time it gives us more juft, more amiable and worthy ideas of human nature, as originally intended to be actuated by more difintere- fted principles, than thefe philofophers are willing to allow, who labour to reduce all the motions of the human mind to felf-love at bottom, however much they may feem to be different from it at firft appea- rance. According to our Author's views of human na- ture, tho' thefe generous principles may be born down and over-powered in this corrupt ftate, by fenfual and felfifh paffions, fo as not to exert themfelves with fuf- ficient vigour, even when there is proper occafion for them; yet the intention of the Author of Nature is a- bundantly manifeft from this important circumftance, that the moral fenfe is always fo far true to its office, that it never fails to give the higheft and warmeft ap- probation to every inftance of truly difinterefted vir- tue. The lefs fufpicion there is of any view even to future fame in the behaviour of the martyr, the pa- triot, or hero, when he yields up his life in a worthy caufe, fo much louder and ftronger is the applaufe of all fpectators, and fo far as any interefted confiderati- ons are fuppofed to influence him, the approbation given to him is proportionably diminished: according to this reprefentation of things, the foul of man, not only bears a refemblance of the Divine Intelligence in its rational faculties, but alfo of the Divine difin- terefted benignity in its focial and public affections: and thus too our internal conftitution, formed for purfuing the general good, beautifully tallies with the conftitution of the univerfe: we fee thro' the whole of Nature what admirable provifion is made for carry- ing on the general interefts of all the fpecies of living beings. So that it is quite agreeable to the analogy of Nature, that mankind, the higheft order of creatures in this lower world, fhould be formed with difpofiti- ons to promote the general good of their fpecies, and with a difcernment that it is their duty to part with life itfelf, when a public intereft requires it.

But Dr. Hutchefon's character, as a man of parts and learning, does not depend merely on the peculi- arities of a fcheme of morals. His knowledge was by no means confined to his own fyftem: that he was well acquainted with the writings both of the anci- ents and moderns relative to morality, religion, and government will appear evident to every one who peruſes the following work. Nor did the ſtudy of morals, even in this extenſive view, engroſs his whole time and attention. An ardent love of knowledge was natural to him. He loved truth, and ſought after it with impartiality and conſtancy. His apprehenſion was quick and his memory ſtrong: he was not only patient of thought and enquiry, but delighted in it. His mind was never ſubject to that languor which frequently interrupts the ſtudies of worthy men: his faculties were always at his command and ready for exerciſe. A mind endowed and diſpoſed in ſuch a manner, and employed in ſtudy for a long courſe of years, muſt have been furniſhed with a large compaſs of knowledge.

In the earlier part of his life he entered deeply into the ſpirit of the ancients, and was ſoon ſenſible of and admired that juſtneſs and ſimplicity both of thought and expreſſion which has preſerved and diſtinguiſhed their writings to this day. He read the hiſtorians, poets, and orators of antiquity with a kind of enthuſiaſm, and at the ſame time with a critical exactneſs. He had read the poets eſpecially ſo often, that he retained large paſſages of them in his memory, which he frequently and elegantly applied to the ſubjects he had occafion to treat in the courfe of his prelections. His knowledge and tafte in Latin appears from what he has wrote in it. His Synopfis of Metaphyfics, Pneumatics, Natural Theology, and his Compend of Ethics are written with a fpirit and purity of ftyle feldom to be met with in modern Latin compofitions.

He had ftudied all the parts of Philofophy with fuch care as to have attained clear and comprehenfive views of them. He compofed a fmall treatife of Logic, which tho' not defigned for the public eye, yet gives fufficient proof how much he was mafter of that fcience. It appears from his treatife of Metaphyfics, that he was well acquainted with the logomachies, meaninglefs queftions, and trivial debates of the old Scholaftics, which had thrown a thick darknefs on that part of Philofophy: he has fet that branch of knowledge in a clear light, and rendered it inftructive and entertaining. He underftood Natural Philofophy as it is now improved by the affiftance of Mathematics and experiments, and applied his knowledge of it to the noble purpofes of eftablifhing the grand truths of the exiftence, the perfections, and government of God. He was well acquainted with the hiftory of the arts and fciences: he had carefully traced them from their origin, thro' all their various improvements, progreffes, interruptions, and revolutions, and marked the characters of the moft remarkable Philofophers, and the diftinguifhing doctrines and peculiar genius of their Philofophy. Befides he knew the civil and ecclefiaftical hiftory both of antient and modern times with an exactnefs that was furprizing in one fo much converfant in deeper and feverer ftudies. He had ftudied too the original language of the Old Teftament, and tho' his other neceffary ftudies had not permitted him to become a critic in it himfelf, yet he knew the moft important criticifms of the learned in that way.

His great capacity appeared in the ftrongeft light, in his converfation with his friends; there he difcovered fuch a readinefs of thought, clearnefs of expreffion, and extent of knowledge, on almoft every fubject that could be ftarted, as gave delight to all who heard him. There are fome men who have amaffed great ftores of learning, but it is repofited as it were in fome corner of the mind, and requires time to recollect it and bring it forth. In others you fee their great erudition feems to darken their conceptions and disturb their views of things, by the different ideas which crowd into their minds at once. But the whole compass of his knowledge lay as it were always before him, and was at his command at all times; and he saw at once whatever was connected with his present subject, and rejected what did not belong to it. He spoke on the most difficult and abstruse subjects without any labour and with a degree of perspicuity which would have cost other men of no mean parts repeated efforts, without equal success: he exposed and took to pieces deceitful reasonings with the greatest facility; and distinguished at once, betwixt true learning and false, betwixt subjects which admit of demonstration, and such as do not, and betwixt questions which are useful and important, and such as are only curious and amusing. He gave an habitual attention to the real uses to which knowledge could be applied in life. He did not chuse to amuse with insignificant speculations, but in all his enquiries having the real good and utility of mankind in view, he took occasion even from metaphysical disputes, (of which no other use could be made) to repress that pride and vanity that is apt to puff up young minds from a notion of their superior knowledge, by shewing how uncapable the acutest of mankind are of penetrating into the intimate nature and essences of things.

Thefe singular abilities and talents were united in Dr. Hutchefon with the most amiable dispofitions and most useful virtues: the purity of his manners was unspotted from his youth: as he always expreft the higheft indignation against vice, he kept at the greatest diftance from it, avoiding even the fmalleft indecencies of conduct: but this severity of virtue was without any thing of that fournefs, ftiffnefs, or unfociablenefs which fometimes accompanies it, and renders characters, otherwife valuable, in fome refpects difagreeable, and prevents the good effects that the example of their virtues might produce upon others. His integrity was ftrict and inviolable: he abhorred the leaft appearance of deceit either in word or action: he contemned thofe little artifices which too frequently pafs in the world for laudable arts of addrefs, and proofs of fuperior prudence: his nature was frank, and open, and warmly difpofed, to fpeak what he took to be true: you faw at firft fight his fincere and upright foul, and in all further intercourfe with him you found

him always the fame. He was all benevolence and affection; none who faw him could doubt of it; his air
and countenance befpoke it. It was to fuch a degree
his prevailing temper, that it gave a tincture to his
writings, which were perhaps as much dictated by his
heart as his head: and if there was any need of an a-
pology for the ftrefs that in his fcheme feems to be
laid upon the friendly and public affections, the prevalence of them in his own temper would at leaft form
an amiable one.

His heart was finely turned for friendfhip; he was
fparing indeed of the external profeffions of it, but
liberal of its moft important offices: he was the refuge
of his friends for advice and affiftance in all cafes of
perplexity and diftrefs. The ardor of his affection for
his friends got the better of a natural reluctance he
had to ask favours, which no regard for his own interefts could have overcome: his kind offices were far
from being confined to the circle of his particular
friends and relations; his heart overflowed with good-
will to all around him, and prompted him to embrace
every opportunity of doing kind and obliging things.
Tho' there are but few to be found who had fuch a

keen thirft for knowledge, or who purfued it with fuch unremitting attention and vigour; yet even this tafte yielded on all occafions to the more important one of doing good. Among many other acts of beneficence, he took a peculiar delight in affifting worthy young men, in ftraitened circumftances, to profecute their ftudies with his money, and admitting them to attend his colleges without paying the cuftomary fees.

A remarkable degree of a rational enthufiafm for the interefts of learning, liberty, religion, virtue, and human happinefs, which animated him at all times, was a diftinguifhing part of his character: he was vifibly moved by fome of thefe noble principles in whatever he faid or did. They had fuch an afcendency over him as gave a peculiar caft to his whole converfation and behaviour, and formed in him a public fpirit of a very extenfive kind. Public fpirit in him was not a vague and undetermined kind of ardor, for fomething unknown or not diftinctly underftood; but it was an enlightened and univerfal zeal for every branch of human happinefs, and the means of promoting it. His love of valuable knowledge, his unabating activity in purfuing it and fpreading a tafte for it, fitted him, in a

very fingular manner, for that ftation which Providence had affigned him. And perhaps very few men,
even in fimilar ftations, have difcovered equal zeal, or
had equal fuccefs, in promoting a tafte for true literature: but his zeal was not confined to what peculiarly belonged to his own profeffion, but extended to every thing that could contribute to the improvement of
human life. When he fpoke, you would have imagined that he had been employed in almoft all the different ftations in fociety, fo clearly did he appear to
underftand the interefts of each, and fuch an earneft
defire did he exprefs for promoting them. His benevolent heart took great delight in planning fchemes for
rectifying fomething amifs, or improving fomething
already right, in the different orders and ranks of
mankind. Thefe fchemes were not airy and roman-
tic, but fuch as were practicable, and might have de-
ferved the attention of thofe whofe power and influence in fociety could have enabled them to carry them
into execution. This warm zeal for public good appeared uppermoft in his thoughts not only in his more
ferious, but alfo in his gayer hours. But while he a-
bounded in projects for the interefts of others, none

ever heard of one which centered in himself. It has already been obferved, that in the earlier part of life, when the tafte for external enjoyments is commonly ftrongeft, he did not liften to propofals which offered profpects of rifing to wealth and preferment: in a more advanced age, but when he was ftill in fuch a vigorous ftate of health, as he might have hoped for many years longer of life, he had offers made of removing him to the Univerfity of Edinburgh, to be Profeffor of Moral Philofophy there, which might have been a more lucrative place to him, and given him better opportunities of forming connections with people of the firft rank and diftinction in this country, but he was contented with his prefent fituation, and difcouraged all attempts to change it.

Thefe fingular accomplifhments and moral endowments rendered his converfation, efpecially among his friends, fo entertaining and inftructive, that it was a fchool of wifdom to thofe who had the happinefs to enjoy it. It muft have been an undifcerning company which did not receive both pleafure and improvement from him. A remarkable vivacity of thought and expreffion, a perpetual flow of chearfulnefs and good-will, and a vifible air of inward happinefs, made him the life and genius of fociety, and fpread an enlivening influence every where around him. He was gay and pleafant, full of mirth and raillery, familiar and communicative to the laft degree, and utterly free from all ftatelinefs or affectation. No fymptoms of vanity or felf-conceit appeared in him. He fought not after fame, nor had he any vain complacency in the unfought poffeffion of it. While he was vifibly fuperior to others about him, he was the only one that was quite infenfible of it. His own talents and endowments were not the objects on which his thoughts were employed: he was always carried away from attending to himfelf, by the exercife of kind affections, zeal for fome public generous defigns, or keen enquiries after truth. This was fuch an acknowledged part of his character, that even thofe who were leaft difpofed to think well of him, never infinuated that he was proud or vain: the natural modefty of his temper was heightened and refined by his religious fentiments.

He had a full perfuafion and warm fenfe of the great truths of natural and revealed religion, and of the importance of juft and rational devotion to the happi-

nefs of human life, and to the ftability and purity of
a virtuous character. The power of devout fentiments
over his mind appeared in his converfation : in his
public prelections he frequently took occafion from
any hints which his fubject afforded him, as well as
when it was the direct fubject itfelf, to run out at great
length, and with great ardor, on the reafonablenefs
and advantages of habitual regards to God, and of
referring all our talents, virtues, and enjoyments to
his bounty. Such habitual references appeared to him
the fureft means of checking thofe emotions of pride,
vain complacency, and felf-applaufe, which are apt to
fpring up in the minds of thofe, who do not ferioufly
and frequently reflect, that they did not make themfelves *to differ from others, and that they have nothing
but what they received.* Such fentiments deeply rooted
in the mind, he looked upon as the proper foundation of that fimplicity of heart and life, which is the
higheft perfection of a virtuous character.

Such abilities, fuch difpofitions, and fuch ftores of
knowledge,as have been mentioned,accompanied with
a happy talent of fpeaking with eafe, with propriety
and fpirit, rendered him one of the moft mafterly and

engaging teachers that has appeared in our age. He had a great fund of natural eloquence and a perfuafive manner: he attended indeed much more to fenfe than expreffion, and yet his expreffion was good: he was mafter of that precifion and accuracy of language which is neceffary in philofophical enquiries. But he did not look upon it as his duty, either in his prelections, or in his writings upon moral and religious fubjects, to keep up ftrictly at all times to the character of the didactive teacher, by confining himfelf to all the precifion requifite in accurate explication and ftrict argument. He apprehended that he was anfwering the defign of his office as effectually, when he dwelt in a more diffufive manner upon fuch moral confiderations as are fuited to touch the heart, and excite a relifh for virtue, as when explaining or eftablifhing any doctrine, even of real importance, with the moft philofophical exactnefs: he regarded the culture of the heart as a main end of all moral inftruction: he kept it habitually in view, and he was extremely well qualified for fucceeding in it, fo far as human means can go: he had an uncommon vivacity of thought and fenfibility of temper, which rendered him quickly fufceptible of the warmeſt emotions upon the great ſubjects of morals and religion: this gave a pleaſant unction to his diſcourſes, which commanded the attention of the ſtudents, and at the ſame time left ſtrong impreſ-ſions upon their minds: he filled their hearts with a new and higher kind of pleaſure than they had any experience of before, when he opened to their view, in his animated manner, large fields of ſcience of which hitherto they had no conception: when, for inſtance, he pointed out to his pupils, in his lectures on Natu-ral Theology, the numberleſs evidences of wonderful art and kind deſign in the ſtructure of particular things, and the ſtill more aſtoniſhing evidences of the wiſeſt contrivance, and of the moſt benign intention, in the whole material ſyſtem conſidered as one thing, it is eaſy to conceive that their tender minds, warm with the love of knowledge, would be greatly ſtruck. Such views of nature were new diſcoveries to them, which filled them with delight and aſtoniſhment, and gave them at the ſame time the moſt joyful and ſatisfying conviction of the being and perfections of the great Author of all. In like manner, when he led them from the view of the external world to the contemplation of the internal one, the foul of man, and fhewed them like inftances of Divine wifdom and benignity in the contrivance of its moral conftitution, they were filled with frefh delight and wonder, and difcerned new and encreafing proofs of the glorious perfections of the Father of our fpirits. And when he defcribed the feveral virtues exercifed in real life, as beautiful in themfelves, as the nobleft employment of our rational and moral powers, as the only fources of true dignity and happinefs to individuals and to communities, they were charmed with the lovely forms, and panted *to be* what they beheld. The pleafure fpringing from the light of truth and beauty of virtue breaking in upon ingenious and well-difpofed minds, excited fuch a keen defire of knowledge, and fuch an ardor of purfuing it, as fufpended for a time thofe impulfes of youthful paffions which are apt to hurry young men away, in that period of life. But that it may not be imagined thefe ftrong effects are entirely to be afcribed to the charms of novelty, it deferves to be taken notice of, that ftudents advanced in years and knowledge chufed to attend his lectures on Moral Philofophy, for four, five, or fix years together, ftill finding frefh entertainment, tho' the fubject in the main was the fame every feafon.

It was a great addition to the ufefulnefs of his leffons, that they were not confined to high fpeculations, and the peculiarities of a fcheme, but frequently defcended to common life, fometimes pointing out and expofing fashionable vices and follies in the upper part of the world, departures from real juftice and equity in the bufy and commercial part of it, and the dangerous rocks on which youth is apt to fplit and make fhipwreck both of virtue and happinefs; and at other times infifting upon matters acknowledged by all, to be of the higheft importance. The grand maxims he dwelt upon, and laboured to inftil into the minds of his pupils, were to rejoice above all things in the firm perfuafion of the univerfal Providence of a Being infinitely wife and good, who loves all his works, and cannot be conceived as hating any thing he hath made. This he conftantly inculcated in the warmeft manner, " as a fteady foundation of entire truft and " confidence in him, and chearful fubmiffion to his " will in all events. That fufferings may be confidered " as our greateft bleffings, by giving us an opportu-

" nity of practising the moft fublime virtues, fuch as
" refignation to the will of God, forgiving of injuries,
" returning good for evil, and by leading us to form
" juft notions of the vanity of all things, except the
" love of God, and the love and practice of univerfal
" goodnefs: that all our advantages, of all kinds, are
" things which ought never to be afcribed to ourfelves,
" but to God the giver of all. That love and gratitude
" afcribing to him the glory of all that is excellent,
" joined to a vigorous zeal of doing good, feems to
" be the height of human perfection." He delivered
himfelf on thefe grand topics in that fimple but ftriking manner which immediately touches the heart, and
prefents the imagination with the moft beautiful and
engaging forms.

As he had occafion every year in the courfe of his
lectures to explain the origin of government, and compare the different forms of it, he took peculiar care,
while on that fubject, to inculcate the importance of
civil and religious liberty to the happinefs of mankind:
as a warm love of liberty, and manly zeal for promoting it, were ruling principles in his own breaft, he always
infifted upon it at great length, and with the greateft

ftrength of argument and earneftnefs of perfuafion : and he had fuch fuccefs on this important point, that few, if any, of his pupils, whatever contrary prejudices they might bring along with them, ever left him without favourable notions of that fide of the queftion which he efpoufed and defended.

Befides his conftant lectures five days of the week, on Natural Religion, Morals, Jurifprudence, and Government, he had another lecture three days of the week, in which fome of the fineft writers of antiquity, both Greek and Latin, on the fubject of Morals, were interpreted, and the language as well as the fentiment explained in a very mafterly manner.

Befides thefe fetts of lectures he gave a weekly one on the Sunday-evening, on the truth and excellency of Chriftianity, in which he produced and illuftrated, with clearnefs and ftrength, all the evidences of its truth and importance, taking his views of its doctrines and divine fcheme from the original records of the New Teftament, and not from the party-tenets or fcholaftic fyftems of modern ages: this was the moft crowded of all his lectures, as all the different forts and ranks of ftudents, being at liberty from their peculiar purfuits on this day, chufed to attend it, being always fure of finding both pleafure and inftruction.

A Mafter, of fuch talents, fuch affiduity in the duties of his office, with the accomplifhments of the gentleman, and fond of well difpofed youth, entering into their concerns, encouraging and befriending them on all occafions, could not fail to gain their efteem and affections in a very high degree. This gave him a great influence over them, which he employed to the excellent purpofes of ftamping virtuous impreffions upon their hearts, and awakening in them a tafte for literature, fine arts, and every thing that is ornamental or ufeful to human life. And he had remarkable fuccefs in reviving the ftudy of ancient literature, particularly the Greek, which had been much neglected in the Univerfity before his time : he fpread fuch an ardor for knowledge, and fuch a fpirit of enquiry every where around him, that the converfation of the ftudents at their focial walks and vifits turned with great keennefs upon fubjects of learning and tafte, and contributed greatly to animate and carry them forward in the moft valuable purfuits. He did not confine his attention to the pupils immediately under his care, but laid

himſelf out to be uſeful to the ſtudents in all the different faculties, whenever any opportunity offered: and
he was eſpecially ſolicitous to be ſerviceable to the ſtudents of divinity, endeavouring, among other important
inſtructions, to give them juſt notions of the main deſign of preaching. High ſpeculations on diſputable
points, either of Theology or Philoſophy, he looked
upon as altogether improper for the pulpit, at leaſt on
all ordinary occaſions. He particularly inſiſted upon
the uſeleſſneſs and impropriety of handling in the pulpit ſuch ſpeculative queſtions, as, whether human nature is capable of diſintereſted affections, whether the
original of duty or moral obligation is from natural
conſcience, or moral ſenſe, from law, or from rational views of intereſt, and ſuch like enquiries. Tho'
ſuch diſquiſitions might be proper and even neceſſary
in a ſchool of philoſophy *, yet in his view of things

* According to our Author's ſcheme
it is only vindicating the Divine Wiſdom and Goodneſs, manifeſted in the conſtitution of our nature, to aſſert the exiſtence and binding authority of the moral ſenſe; becauſe whatever other obligations we may be under, this internal one
will co-operate with them, when the mind
perceives them, and will exerciſe its authority without them, when thro' a variety of
cauſes we may be hindered from attending
to them. Is the law of God duely promulgated the ſupreme obligation on all intelligent beings? in this view of obligation,
the internal law will co-operate with the
external one, when we are attentive to its
authority; and when we are not, it will
be a rule of action, in ſome degree at leaſt,
without it. Beſides it may be obſerved,
that if the obligation of the moral ſenſe be
admitted to be a real one, men of the moſt
ſceptical turn of mind muſt be conſidered

they did not fall within the province of the preacher, whofe office is not to explain the principles of the human mind, but to addrefs himfelf to them, and fet them in motion: befides, as to the philofophical quefti-on concerning moral obligation, all the different ways of explaining it confpire to prefs the fame virtuous courfe of action, which is the main thing the facred orator fhould be concerned about. The general plan of preaching which he recommended was to this pur-pofe: As mankind are weak, ignorant, guilty creatures, altogether infufficient for their own happinefs, and eve-ry moment expofed to many unavoidable calamities, let them be called upon to reflect upon themfelves as fuch, and let thefe doctrines of natural and revealed religion, which will impart confolation to them un-der thefe humbling views of themfelves, be fet be-fore them in the ftrongeft light: As they are apt to

---

as remaining under its authority when they have fet themfelves at liberty from all other ties. Let us fuppofe a perfon fo un-happy as not to believe that there is a God, or a future ftate of rewards and punifh-ments, or that it is his intereft upon the whole in this life to act the virtuous part; even fuch a perfon is ftill under the power of the internal fentiment, that one thing is right and another wrong. If he acts con-trary to it he violates a known obligation, and muft be confcious that he deferves punifhment, and that it awaits him, if there is a judge and punifher. If we fup-pofe that the fenfe of right and wrong is entirely erazed, then on our Author's fcheme, as well as that of others, he is ftill accountable at leaft for the previous fteps he had taken to bring himfelf into this ftate of total infenfibility as to all moral perceptions and views.

be feduced both from their duty and happinefs by felfifh and fenfual paffions, let both the awful doctrines
of religion, which may ftrike a dread and check the impulfes of bad paffions, and the joyful ones, which may
excite and encourage to the practice of purity, fincerity, and all goodnefs, be difplayed before them in all
their force. And as they are prone to reft in the general knowledge of their duty, without ferioufly ap-
plying it to the government of their hearts and lives,
let the religious inftructor take care not to dwell too
much upon fuch general topics as the beauty, excellency, and reafonablenefs of the Divine Laws, but
commonly defcend, in a minute and particular manner, to direct their conduct in all the relations and
ftations of life, even the loweft, and in the ordinary
bufinefs and intercourfes of it. And let all thefe things
be done without laboured elevation of language, in
that plain and fimple manner which touches the heart,
and brings things home to the confcience and immediate feeling of every one.

    To all which it is but juft to add, that he was a
moft valuable member of the Univerfity in all other
refpects as well as that of an inftructor of youth, his

great talents qualifying him, and his unwearied zeal prompting him on all occafions to promote all its civil as well as literary interefts.

Such was the life of this worthy perfon, fpent in a courfe of affiduous but not painful ftudy, in continually doing good to the utmoft of his power, and propagating truth, virtue, and religion among mankind. To conclude, he had uncommon abilities, uncommon virtues, and fmall failings, and thefe arifing from good qualities; if he was at any time too much or too foon heated, it was owing to the quicknefs of his parts and fenfibility of his temper; if his indignation was ftrong, it was only provoked by fuch bafenefs or malignity as his heart abhorred; if at any time he was open, when referve might have been more proper, it proceeded from an honefty and fincerity of heart unaccuftomed to diffemble. Some were difpleafed with his honeft freedom, fome might emulate his reputation, fome traduce him thro' prejudice, fome thro bigotry; but his parts, his fpirit, and his worth, will be remembered, when any prejudices that were raifed againft him will be entirely forgotten.

A firm conftitution and a pretty uniform ftate of

good health, except some few slight attacks of the gout, till some months before his death, seemed to promise the world much longer enjoyment of so valuable a life; but it pleased all-wise Providence to cut him off, after a few months of an uncertain state of health, and a few days of a fever, in the fifty-third year of his age, and about sixteen years after his coming to Glasgow, to the great regret of the lovers of learning and virtue, and the irreparable loss of the society of which he had been a most excellent member, and of all who were connected with him, either by blood, friendship, or acquaintance.

He was married, soon after his settlement in Dublin, to Mrs. Mary Wilson, a daughter of Francis Wilson, Esq; a gentleman of estate in the county of Langford, who distinguished himself at the Revolution as a Captain in the service of the late King William of glorious and immortal memory. He showed the same liberal and generous principles in this transaction, which appeared in all the other steps of his life. He had an abhorrence of that spirit of traffick which often mingles so deeply in forming this alliance: he was determined solely by the good sense, lovely dispositions, and virtuous accomplifhments of the lady: and the uniform happinefs of their whole conjugal ftate juftified the wifdom and virtue of his choice: he has left behind him one fon, Francis Hutchefon, Doctor of Medicine, who gave early marks of genius, and is the publifher of this Work. If any one fhould wifh to know any thing about Dr. Hutchefon's external form; it may be faid it was an image of his mind. A ftature above middle fize, a gefture and manner negligent and eafy, but decent and manly, gave a dignity to his appearance. His complexion was fair and fanguine, and his features regular. His countenance and look befpoke fenfe, fpirit, kindnefs and joy of heart. His whole perfon and manner raifed a ftrong prejudice in his favour at firft fight.

It only remains to be added, that it has been intended, in any thing that is faid of the Author's Philofophy, to deliver his fentiments without any regard to what may be the writer's own views of thefe fubjects. The Author was a lover of truth and freedom of thought, and did not wifh that any one fhould efpoufe his opinions, farther than the evidence with which they were fupported, determined him. There

appears thro' the work fuch a manifeft aim of promoting piety and virtue, and the good of mankind,
that it is hoped the main of it muft be approven of
by all unprejudiced and well-difpofed perfons, however the writer of thefe memoirs or others may differ
from the Author, as to particular fentiments, or the
decifion of particular queftions.

Some very good judges may think, and perhaps not
without reafon, that by any thing yet faid, juftice has
not been done to Dr. Hutchefon's character as an author: " That he has been reprefented only as en-
" quiring into the mind of man as a moral conftitu-
" tion, and afferting a diftinct order of affections in
" it terminating ultimately on the good of others, and
" a Moral Senfe, by which we inftantaneoufly perceive
" a certain fet of affections, characters, and actions
" as good, and a contrary one as bad; all which is com-
" monly done by that whole order of Philofophers
" who agree with him in admitting generous princi-
" ples in human nature: whereas he juftly deferves to
" be exhibited to the public in the light of an ori-
" ginal, original in the moft capital of all articles re-
" lative to the fcience of human nature and morality:

" for tho' all the difciples of the generous philofophy
" affert, in the ftrongeft manner, a diftinct order of
" affections in our nature, having the happinefs of
" others for their ultimate object, yet when the agent
" is put upon determining the moft important mea-
" fure of human conduct, Why am I to gratify this
" prefent defire? or why fhould I rather chufe to con-
" troul it in favour of another? the anfwer which this
" order of philofophers has given, is very different
" from that which is and muft be given by Dr. Hut-
" chefon: according to the former the agent is refer-
" red to the confideration of his perfonal happinefs *
" (arifing indeed from the prevalence of virtuous af-
" fections) as the determiner of his choice; taking it
" for granted, that there can be but one ultimate
" end of the agent's cool and deliberate purfuit, viz.
" his own higheft intereft or perfonal happinefs: but
" Dr. Hutchefon's doctrine is far otherways; accord-
" ing to him, there are three calm determinations in
" our nature, namely, the calm defire of our own
" happinefs, the calm defire of the happinefs of other
" beings, and the calm defire of moral perfection,

---

* Shaft. Inq. from p; 77 to 174, and p. 69 middle fect. Lond. Ed.

" each of them alike ultimate; that betwixt the fe-
" cond and third determination there can fcarce hap-
" pen any oppofition, but that it is quite otherwife
" betwixt the firft and the other two, where an appa-
" rent oppofition at leaft may often fall out, and in
" all fuch cafes it is fo far from being intended by the
" conftitution of our nature, that the defire of pri-
" vate happinefs fhould controul the other defires, that
" the Moral Senfe never fails to dictate to the agent
" the voluntary facrifice of the firft, to either of the
" other two †: the whole is a queftion of fact, and
" every one muft judge of it for himfelf: but the diffe-
" rence is the greateft imaginable, whether the defire
" of moral excellence, or the defire of private happi-
" nefs is deftined to be the fupreme controuling prin-
" ciple according to the actual conftitution of our na-
" ture: and none of the Philofophers before our Au-
" thor has ever hinted at fuch a reprefentation of our
" nature as pleads for the former as the juft account
" of the matter: nature has formed the union be-
" tween the latter two of the three great ultimate de-
" terminations of the human mind; but it is religion

† Book I. chap. iv. § 12. of this work.

" alone, according to him, that can render all the
" three invariably harmonious, and incapable of ac-
" ting in different and oppofite directions."

It may be acknowledged that Dr. Hutchefon has
taught this doctrine more fully and explicitly than
any of the Philofophers either antient or modern ‡;
but that none of them have *ever hinted at it,* tho' it
fhould be fo, cannot well be pofitively afferted without a very extenfive, and at the fame time a very particular furvey of their works. Our Author has indeed
made no pretenfions to new difcoveries, but rather
exprefsly difclaimed them *: but this may be owing
to the particular modefty of his genius and difpofition: it was probably owing, in fome degree, to this
amiable turn of mind, that he chufed to confider morals rather in the humbler way of a matter of fact,
than in the more pompous one of fcientifical knowledge: and this too made him always more folicitous
that his doctrine fhould in the main coincide with
that of other good Moralifts, than that it fhould be
different or oppofite: thus he endeavoured to fhew,

‡ Book I. chap. iv. § 1 2. of this work.
* Pref. to Effay on the Paff. p. 18 and 19.

that once admitting the generous affections into human nature and the Moral Senſe, the doctrine of the
eternal fitneſs and unfitneſs of things, and of immutable moral truths was very juſt and ſolid. But it is
time to leave the candid reader to the peruſal of the
Work itſelf, and to form ſuch judgments of the Author's doctrine in all reſpects, as upon ſerious examination ſhall appear to him to be well founded.

W. LEECHMAN.

GLASGOW-COLLEGE,⎱
  Dec. 24. 1754. ⎰

A
SYSTEM
OF
MORAL PHILOSOPHY.

B O O K I.

Concerning the Conſtitution of HUMAN NATURE, *and the* SUPREME GOOD.

C H A P T E R I.

Of the Conſtitution of Human Nature and its Powers, and firſt the Underſtanding, Will and Paſſions.

I. THE INTENTION OF MORAL PHILOSOPHY IS TO direct men to that courſe of action which tends moſt effectually to promote their greateſt happineſs and perfection; as far as it can be done by obſervations and concluſions diſcoverable from the conſtitution of nature, without any aids of ſupernatural revelation: theſe maxims, or rules of conduct are therefore reputed as laws of nature, and the ſyſtem or collection of them is called the LAW of NATURE.

As human happineſs, which is the end of this art, cannot be diſtinctly known without the previous knowledge of the conſtitution of this ſpecies, and of all its perceptive and active powers, and their natural objects; (ſince happineſs denotes the ſtate of the ſoul ari-

Moral Philoſophy, what.

Knowledge of the human powers neceſſary to it.

BOOK I. fing from its feveral grateful perceptions or modifications;) the moft natural method in this fcience muft
be firft to inquire into the feveral powers and difpofitions of the fpecies, whether perceptive or active, into
its feveral natural determinations, and the objects from
whence its happinefs can arife; and then to compare
together the feveral enjoyments this fpecies is capable
of receiving, that we may difcover what is its fupreme
happinefs and perfection, and what tenor of action is
fubfervient to it.

In this inquiry we fhall but briefly mention fuch
parts of our conftitution, whether in body or mind, as
are not of great confequence in morals; avoiding unneceffary controverfies, and often referring to other authors for thofe points which have been tolerably well
explained by them. Thus we pafs over many ingenious anatomical obfervations upon the advantages and
dignity of the human body above that of other animals. The reader may find them in the anatomical
authors, and Dr. Cumberland.

Early infirmities   II. Confider mankind from their birth, you fee a
of men.   fpecies at firft weaker and lefs capable of fubfifting,
without the aid of the adult, than any other; and con-
tinuing longer in this infirm ftate. Animals of feveral
other kinds attain to their full vigour and the perfect
ufe of all their powers in a few months; and few require more than four or five years to their maturity.
Ten or twelve years are neceffary to mankind before
they can obtain fubfiftence by their own art or labour,
even in civilifed focieties, and in the fineft climates af-

ter they have been cleared of all beasts of prey. Many CHAP. I. other animals are both cloathed and armed by nature, and have all that is neceſſary for their defence or convenient ſubſiſtence without any care or contrivance of their own: the earth uncultivated offers them their food, and the woods or rocks their ſhelter. Mankind are naked and unarmed; their more ſalutary and agreeable food is more rare, requiring much art and labour: their bodies are leſs fit to reſiſt the injuries of weather, without more operoſe contrivances for cloathing and ſhelter. Their preſervation therefore, in their tender years, muſt depend on the care of the adult; and their lives muſt always continue miſerable if they are in ſolitude, without the aids of their fellows.

This is no unreaſonable ſeverity in the Author of *their final cauſes.* Nature to our ſpecies. We ſhall ſoon diſcover the natural remedy provided for this laſting imbecillity of our younger years, in the tender parental affection of a rational ſpecies; and the final cauſes of it, in the ſeveral improvements we are capable of receiving. The means of ſubſiſtence to our ſpecies require much contrivance and ingenuity: we are capable of many noble enjoyments unknown to other animals, and depending on uſeful and delightful arts, which we cannot attain to without a long education, much inſtruction and imitation of others. How much time is requiſite for learning our mother-tongues? how much for dexterity even in the commoneſt arts of agriculture, or in domeſtic ſervice? full ſtrength of body, without a mind equally advanced in

BOOK I. knowledge and arts and focial habits, would make us ungovernable and untractable to our parents or inftructors. Since we need to be fo long in fubjection, we fhould not foon be able to fhake off the neceffary and friendly yoke.

Powers which appear firft.   III. The natural principles which firft difcover themfelves are our external fenfes, with fome fmall powers of fpontàneous motion, an appetite for food, and an inftinct to receive and fwallow it. All thefe powers exert themfelves in a way too dark for any of us ever to apprehend completely: much lefs have the brutes any knowledge to direct them to the teats of their dams, or notion of the preffure of the air upon which fucking depends. At firft indeed we all alike act by inftincts wifely implanted by a fuperior hand.

Our external fenfes foon introduce to the mind fome perceptions of pleafure and pain: and along with thefe perceptions there immediately appears a natural conftant determination to defire the one and repel the other; to purfue whatever appears to be the caufe or occafion of pleafure, and to fhun the caufes of pain. Thefe are probably our firft notions of natural good or evil, of happinefs or mifery.

Proper ideas of fenfation.   The external fenfes are thofe " determinations of " nature by which certain perceptions conftantly arife " in the mind, when certain impreffions are made upon " the organs of the body, or motions raifed in them." Some of thefe perceptions are received folely by one fenfe, others may be received by two or more. Of the former clafs, are thefe five forts, viz. colours, founds, taftes, fmells, cold or heat; fome ingenious authors Chap. i. reckon more: thefe we may call the proper ideas of fenfation.

These fenfations, as the learned agree, are not pictures or reprefentations of like external qualities in objects, nor of the impreffion or change made in the bodily organs. They are either *fignals*, as it were, of new events happening to the body, of which experience and obfervation will fhew us the caufe; or *marks*, fettled by the Author of Nature, to fhew us what things are falutary, innocent, or hurtful; or intimations of things not otherways difcernable which may affect our ftate; tho thefe marks or fignals bear no more refemblance to the external reality, than the report of a gun, or the flafh of the powder, bears to the diftrefs of a fhip. The pleafant fenfations of tafte, fmell, and touch, generally arife from objects innocent or falutary, when ufed in a moderate degree; the difagreeable or painful fenfations, from fuch as are pernicious or unfit for common ufe. But fight and hearing feem not to be immediate avenues of pain; fcarcely is any vifible form or any found the immediate occafion of it; tho' the violent motion of light or air may caufe painful feelings; and yet by fight and hearing the exquifite pleafures of beauty and harmony have accefs to the foul, as well as the ideas of magnitudes, figures, fituation, and motion. It is by the former fenfes, and not by thofe, that we receive the pleafures commonly called *fenfual.*

The ideas of two or more fenfes are Duration, num-

Concomitant ideas of fenfation.

ber, extenſion, figure, motion, reſt. Duration and number are applicable to every perception or action of the mind, whether dependent upon bodily organs or not. The ſimpler ideas of this claſs, which ſome call the Concomitant ideas of ſenſation, are not generally either pleaſant or painful. It is from ſome complex modes of figure and motion that pleaſure is perceived: beauty, from ſome proportions of figure with colour: harmony, from ſome proportions of time as well as of tones or notes. The proportions of numbers and figures are the field in which our reaſoning powers have the moſt free and vigorous exerciſe. Of theſe hereafter.

Ideas of conſciouſneſs or reflection.   IV. There is another natural power of perception, always exerciſed but not enough reflected upon, an inward ſenſation, perception, or conſciouſneſs, of all the actions, paſſions, and modifications, of the mind; by which its own perceptions, judgments, reaſonings, affections, feelings, may become its object: it knows them and fixes their names; and thus knows itſelf in the ſame manner that it does bodies, by qualities immediately perceived, tho' the ſubſtance of both be unknown.

judging and reaſonirg.   Theſe two powers of perception, *ſenſation* and *conſciouſneſs*, introduce into the mind all its materials of knowledge. All our primary and direct ideas or notions are derived from one or other of theſe ſources. But the mind never reſts in bare perception; it compares the ideas received, diſcerns their relations, marks the changes made in objects by our own action or that of

others; it inquires into the natures, proportions, caufes, effects, antecedents, confequents, of every thing,
when it is not diverted by fome importunate appetite.
Thefe powers of judging and reafoning are more
known and better examined by all philofophers than
any other, and therefore we pafs them over. All thefe feveral powers, of external fenfation, confcioufnefs, judging, and reafoning, are commonly called the acts of
the *underftanding*.

V. Tho' there are many other forts of finer perceptions to be confidered as natural to men, yet as fome
of them have the acts of the *will*, the affections, and
paffions, for their objects, it is neceffary to take a fhort
view of the will and its natural determinations, before
we proceed to thefe finer perceptions.

Here it is plain, as foon as any fenfe, opinion, or
reafoning, reprefents an object or event as immediately good or pleafant, or as the means of future pleafure, or of fecurity from evil, either for ourfelves or
any perfon about whom we are follicitous, there arifes
immediately a new motion of the foul, diftinct from
all fenfation, perception, or judgment, a *defire* of that
object or event. And upon perception or opinion of
an object or event as the occafion of pain or mifery, or
of the lofs of good, arifes a contrary motion called
averfion; on all occafions of this fort, thefe primary
motions of the will naturally arife without any previous choice or command, and are the general fprings of
action in every rational agent.

To the *will* are commonly referred alfo two other

Book I. modifications, or new ftates, arifing from our apprehenfions of objects or events, as obtained or not obtained, according to our previous defire; or repelled and prevented, or not, according to our previous averfions; which are called *joy* and *forrow*. But
as they do not immediately move the foul to action, they feem rather new *feelings* or *ftates* of the foul,
than acts of the will, more refembling fenfations than
volitions. Thefe words however are often ufed promifcuoufly, as are many other names of the actions
and paffions of the foul. Thus *delight* or *joy*, is often
ufed for the defire of any event which when it befals
will give delight; fo is *forrow*, for fear and averfion.
Thus we have the * old divifion of the motions of the
will into four general fpecies, Defire, Averfion, Joy,
and Sorrow. Nor can we eafily imagine any fpirit without thefe modifications and motions of Will of one
fort or other. The Deity indeed, as he is poffeffed of
all power and all perfection, muft be incapable of every
modification implying pain.

Thefe felfifh or
benevolent.   The acts of the will may be again divided into two
claffes, according as one is purfuing good for himfelf,
and repelling the contrary, or purfuing good for o-
thers and repelling evils which threaten them. The
former we may call *felfifh*, the later *benevolent*. Whatever fubtile debates have been to prove that all moti-

---

* See Cicero's Tufcul. lib. iii. & iv.
Hinc metuunt, cupiuntque, dolent, gaudent-
que. Virg.
The Stoics, the avowed enemies of the
paffions, allowed the βἰλησις and ιὐλἀτεια,
and χαρά, in the perfectest character, even
the Deity; but all thefe of an higher fort
than the turbulent paffions; of which diftinction hereafter.

ons of the *will* ſpring from one fountain, no man can Chap. I.
deny that we often have a real internal undiſſembled
deſire of the welfare of others, and this in very different degrees.

VI. There are two calm natural determinations *The two calm determination of will.*
of the will to be particularly conſidered on this occa- *Self-love.*
ſion. Firſt, an invariable conſtant impulſe toward one's
own perfection and happineſs of the higheſt kind. This
† inſtinct operates in the bulk of mankind very con-
fuſedly; as they do not reflect upon, or attend to, their
own conſtitution and powers of action and enjoyment;
few have conſidered and compared the ſeveral enjoyments they are capable of, or the ſeveral powers of action. But whoſoever does ſo will find a calm ſettled
deſire of the perfection of all our active powers, and of
the higheſt enjoyments, ſuch as appear to us, upon
compariſon, of the greateſt importance to our happineſs. Thoſe who have not made ſuch reflections and
compariſons, naturally deſire all ſorts of enjoyments
they have any notion of by their ſenſes or any higher
powers they have exerciſed, as far as they are conſiſtent with each other, or appear to be ſo; and deſire the
perfection of ſuch powers as they attend to. Where
ſeveral enjoyments appear inconſiſtent, the mind,
while it is calm, naturally purſues, or deſires in preference to others, thoſe which ſeem of the greateſt importance to its happineſs.   So far all agree.

The other determination alleged is toward the *Benevolence.*

---

† We need no apology, for uſing the word inſtinct for our higheſt powers, to thoſe who know the Latin language. Ap- | petite is in our language much confined to lower powers; but in Latin the word is applied to the higheſt.

univerſal happineſs of others. When the ſoul is calm and attentive to the conſtitution and powers of other beings, their natural actions and capacities of happineſs and miſery, and when the ſelfiſh appetites and paſſions and deſires are aſleep, 'tis alleged that there is a calm impulſe of the ſoul to deſire the greateſt happineſs and perfection of the largeſt ſyſtem within the compaſs of its knowledge. Our inward conſciouſneſs abundantly teſtifies that there is ſuch an impulſe or determination of the ſoul, and that it is truly ultimate, without reference to any ſort of happineſs of our own. But here again, as few have conſidered the whole ſyſtem of beings knowable by men, we do not find this determination exerted generally in all its extent; but we find natural deſires of the happineſs of ſuch individuals, or ſocieties, or ſyſtems, as we have calmly conſidered, where there has intervened no prejudice againſt them, or notion that their happineſs is any way oppoſite to our own.

As the notion of one's own higheſt happineſs, or
Affections exten-
five or limited. the greateſt aggregate or ſum of valuable enjoyments, is not generally formed by men, it is not expreſsly deſired or intended. And therefore we cannot ſay that every particular calm deſire of private good is aiming directly at that ſum, and purſuing its object under the notion of a neceſſary part of that ſum. Men naturally deſire, even by calm motions of the ſoul, ſuch objects as they conceive uſeful or ſubſervient to any valuable enjoyment, ſuch as wealth, power, honour, without this conception of their making a part

of this greateſt ſum. In like manner we have calm benevolent affections toward individuals, or ſmaller ſocieties of our fellows, where there has not preceeded
any conſideration of the moſt extenſive ſyſtem, and
where they are not conſidered formally as parts of this
largeſt ſyſtem, nor their happineſs purſued as condu-
cing to the greateſt ſum of univerſal happineſs. Such
are our calm benevolent affections to friends, countries, men of eminent worth, without any reference
in our thoughts to the moſt extenſive ſyſtem. We
can make theſe references of all ſelfiſh enjoyments purſued by us to the greateſt ſum of private happineſs,
whenever we pleaſe; and we can in like manner refer
all our calm particular kind affections to the general
extenſive benevolence; and 'tis of great conſequence
to have theſe large conceptions, and to make theſe references. But 'tis plain the ſeveral particular affections,
whether ſelfiſh or benevolent, operate, and that too
without turbulent or paſſionate commotions, where no
ſuch references have preceeded.

VII. But beſide all theſe calm motions of the will *Turbulent paſ-*
more or leſs extenſive, there are many particular paſ- *ſions ſelfiſh or be-*
ſions and appetites which naturally ariſe on their pro- *nevolent.*
per occaſions, each terminating ultimately on its own
gratification, without further reference; and attended
with violent, confuſed, and uneaſy ſenſations, which
are apt to continue till the object or gratification is obtained. Of theſe turbulent paſſions and appetites ſome
are ſelfiſh, ſome benevolent, and ſome may partake of
both characters. Of the ſelfiſh are hunger, thirſt, luſt,

BOOK I. paffions for fenfual pleafure, wealth, power, or fame.
Of the benevolent kind are pity, condolence, congratulation, gratitude, conjugal and parental affections,
as often as they become violent and turbulent commotions of the foul. Anger, envy, indignation, and
fome others, may be of either kind, according as they
arife either on account of fome oppofition to our own
interefts, or to thofe of our friends or perfons loved
and efteemed. Thefe all arife on their natural occafions, where no reference is made by the mind to its
own greateft happinefs, or to that of others.

The difference between the calm motions of the
will and the paffionate, whether of the felfifh or benevolent kinds, muft be obvious to any who confider
how often we find them acting in direct oppofition. *
Thus anger or luft will draw us one way; and a calm
regard, either to our higheft intereft the greateft fum
of private good, or to fome particular intereft, will
draw the oppofite way: fometimes the paffion conquering the calm principle, and fometimes being conquered by it. The calm defire of wealth will force one, tho'
with reluctance, into fplendid expences, when neceffary to gain a good bargain or a gainful employment;
while the paffion of avarice is repining at thefe ex
pences. The fedate defire of a child's or a friend's virtue and honour and improvement, will make us fend
them abroad amidft dangers; while the parental and
friendly paffions are oppofing this purpofe. Gratitude, pity, and friendly paffions, folicite to one fide;

* See this well defcribed in *Plato. Rep. l. 9.* and *Ariftot. Eth. Nicom.*

and love of a country, or a yet more extensive benevolence, may be soliciting on the other side. We correct and restrain our children, we engage them in uneasy studies and labours, out of calm good-will, while this tender passion is opposing every thing that is uneasy to them. Desire of life persuades to abstinence, to painful cures and nauseous potions, in opposition to the appetites destined to preserve life in the order of nature.

As there belong to the understanding not only the lower powers of sensation, common to us with the brutes, but also those of reasoning, consciousness, and *pure intellect*, as 'tis called; so to the will belong not only the bodily appetites and turbulent passions, but the several calm and extensive affections of a nobler order.

VIII. To the Will we also ascribe the power of Spontaneous Motion; since, in consequence of our willing it, we find many parts of the body move as we incline. All its parts are not thus subjected to be moved as we please; but only such as 'tis necessary or useful in life for us to have thus subjected. The inward parts go on, in those motions upon which the continuance of life immediately depends, without any acts of our will; nor can we directly, by any volition, accelerate or retard them. To superintend motions continually necessary would engross the mind perpetually, and make it incapable of any other business. Nor does every motion or impression on the parts of the body excite sensations in the soul. There is no sensation of the internal motions on which life immediately depends, while the body is in good order. Such fenfation would be an uneafy ufelefs diftraction of the mind from all valuable purpofes; as we experience, when a difeafe makes the contraction of the heart, or beatings of the pulfe, become fenfible. Senfations indicate only fuch changes, and new events, or objects, as 'tis convenient we fhould be apprized of. Thus volitions move the head, the eyes, the mouth, the tongue, the limbs, and, that exquifite inftrument of a rational inventive and artful fpecies, the hand. All thefe are plain indications of the wife and benign counfel of our Creator. Nay our limbs are moved immediately in confequence of the contraction of mufcles, and of fome power fent down by nerves from the head. But in our fpontaneous motions we neither know nor will thefe intermediate fteps: we intend the laft motion; and thofe other motions are performed without any knowledge or will of ours. Senfation in like manner immediatly enfues upon fome motion in a nerve continued to the brain: we perceive no motion in the brain; but have a fenfation immediatly referred to the extremity of the body where the impreffion was made, and feeming to occupy that place; in a manner quite inexplicable. Thefe confiderations have led fome ingenious and pious men to conclude that a fuperior Being, or the Deity himfelf, is the fole phyfical caufe of all our motions; according to certain general laws; and the fole efficient caufe of all our fenfations too, in the like manner.

CHAP. II.

Concerning the finer Powers of Perception.

I. AFTER the general account of the perceptive powers, and of the will, we proceed to confider fome finer powers of perception, and fome other natural determinations of will, and general laws of the human conftitution.

To the fenfes of feeing and hearing, are fuperadded in moft men, tho' in very different degrees, certain powers of perception of a finer kind than what we have reafon to imagine are in moft of the lower animals, who yet perceive the feveral colours and figures, and hear the feveral founds. Thefe we may call the fenfes of beauty and harmony, or, with Mr. Addifon, the *imagination*. Whatever name we give them, tis manifeft that, the feveral following qualities in objects, are fources of pleafure conftituted by nature; or, men have natural powers or determinations to perceive pleafure from them. *Pleafures of imagination.*

1. Certain forms are more grateful to the eye than others, even abftracting from all pleafure of any lively colours; fuch complex ones, efpecially, where, uniformity, or equality of proportion among the parts, is obfervable; nor can we, by command of our will, caufe all forms indifferently to appear pleafant, more than we can make all objects grateful to the tafte. *Beauty.*

2. As a difpofition to imitate is natural to man- *Imitation.*

BOOK I. kind from their infancy, so they universally receive pleasure from imitation*. Where the original is beautiful, we may have a double pleasure; but an exact imitation, whether of beauty or deformity, whether by colours, figures, speech, voice, motion or action, gives of itself a natural pleasure.

Harmony. 　3. Certain compositions of notes are immediatly pleasant to the generality of men, which the artists can easily inform us of. The simpler pleasures arise from the concords; but an higher pleasure arises from such compositions as, in sound and time, imitate those modulations of the human voice, which indicate the several affections of the soul in important affairs. Hence PLATO† and LYCURGUS ‡ observed a moral character in musick, and looked upon it as of some consequence in influencing the manners of a people.

Design. 　4. As we are endued with reason to discern the fitness of means for an end, and the several relations and connexions of things; so, there is an immediate pleasure in knowlege ‖, distinct from the Judgment itself, tho naturally joined with it. We have a pleasure also in beholding the effects of art and design, in any ingenious machinery adapted to valuable purposes, in any utensil well fitted for its end; whether we hope to have the use of it or not. We have delight in exercising our own rational, inventive, and active powers; we are pleased to behold the like exercises of others, and the artful effects of them. In such works of art

* *Ariflot.* Poet. c. 4. calls man ζωον μιμητικωτατον.　† De Repub. l. 3.　‡ Plut. in Lycurgo.　‖ *Inquiry* b. i. c. 3. and *Ariflot. Ethic.* there cited.

we are pleafed to fee intermixed the beauty of form,
and imitation, as far as it confifts with the defign; but ∿
the fuperior pleafure from the execution of the defign makes us omit the inferior when it is inconfiftent

II. Granting all thefe difpofitions to be natural, we *Caufe of variety of taftes.*
may account for all that diverfity of fancies and taftes
which we obferve; fince fo many qualities are naturally pleafing, fome of which may be chiefly regarded by
one, and others by others. The neceffitous, the bufy,
or the floathful, may neglect that beauty in drefs, architecture, and furniture, which they might obtain,
and yet not be infenfible to it. One may purfue only
the fimpler kind in the uniformity of parts; others
may alfo interfperfe imitation of the beautiful works
of nature; and, of thefe, fome may chufe one fet of
natural objects, and others may chufe other objects
of greater beauty or dignity: the manner too of imitation may be more or lefs perfect. Again, fome in
their works may chiefly regard the pleafure from appearance of defign, and ufefulnefs, admitting only the
pleafures of beauty and imitation as far as they confift with it. In the moft fantaftick dreffes there is uniformity of parts, and fome aptitude to the human
fhape, and frequently imitation. But our modern dreffes are lefs fitted for eafy motion, and the difplaying
of the human fhape, than the antient. Spectators who
regard thefe ends may prefer the ancient dreffes; thofe
who do not think of them, or regard them, may prefer the modern.

In like manner as to architecture; they who dif-

BOOK I. cern the imitation of the proportions of the human body in certain parts, may relish one manner on that account. Others, who know the uses of which certain parts present the appearance, may relish this design; others, without these views, may be pleased with the uniformity of the parts: others may like or dislike through some * associations of ideas; of which hereafter.

not reducible to usefulness.

One who would reduce all sense of beauty in forms to some real or apparent usefulness discerned, will never be able to explain how the spectator relishes those useful forms from which he gets no benefit, nor expects any beyond the pleasure of beholding them; nor how we are pleased with the forms of flowers, of birds, and wild beasts, when we know not any real or apparent uses indicated by them; nor how any spectator, quite a stranger to the views of the architect, shall be pleased with the first appearance of the work; nor whence it is that we are all pleased with imitations of objects, which, were they really placed where their images are, would be of no advantage; one may as well assert that, before we can be pleased with a favour, we must know the figures of the minute particles, and see their inoffensive nature to our nerves.

of great consequence in life.

The pleasures of these † finer senses are of no small importance in life. How much soever they seem ne-

---

* See the *Inquiry* into Beauty. b. i. c. 7. §. 4.

† One who would make all these to be perceptions of the external senses, and deny that we have any distinct powers of perception, may as well assert that the pleasures of geometry, or perspective, are sensual, because 'tis by the senses we receive the ideas of figure.

glected by the votaries of wealth and power, they are Chap. 2.
generally much in their view for themſelves, in ſome
future period of life, or for their poſterity: as for o-
thers who have a more elegant taſte, they are the
end of a great part of their labours: and the greateſt
part of men, when they are tolerably provided againſt
the uneaſy cravings of appetite, ſhew a reliſh for theſe
pleaſures: no ſooner are nations ſettled in peace than
they begin to cultivate the arts ſubſervient to them, as
all hiſtories will inform us.

To theſe pleaſures of the imagination may be ad- *Reliſh for grandeur and novelty.*
ded two other grateful perceptions ariſing from no-
velty and grandeur. The former ever cauſes a grateful commotion when we are at leiſure; which perhaps
ariſes from that curioſity or deſire of knowlege which
is deeply rooted in the ſoul; of which hereafter. Grandeur alſo is generally a very grateful circumſtance in
any object of contemplation diſtinct from its beauty
or proportion. Nay, where none of theſe are obſerved, the mind is agreeably moved with what is large,
ſpacious, high, or deep, even when no advantage ariſing from theſe circumſtances is regarded. The final
cauſes of theſe natural determinations or ſenſes of
pleaſure may be ſeen in ſome * late authors.

III. Another important determination or ſenſe of *The ſympathetick ſenſe. Compaſſion.*
the ſoul we may call the *ſympathetick,* different from all
the external ſenſes; by which, when we apprehend the
ſtate of others, our hearts naturally have a fellow-feeling with them. When we ſee or know the pain, diſ-

* See *Spectator* N. 412. and the *Inquiry* into *Beauty,* laſt ſection.

BOOK I. trefs, or mifery of any kind which another fuffers, and turn our thoughts to it, we feel a ftrong fenfe of pity, and a great pronenefs to relieve, where no contrary paffion with-holds us. And this * without any artful views of advantage to accrue to us from giving relief, or of lofs we fhall fuftain by thefe fufferings. We fee this principle ftrongly working in children, where there are the feweft diftant views of intereft; fo ftrongly fometimes, even in fome not of the fofteft mould, at cruel executions, as to occafion fainting and ficknefs. This principle continues generally during all our lives.

Congratulation. We have a like natural difpofition to Congratulation with others in their joys; where no prior emulation, imagined oppofition of intereft, or prejudice, prevents it. We have this fympathy even with the brute animals; and hence poets fo fuccefsfully pleafe us with defcriptions of their joys. But as our own felfifh paffions which repel evil, fuch as fear, anger, refentment, are generally ftronger commotions of foul than the paffions purfuing private good; fo pity is a ftronger benevolent paffion than congratulation. And all this is wifely contrived, fince immunity from pain feems previoufly neceffary to the enjoyment of good. Thus the ftronger motions of the mind are directed toward that which is moft neceffary. This fympathy feems to extend to all our affections and paffions. They all feem naturally contagious. We not only forrow with the diftreffed, and rejoice with the profpe-

* See *Inquiry* into *Virtue* fect. 2.

rous; but admiration, or furprife, difcovered in one,
raifes a correfpondent commotion of mind in all who
behold him.   Fear obferved raifes fear in the *obferver*
before he knows the caufe, laughter moves to laugh,
love begets love, and the devout affections difplayed
difpofe others to devotion. One eafily fees how directly fubfervient this fympathy is to that grand determination of the foul toward univerfal happinefs.

IV. Before we mention fome other finer fenfes, *A natural pro-*
penfity to action
which have actions of men for their objects, we muft *in moft animals,*
obferve one general determination of the foul to exercife all its active powers. We may fee in our fpecies,
from the very cradle, a conftant propenfity to action
and motion; children grafping, handling, viewing,
tafting every thing. As they advance they exert other
powers, making all tryals poffible; obferving all changes, and inquiring into their caufes; and this from an
impulfe to action and an implanted inftinct toward
knowledge, even where they are not allured by any profpects of advantage. Nay we fee almoft all other animals, as foon as they come to light, exercifing their feveral powers by like inftincts, in the way that the Author of Nature intended; and by this exercife, tho' often laborious and fatiguing, made happier than a-
ny ftate of flothful fenfuality could make them. Ser-
pents try their reptile motions; beafts raife themfelves
and walk or run; birds attempt to raife themfelves
with their wings and foar on high; water-fowl
take to the water as foon as they fee it. The colt is
practifing for the race, * the bull is butting with his

* *Dente lupus,* &c. Hor. lib: i. fat. 1. l. 52.

horns, and the hound exercifing himfelf for the chace. Children are ever in motion while they are awake, nor do they decline wearinefs and toil: they fhew an averfion to fleep till it over-powers them againft their wills - they obferve whatever occurs, they remember and inquire about it; they learn the names of things, inquire into their natures, ftructures, ufes, and caufes; nor will their curiofity yield to rebukes and affronts. Kind affections foon break out toward thofe who are kind to them; ftrong gratitude, and an ardor to excel in any thing that is praifed; in vying with their fellows they are tranfported with fuccefs and victory, and exceedingly dejected when they are out-done by others. They are foon provoked to anger upon any imagined injury or hurt; are afraid of experienced pain, and provoked at the caufe of it; but foon appeafed by finding it undefigned, or by profeffions of repentance. Nothing do they more refent than falfe accufation or reproach. They are prone to fincerity, and truth, and opennefs of mind, until they have experienced fome evils following upon it. They are impatient to relate to others any thing new or ftrange, or apt to move admiration or laughter; ready to gratify any one with what they have no ufe for themfelves; fond of pleafing, and void of fufpicion, till they have had experience of injuries.

This impulfe to action continues during life, while we retain the ufe of our powers. The men who are moft worthlefs and flothful yet are not wholly idle - they have their games, their cabals and converfation

to employ them, or some mean ingenuity about sensual pleasures. We see in general that mankind can
be happy only by action of one kind or other; and
the exercise of the intellectual powers is one source
of natural delight from the cradle to the grave. Children are transported with discoveries of any thing
new or artificial, and impatient to shew them to o-
thers. Publick shows, rarities, magnificence, give
them high entertainment: but above all, the important actions of great characters; the fortunes of such
men, and of the states where they lived, whether related, read, or represented by action, are the delight
of all ages. Here the pleasure is heightened by our social feelings of joy, and the keeness of inquiry increased by our impulse to compassion, and our concern a-
bout the persons we admire.

When men have the proper genius, and access to
more laborious knowlege, what ardour of mind do
some shew for geometry, numbers, astronomy, and
natural history? All toils and watchings are born with
joy. Need we mention even fabulous history, mytho-
logy, philology? 'Tis manifest there is an high natural pleasure in knowledge without any allurements of
other advantage. There is a like pleasure in practical
knowlege about the business of life, and the effects of
actions upon the happiness of individuals, or that of
societies. How contrary are all these appearances of
Nature to that Philosophy which makes the sole
impulse or determination of the soul to be a desire of

such pleasures as arise from the body and are referred to it, or of immunity from bodily pain!

     V. Action is constituted to mankind the grand
source of their happiness by an higher power of perception than any yet mentioned; namely, that by which
they receive the moral notions of actions and characters. Never was there any of the human species, except ideots, to whom all actions appeared indifferent.
Moral differences of action are discerned by all, even
when they consider no advantage or disadvantage to
redound to themselves from them. As this moral
sense is of high importance, it shall be more fully considered in a subsequent chapter. It may suffice at present to observe what we all feel, that a certain temper, a set of affections, and actions consequent on them,
when we are conscious of them in ourselves, raise the
most joyful sensations of approbation and inward satisfaction; and when the like are observed in others, we
have a warm feeling of approbation, a sense of their
excellence, and, in consequence of it, great good-will
and zeal for their happiness. If we are conscious of
contrary affections and actions, we feel an inward remorse, and dislike to ourselves; when we observe the
like in others, we dislike and condemn their dispositions, reputing them base and odious.

     The affections which excite this moral approbati-
on are all either directly benevolent, or naturally connected with such dispositions; those which are disapproved and condemned, are either ill-natured, by
which one is inclined to occasion misery to others; or

such selfish dispositions as argue some unkind affecti- CHAP. 2.
on, or the want of that degree of the benevolent affections which is requisite for the publick good, and
commonly expected in our species.

This moral difcernment is not peculiar to persons *universal in*
of a fine education and much reflection. The rudeft *mankind.*
of mankind fhew fuch notions; and young minds,
who think leaft of the diftant influences of actions u-
pon themfelves or others, and have fmall precaution
about their own future interefts, are rather more moved
with *moral forms* than others. Hence that ftrong inclination in children, as foon as they underftand the
names of the feveral affections and tempers, to hear
fuch ftories as prefent the moral characters of agents
and their fortunes. Hence that joy in the profperity
of the kind, the faithful, and the juft; and that indignation and forrow upon the fuccefles of the cruel and
treacherous. Of this power we fhall treat more fully
hereafter.

VI. As by the former determination we are led to *A fenfe of ho-*
approve or condemn ourfelves or others according to *nour ;*
the temper difplayed, fo by another natural determination, which we may call a fenfe of honour and fhame,
an high pleafure is felt upon our gaining the approbation and efteem of others for our good actions, and
upon their expreffing their fentiments of gratitude; and
on the other hand, we are cut to the heart by cenfure,
condemnation, and reproach. All this appears in the
countenance. The fear of infamy, or cenfure, or con
tempt, difplays itfelf by blufhing.

Vol. I.   D

'Tis true, we may obferve from our infancy, that men are prone to do good offices to thofe they approve and honour. But we appeal to the hearts of men, whether they have not an immediate pleafure in being honoured and efteemed, without thinking of any future advantages, and even when they previoufly know that they can receive none. Are not we generally folicitous about our characters after our death? And whence is it that blufhing accompanies this fort of fear, and not the fears of other difadvantages, if this is not an immediate principle?

* Aristotle's account of this pleafure, tho' more elegant, is not juft: " that we relifh honour as it is a " teftimony to our virtue, which we are previoufly " confcious is the greateft good." This confideration may fometimes make honour very grateful to men who are doubtful and diffident of their own conduct. But have not alfo the men of greateft abilities, who are perfectly affured of the goodnefs of their conduct, a like natural joy in being praifed, diftinct from their inward felf-approbation?

The kind intention of God in implanting this principle is obvious. 'Tis a ftrong incitement to every thing excellent and amiable: it gives a grateful reward to virtue: it often furmounts the obftacles to it from low worldly interefts: and even men of little virtue are excited by it to fuch ufeful fervices as they would have otherways declined. The felfifh are thus, beyond their inclination, made fubfervient to a publick intereft; and fuch are punifhed who counteract it.

* *Ethic. ad Nicom.* l. i. c. 5.

What may further prove that this sense of honour CHAP. 2.
is an original principle, is this; we value the praise of ⌇⌇
others, not in proportion to their abilities to serve us,
but in proportion to their capacity of judging in
such matters. We feel the difference, between the in-
terested desire of pleasing the man in power who can
promote us; and the inward joy from the approbation
of the judicious or ingenious, who cannot do us any
other good offices. The desire of praise is acknow-
leged to be one of the most universal passions of the
soul.

VII. Tho' it is by the moral sense that actions be- *A sense of decen-*
come of the greatest consequence to our happiness or *cy and dignity.*
misery; yet 'tis plain the mind naturally perceives some
other sorts of excellence in many powers of body and
mind; must admire them, whether in ourselves or others;
and must be pleased with certain exercises of them, without conceiving them as moral virtues. We often use
words too promiscuously, and do not express distinctly
the different feelings or sensations of the soul. Let us
keep *moral approbation* for our sentiments of such dispositions, affections, and consequent actions, as we repute virtuous. We find this warm approbation a very
different perception from the admiration or liking
which we have for several other powers and dispositions; which are also relished by a sense of *decency* or
dignity. This sense also is natural to us, but the perceptions very different from moral approbation. We
not only know the use of such valuable powers, and
of their exercise, to the person possessed of them; but

Book I. have agreeable commotions of admiration and liking, and thefe in feveral degrees. Thus beauty, ftrength, fwiftnefs, agility of body, are more decent and efteemable than a ftrong voracious ftomach, or a delicate palate. The manly diverfions of riding, or hunting, are beheld with more pleafure and admiration than eating and drinking even in a moderate degree. A tafte for thefe manly exercifes is often valued; whereas purfuits of mere fenfuality appear defpicable even when they do not run into excefs, and at beft are only innocent. Nay there is fomething graceful, in the very fhape gefture and motion, and fomething indecent and uncomely; abftracting from any indications of advantage difcerned by the fpectators.

in different de-grees. But this is ftill more obvious about the powers of the mind and their exercife. A penetrating genius, capacity for bufinefs, patience of application and labour, a tenacious memory, a quick wit, are naturally admirable, and relifhed by all obfervers; but with a quite different feeling from moral approbation. To every natural power there feems to be a correfponding fenfe or tafte, recommending one fort of exercife, and difliking the contrary. Thus we relifh the exercife of all the ingenious arts, machinery of every kind, imitation in painting, fculpture, ftatuary, poetry; gardening, architecture, mufick. We not only behold the works with pleafure, but have a natural admiration of the perfons in whom we difcern a tafte and genius for thefe arts. Whereas the exercife of our lower powers, merely fubfervient to fenfual gratification, are at beſt beheld with indifference, are often matter of ſhame, and the cauſe of contempt.

Thus according to the juſt obſervation of ARISTOTLE, "The chief happineſs of active beings muſt "ariſe from action; and that not from action of eve-"ry ſort, but from that ſort to which their nature is "adapted, and which is recommended by nature." When we gratify the bodily appetites, there is an immediate ſenſe of pleaſure, ſuch as the brutes enjoy, but no further ſatisfaction; no ſenſe of dignity upon reflection, no good-liking of others for their being thus employed. There is an exerciſe of ſome other bodily powers which ſeems more manly and graceful. There is a manifeſt gradation; ſome fine taſtes in the ingenious arts are ſtill more agreeable; the exerciſe is delightful; the works are pleaſant to the ſpectator, and reputable to the artiſt. The exerciſe of the higher powers of the underſtanding, in diſcovery of truth, and juſt reaſoning, is more eſteemable, when the ſubjects are important. But the nobleſt of all are the virtuous affections and actions, the objects of the moral ſenſe.

Happineſs of active beings is in action.

Some other abilities and diſpoſitions of ſoul, which are naturally connected with benevolent diſpoſitions, and inconſiſtent with the higheſt ſelfiſhneſs and ſenſuality, ſeem to be immediatly approved by the moral ſenſe itſelf. Theſe we refer to another place. We ſhall only take notice here, that by certain aſſociations of ideas, and by frequent compariſons made in ſimilies and metaphors, and by other cauſes, ſome ina-

Additional ideas.

nimate objects have obtained additional ideas of dignity, decency, sanctity; some appear as mean and despicable; and others are in a middle state of indifference. Our relish for imitation and observing resem-
blances has made all languages full of metaphors:
and similitudes and allegories give no small pleasure
in many compositions: hence we cloath many objects
with additional ideas of qualities they are not naturally capable of; some of these ideas are great and ve-
nerable, others low and contemptible. Some attempt
to explain the natural cause or occasion of laughter,
a commotion of mind generally agreeable, of which
all are susceptible, from a natural sense of the *ridicu-*
lous in objects or events.

Association of i-
deas very necef-
fary. VIII. Before we pass to the dispositions of the will,
we may observe a natural involuntary determination
to associate or bind together all such perceptions as
have often occurred together, or have made at once a
strong impression on the mind, so that they shall still
attend each other, when any object afterwards excites
any one or more of them. As this is experienced in
smaller matters, so it affects our apprehensions of good
and evil natural and moral. When the strain of con-
versation and popular maxims have long represented
certain actions or events as good, and others as evil; we
find it difficult to break the association, even after our
reason is convinced of the contrary. Thus certain actions are confusedly imagined honourable, others dif-
honourable; certain stations miserable, and others
happy; as spectres are imagined in church-yards. Tho'

many miferies and vices fpring from this fountain, we
may fee the abfolute neceffity of this determination. ∽∾∽
Without it we could have little ufe of memory, or
recollection, or even of fpeech. How tedious would
it be to need a particular recollection, upon each word
we hear or defire to fpeak, to find what words and
ideas are joined by the cuftom of the language? it muft
be as tedious a work as decyphering after we had found
an alphabet. Whereas, now, the found and idea are
fo affociated, that the one ever is attended with the
other. Nay, how is it we remember? when we are examined about a paft event, the time, or place, fome
circumftance, or perfon then prefent, is fuggefted in
the queftion, and thefe bring along with them the
whole train of the affociated ideas. The fubject of a
debate is fuggefted; a man converfant in it finds, previous almoft to volition, the principal reafonings on
both fides arifing in his mind. To this difpofition
in a great meafure is owing the power of education,
which forms many affociations in our early years; and
few have the patience or courage to examine, whether
they are founded in nature, or in the weaknefs of our
inftructors.

IX. Many of the natural determinations of the
will are abundantly explained by fuch as treat defign-
edly upon that fubject, and point out the natural occafions of the feveral paffions and affections. To thefe
authors we may refer much of this fubject. We confidered, above, the ftrong natural propenfity to action.
We may alfo obferve another determination, or law

BOOK I. of our nature, by which the frequent repetition of actions gives not only a facility in performing them, by encreaſing our active powers, but makes the mind more prone to them for the future, or more uneaſy when it is by violence reſtrained from them. And this is called an Habit. In our paſſive ſenſations the pleaſures and pains are rather abated by frequent feelings: and yet the uneaſineſs under the want of pleaſures is increaſed by our being long enured to them. If we find much detriment from habits of vice, equally great is the advantage of the habits of virtue. It is of general advantage to a rational ſpecies, that it thus can increaſe any of its powers as it chuſes, and make them more ſtable and vigorous. It is ſtill in our power, too, to wear out any habits, by abſtaining from their acts, or reſolutely acting in oppoſition to them. Could we acquire no habits, our powers muſt remain miſerably weak, and all artificial action continue as uneaſy as we found our firſt eſſays.

No habit or cuſtom gives new ideas.　　But all theſe aſſociations, habits, cuſtoms, or prejudices, recommend objects to our liking, or raiſe averſions to them, under the notion of ſome quality or ſpecies perceivable by the ſenſes we are naturally endued with, nor can they raiſe any new ideas. No ſentiments therefore of approbation or condemnation, no liking or diſliking, are ſufficiently explained by attributing them to prejudice, cuſtom, or education, or aſſociation of ideas; unleſs we can fully ſhew what theſe ideas or notions are, and to what ſenſe they be-

long, under which thefe objects are approved or condemned, liked or difliked.

X. At a certain age arifes a new defire between the
fexes, plainly deftined for the continuance of our
race; which, as it would be pernicious or ufelefs in
our firft years, before we had acquired knowledge and
experience fufficient for the prefervation of offspring,
is wifely poftponed in the order of nature. This defire in mankind does not terminate merely on fenfual pleafure, as in the brutes; nor is it in mankind only a blind impulfe, fuch as excites the brutes, previoufly to experience of pleafure. There is a natural
liking of beauty as an indication of a temper and manners. A character is apprehended, and thence good-
will and efteem arifes, and a defire of fociety for life,
with friendfhip and mutual love, and united interefts.
Thus thefe fentiments and defires, in mankind, always accompany the natural impulfe. They have alfo univerfally a defire of offspring, where no ftronger
inconfiftent views reftrain them.

Toward offspring there is in man, as in other animals, a peculiar ftrong affection, and a tender folici-
tude for their prefervation and happinefs. In mankind this affection continues during life, as parents
may always do fome good to their pofterity. It de-
fcends to grandchildren, and their children, almoft
undiminifhed. In the brutes it is found where the
young need affiftance; where they don't, it is not
found. It lafts till the young can fupport themfelves,
and then generally ceafes. All this carries with it ma-

Bᴏᴏᴋ I. nifeſt evidences of deſign in the Author of Nature
Like affections, but weaker, are found generally to
attend the tyes of blood among collaterals. Theſe
tender affections are the ſprings of more than one
half of the labours and cares of mankind: and, where
there is any ability, they rouſe the mind to diligence
and induſtry, and to things great and honourable.
By means of them the heart is made more ſuſcep-
tible of every tender kind and ſocial affection.

Men ſocial, and fit for civil ſo-ciety.   XI. One can ſcarce deny to mankind a natural im
pulſe to ſociety with their fellows, as an immediate
principle, when we ſee the like in many ſpecies of
animals; nor ſhould we aſcribe all aſſociating to
their indigence. Their other principles, their curioſity, communicativeneſs, deſire of action; their
ſenſe of honour, their compaſſion, benevolence, gai-
ety, and the moral faculty, could have little or no
exerciſe in ſolitude, and therefore might lead them
to haunt together, even without an immediate or
ultimate impulſe, or a ſenſe of their indigence. The
tyes of blood would have the ſame effect, and have
probably firſt united large numbers for mutual aſ-
ſiſtance and defence, upon a common apprehenſion
of their indigence in ſolitude. When many were
thus aſſociated, the ſuperior goodneſs, prudence, or
courage of ſome, would naturally procure them a ſuperior eſteem and confidence from all around them.
Controverſies would ariſe; the miſchief of deciding
them by violence would ſoon appear. They would
ſoon ſee the danger of divided counſels, either about

improving their condition, or common defence; tho' CHAP. 2.
all agreed in the general end. The moft efteemed
would foon be chofen *arbitrators* of their controverfies, and *directors* of the whole body in matters concerning their common intereft; and, as their prudence
fuggefted, laws and political inftitutions would be
eftablifhed. The reft, finding the fweets of good order,
fafety, and laws, would have a veneration for the fociety, and its governors, and conftitution. The finer fpirits would feel patriotifm and the love of a
country in their breafts: and all, in fome meafure,
by bonds of acquaintance, and intercourfe of bufinefs,
and the enjoyments of protection for themfelves and
their fortunes, would acquire a love to the community and zeal for its interefts.

XII. As the order, grandeur, regular difpofitions *Religion natural.*
and motions, of the vifible world, muft foon affect the
mind with admiration; as the feveral claffes of animals and vegetables difplay in their whole frame exquifite mechanifm, and regular ftructure, evidencing
counfel, art, and contrivance for certain ends; men of
genius and attention muft foon difcover fome intelligent beings, one or more, prefiding in all this comely
order and magnificence. The great and the beautiful ftrikes the mind with veneration, and leads us to
infer intelligence as refiding in it, or directing it: a
careful attention to the ftructure of our own nature
and its powers leads to the fame conclufion. Our
feeling moral fentiments, our fenfe of goodnefs and
virtue, as well as of art and defign; our experience of

Book I. some moral diftribution within, by immediate happineſs or miſery conſtantly attending virtue and vice, and of a like diftribution generally obtaining even in external things by a natural tendency, muſt ſuggeſt that there is a moral government in the world: and as men are prone to communicate their knowledge, inventions, conjectures, the notions of a Deity and providence muſt ſoon be diffuſed; and an eaſy exerciſe of reaſon would confirm the perſuaſion. Thus ſome devotion and piety would generally obtain, and therefore may juſtly be called natural to a rational ſyſtem. An early revelation and tradition generally anticipated human invention in this matter: but theſe alone could ſcarce have diffuſed the belief ſo univerſally, without the aids of obvious reaſons from ſtrong appearances in Nature. Notions of Deity and ſome ſort of worſhip have in fact as univerſally obtained among men, as living in ſociety, the uſe of ſpeech, or even propagating their kind; and thus may be counted as natural.

The ſeveral powers diſpoſitions or determinations above-mentioned are univerſally found in mankind, where ſome accident hath not rendered ſome individual monſtrous, or plainly maimed and deficient in a natural faculty. But, in the different individuals, theſe diſpoſitions are not in the ſame proportion as to ſtrength; one being prevalent in one, and another in another: and hence the great diverſity of characters. Yet, upon a proper occaſion, when there is no oppoſi tion from some stronger principle, each of these powers will exert itself, and have its effect.

XIII. Notwithstanding that all these nobler powers we mentioned are natural to us, the causes of that vice and depravity of manners we observe, are pretty obvious. Not to say any thing of causes not discoverable by the light of nature, mankind spend several of their first years, where there is not a careful education, in the gratification of their sensual appetites, and in the exercise of some lower powers, which, by long indulgence, grow stronger: reflecting on moral notions, and the finer enjoyments, and comparing them with the lower, is a laborious exercise. The appetites and passions arise of themselves, when their objects occur, as they do frequently: the checking, examining, and ballancing them, is a work of difficulty Prejudices and groundless associations of ideas are very incident to men of little attention. Our selfish passions early gain strength by indulgence. Hence the general tenor of human life is an incoherent mixture of many social, kind, innocent actions, and of many selfish, angry, sensual ones; as one or other of our natural dispositions happens to be raised, and to be prevalent over others.

C H A P. III.

Concerning the Ultimate Determinations of the Will, and Benevolent Affections.

I. **A**FTER this long enumeration of the several fenfes or powers of perception, by which a great
multitude of objects may be the occasion of pleasure
or pain, or of some sorts of happiness or misery; and a
like enumeration of many dispositions of will, or determinations of desire; human nature must appear a
very complex and confused fabrick, unless we can difcover some order and subordination among these
powers, and thus discern which of them is naturally
fit to govern. Of this we shall treat in some following
chapters. In the first place the *Understanding*, or the
power of reflecting, comparing, judging, makes us
capable of discerning the tendencies of the several
senses, appetites, actions, gratifications, either to our
own happiness, or to that of others, and the comparative values of every object, every gratification.
This power judges about the means or the subordinate ends: but about the ultimate ends there is no reasoning. We prosecute them by some immediate dif-
position or determination of soul, which in the order
of action is always prior to all reasoning; as no opinion or judgment can move to action, where there is no
prior desire of some end.

*The selfish gene-
ral determina-
tion alleged the
only one.* Were there no other ultimate determination or defire in the human soul than that of each one toward

his own happineſs; then calm * ſelf-love would be the CHAP. 3.
ſole leading principle, plainly deſtined by Nature to 〰
govern and reſtrain all other affections, and keep them
ſubſervient to its end; having reaſon for its miniſter
or counſellor, to ſuggeſt the means. But the *end*
would be conſtituted by that ultimate determination,
without any reaſoning.

This is a favourite tenet of a great many authors, *Various accounts of it.*
and pleaſes by its ſimplicity. But very different and
contrary accounts are given, by theſe authors, of the
private enjoyments or happineſs purſued in the offices we commonly repute virtuous. Some make the
ſole motive to all offices or actions even the moſt honourable, the ſole end ultimately intended by them,
to be ſome worldly advantage, ſome bodily pleaſures
or the means of them. This was the tenet of the *Cyrenaicks*, and probably of the *Epicureans* too, and of
ſome moderns. Others ſay, that we deſire the good of
others, or of ſocieties, merely as the means of our own
ſafety and proſperity; others, as the means of ſome
ſubtiler pleaſures of our own by ſympathy with others
in their happineſs: others make our end to be the
pleaſures we enjoy in being honoured, or ſome rewards we expect for our ſervices, and theſe either
from GOD, or men.

But there is ſtill an higher ſcheme; allowing indeed no other calm ſetled determination of ſoul but

---

* By *ſelf-love* we mean, one's *deſire of* | or preference of our moral character and
his own happineſs, and this only. By a fre- | accompliſhments to thoſe of others, which
quent uſe of the word *love*, for *eſteem*, | is contrary to what the modeſt and ſelf-
ſome have imagined an univerſal *ſelf-eſteem*, | diffident continually experience.

BOOK I. that in each one toward his own happiness; but granting that we have a *moral faculty*, and many particular kind affections truly difinterefted, terminating u-
pon the happiness of others, and often operating when
we have no reference of it in our minds to any enjoyment of our own. But, fay they, " the fole original
" fpring of all calm deliberate purpofes of cultivating
" thefe generous affections, and of gratifying them
" in oppofition to any felfifh affections, is this; we ex-
" perience the fublimeft joys of felf-approbation in
" gratifying thefe generous motions; thefe joys are a
" nobler happinefs than any other; and the defire of
" them, flowing from the *calm felfifh determination*,
" is the view of all deliberate purpofes of virtue; tho'
" the kind paffions themfelves often hurry us into
" friendly and generous actions without this thought."

This confiftent
with many difin-
terefted affecti-
ons.
This laft account gives a lovely reprefentation of
human nature and its affections, and leaves a great
deal of room for moft of the generous virtues of life;
but it does not pleafe us with fuch fimplicity as the
other fchemes, which directly deduce every motion of
the heart from *felf-love*. This is not to be reckoned
among the felfifh fchemes, fince it makes all the eminent virtues flow from difinterefted affections, natural to the heart, however in our calmer hours they
may be corroborated by the calm views and defires of
our own happinefs. But our bufinefs is to find the
truth, let the fchemes, or their authors, be claffed as
they will: and, for this purpofe, 'tis neceffary to confider well, both thefe affections alledged to be difinte-

refted, and the *moral faculty* by which we judge of all the motions of the *will;* that we may fee, whether there be in the foul, as we alledged above, another *calm determination,* befide that one toward our own happinefs; as well as many particular affections, terminating upon the good of others, as their immediate and ultimate object, without reference to private intereft of any kind.

II. The *calm felf-love,* or the determination of each *In defires, the* individual toward his own happinefs, is a motion of *uneafinefs differs* the *will* without any uneafy fenfation attending it. *from the motives.* But the feveral felfifh defires, terminating on particular objects, are generally attended with fome uneafy turbulent fenfations in very different degrees: yet thefe fenfations are different from the act of the will to which they are conjoined; and different too from the motives of defire. The motive is fome good apprehended in an object or event, toward which good the defire tends; and, in confequence of defire, fome uneafinefs arifes, till the good is obtained. To averfion, the *motive* is fome evil apprehended or feared, and perhaps not yet felt. Uneafinefs too attends the averfion, untill the evil is repelled. Profpects of the pleafures or powers attending opulence are the motives to the defire of wealth, and never the uneafy feelings attending the defire itfelf. Thefe feelings are, in nature, fubfequent to the defire.

Again, when we obtain the thing defired; befide the pleafures to be obtained from this object, which were the motives of the defire, and often before we

Book I. enjoy them, there is one pleasure immediatly arising from the success, at least in those cases where there was any difficulty in the pursuit, or fear of disappointment. It would be absurd to say that this joy in the success was the motive to the desire. We should have no joy in the success, nor could we have had any desire, unless the prospect of some other good had been the motive. This holds in all our desires, benevolent or selfish, that there is some motive, some end intended, distinct from the joy of success, or the removal of the pain of desire; otherways all desires would be the most fantastick things imaginable, equally ardent toward any trifle, as toward the greatest good; since the joy of success, and the removal of the uneasiness of desire, would be alike in both sorts of desires. 'Tis trifling therefore to say that all desires are selfish, because by gratifying them we obtain the joy of success, and free ourselves from the uneasy feelings of desire.

Subordinate good-will is not virtue.   III. 'Tis owned by all, that many actions, beneficial to others, may directly spring from selfish desires of rewards, of returns of good offices, of honour. One may serve others from fear of unjust violence, or of just punishment. Nay, from the desire of our own happiness we may have an inward undissembled desire of another's happiness, which we conceive to be the means of our own. Thus, one desires the success of a partner in managing the common stock; the prosperity of any country or society upon which his fortunes depend; the advancement of a friend from whom we expect promotion; the fuccefs and good CHAP. 3. conduct of a pupil, which may redound to the honour of the mafter or tutor. Thefe real defires of the welfare of others may all be fubordinate to one's own felfifh defires.

Here tis agreed by all, that defires of the welfare *Whether kind af-* of others, fubordinated to one's defires of his own *fections are ul-timate;* worldly advantages, without any other affection, have nothing virtuous in them. A change of outward circumftances, without any change of temper, would raife defires of the adverfity of others, in the fame manner. The main queftion is, whether the affections reputed benevolent are fubordinated to fome finer interefts than worldly advantages, and ultimately terminate upon them: or, if there are not kind affections ultimately terminating on the good of others; and thefe conftituted by nature, (either alone, or perhaps fometimes corroborated by fome views of intereft,) the immediate caufe of moral approbation. Now 'tis plain,

IV. 1. That all hopes or fears from men, whether *they do not ter-* about wealth or poverty, honour or infamy, bodily *minate upon re-wards from men;* pleafure or pain, can only be motives to external actions or fervices, and not to any inward good-will or defire of their happinefs; fince we all know that our internal affections are hid from others. External deportment alone can be the means of obtaining what we hope from them, or of avoiding what we fear.

2. As felf-love can make us defire only what ap-*nor on thofe from God, or from* pears the means of our own happinefs, one can fcarce *felf-approbati-on.*

BOOK I. alledge that even the fubtileſt intereſts are the ſprings of real good-will to others. If one is aware of the high pleaſures of ſelf-approbation, ariſing upon conſciouſneſs of inward good-will and kind affections, or is convinced that the Deity will confer rewards upon men of ſuch tempers; theſe two motives may make one deſire to have that uſeful ſet of affections, in order to obtain happineſs. Now, could we by command of the will directly raiſe what affections we deſire, from theſe motives we would raiſe kind affections. But a temper or ſet of affections cannot thus be raiſed. As eſteem cannot be raiſed, by any act of the will, toward an object in which no excellence appears, nor fear where there is nothing formidable, nor anger where there is nothing hurtful, nor pity where there is no ſuffering, nor gratitude where there has been no evidence of prior benevolence; ſo neither can a mind wholly determined toward ſelfiſh good raiſe in itſelf kind affections, by a command of its will. The natural cauſe muſt be preſented before any affection can be raiſed.

How divine laws operate to make men virtuous. If indeed our hearts are ſo conſtituted, as the aſſertors of diſintereſted affections alledge, that upon preſenting the ſtate of any ſenſitive beings to our calm thoughts, when no oppoſition of intereſts or evil diſpoſitions apprehended in them obſtruct the natural motion of our ſouls, a kind good-will naturally ariſes; then the motives of gaining the nobler pleaſures of ſelf-approbation, or rewards from God, will incline us to turn our calm attention to the ſtate of others; will furmount little interfering interefts, and remove even CHAP. 3. the obftacles of anger *. The fame motives will make us inquire alfo into all fuch qualities excellencies or good offices of others as are the natural occafions of the warmer and more endearing affections. And thus it is that the fanctions of the divine laws can influence our affections. But,

3. From felf-love we defire only the means of our own happinefs. Now the *actual happinefs of others* is neither the caufe nor means of obtaining felf-approbation, nor rewards from God. Our hearts approve us, and God promifes rewards to us, not becaufe others are in fact happy, but becaufe we have fuch kind difpofitions, and act our parts well in their behalf, whether in the event they are happy or not. Our defire therefore of the pleafure of felf-approbation, or of divine rewards, can only make us defire to have thefe affections, and to act a fuitable part. But thefe affections cannot be directly raifed by the will: and whereever they are, they plainly terminate upon the good of others, as the ultimate end intended by them; tho' in our previous confultations with ourfelves, or deliberations about the inward culture of the mind, we may have refolved, with a view to our own perfection

---

* This is the reference to our own higheft and moft noble enjoyments and interefts, which we fee made in fome of the beft writings of the antients, and in Lord *Shaftesbury;* " That, confcious of the in " ward delights and dignity of *virtue* fur- " paffing all other enjoyments, we refolve " to follow all the noble and generous " motions of our hearts in oppofition to " the lower interefts of this life." Not that they imagined we can raife any new affection, by command of the *will*, which nature had not planted and connected with its proper caufes: nor that all generous affections have private good in view. This notion they oppofed with the greateft zeal and ftrength of reafon.

and fublimeſt happineſs, to incourage all ſuch affections in ourſelves, and to turn our attention to all
ſuch conſiderations as are naturally apt to raiſe them;
and to defpiſe all the mean interfering intereſts of this
preſent world. Theſe generous affections often operate where there have been no ſuch previous deliberations and purpoſes of cultivating them; and where
there have been ſuch purpoſes, ſtill the generous affection terminates and reſts upon its natural object,
the good of others; and muſt have had its exiſtence
in the ſoul previous to all deſires and intentions of
cultivating it.

The affections do not ariſe imme-diatly upon our wiſhing to have them. There is nothing ſtrange or unuſual in this that
one ſhould want certain tender generous affections, of
love, eſteem, gratitude, pity, repentance for offences; while yet he earneſtly wiſhes to have them. An
inward temper and a ſet of affections do not ſtart up at
once upon a wiſh or command. Men who have been
careleſs about virtue and piety are often obſerved,
upon approach of danger, and on other occaſions,
heartily wiſhing, from ſelf-love or fear of puniſhment,
that they had love and gratitude to God, warm charity and good-will to their neighbours, meekneſs and
a forgiving temper, and ſorrow for their ſins; and yet
they have a diſtreſſing conſciouſneſs that theſe diſpoſitions do not ariſe in them. In good men theſe affections operate without any intentions of intereſts,
without views of ſelf-approbation, or future rewards.

Nay, are not ſome of theſe kind affections ſtrongeſt
where we leaſt expect honour from men, rewards from

God, or even any confiderable felf-approbation; as CHAP. 3.
the conjugal and parental affections, friendfhip, and
gratitude? However the want of them is much condemned, thefe affections are reputed but a lower kind
of virtue, fome of them fcarce any virtue at all.

V. Some plead that our moft generous affections *All kind affecti-*
are fubordinate to private intereft by means of *fympa-* *ons are not from*
thy, which makes the pleafures and pains, the happi- *fympathy.*
nefs or mifery of others, the conftant caufes of pleafure or pain to ourfelves. We rejoice in feeing others
happy, nay in knowing that they are happy tho' at a
diftance. And in like manner we have pain or forrow
from their mifery. To obtain this pleafure therefore
and to avoid this pain, we have from felf-love, fay
they, an inward defire of their happinefs, undiffem-
bled, tho' fubordinate to our defire of our own. But
this fympathy can never account for all kind affections, tho' it is no doubt a natural principle and a beautiful part of our conftitution. Where it operates alone,
it is uniformly proportioned to the diftrefs or fuffering beheld or imagined without regard to other circumftances, whereas our generous affections are in very different degrees and proportions; we may have a
weaker good-will to any perfon unknown; but how
much ftronger is the affection of gratitude, the love
with efteem toward a worthy character or intimate
friend, the parental affection? This fympathy, if it is
the caufe of all love, muft be a very variable difpofition,
increafing upon benefits received, moral excellence obferved, intimacies, and tyes of blood: for the inward

BOOK I. good-will, the kind affection, is plainly increafed by thefe caufes.

Grant it naturally varied from thefe caufes, yet this fympathy could never account for that immediate ardour of love and good-will which breaks forth toward any character reprefented to us as eminent in moral excellence, before we have had any thoughts, or made any inquiries into his ftate in point of happinefs or mifery. Suppofe him in the remoteft parts of the earth, or in fome other planet. Sure we can know the intention of the foul in its purfuits or affections. Is our own future pleafure in fome fympathetick joys the object upon which every kind affection and every friendly wifh terminates? Does parental care, patriotifm, even when it is deliberately facrificing life for its country, terminate upon fome private joy of its own? when and where is it to be obtained? only a moment or two, before death is to carry us off from all human affairs, and few of us think of knowing the ftate of our furvivors. Should God intimate to a brave man that his death is approaching next moment, and that he fhould have no longer fellow-feeling with mortals or memory of them, but that he would grant his laft wifhes about his children, his friends, his country; would he not as ardently defire their profperity as in any former period of life, tho' his joyful fympathetick imagination would ceafe next moment? how will one account upon this fcheme for thofe anxieties, tender recommendations, advices, and ardent prayers of men a-dying for thofe who were dear to them, tho'

they are perfuaded that they fhall prefently be removed from this ftate and know no more of human affairs?

Our compaffion too toward the diftreffed, tis plain, *Compaffion not*
felfifh.
terminates upon their relief, even when we have no
attention to our own pain.   Nor is the termination of
any defire merely upon the removal of the uneafinefs
which accompanies it.   Thus tho' there may be in nature fome connections of intereft between us and the
objects of our tender affections, yet the affection terminates on their good, is previous to this connexion,
and is the caufe of it.   We therefore rejoice in the
happinefs of our child, our friend, our country, becaufe we previoufly had an ultimate good-will to them.
Nor do we therefore love them or wifh them well becaufe we have obferved that we would derive joy from
their happinefs, and forrow from their mifery. Hence
it is that, the ftronger our previous love and efteem
was, the greater fhall our joy be on account of their
happinefs, and our forrow for their mifery.

This may fuffice to eftablifh that important point, *Some affections*
entirely difinte-
that our nature is fufceptible of affections truly difin- *refted.*
terefted in the ftricteft fenfe, and not directly fubordinated to felf-love, or aiming at private intereft of any
kind. The tyes of blood, benefits received, moral excellence difplayed, tho' we apprehend no advantage
redounding to ourfelves from it, are the natural caufes
of thefe particular kind affections; many of them arife
unmerited; all terminate on the good of others; and
all of them often operate in the foul when it has no

BOOK I. views, or rational ground of hoping for any private advantage; nay when they are involving it in trouble and anxiety

Calm affections and paffions. VI. As we obferved formerly that the particular motions of the will toward private good are, either the calm ftable affections, or turbulent paffions; fo are the particular motions of the generous kind: fome of them are calm, fedate, and fteddy; aiming at the happinefs of their object, whether an individual or a fo ciety, attended with no turbulent fenfations, and only caufing uneafinefs when they are defeated in their intention; others are turbulent, and attended with uneafy fenfations. We may proceed further in this comparifon.

Univerfal benevolence. As there is found in the human mind, when it recollects itfelf, a calm general determination toward perfonal happinefs of the higheft kind it has any notion of; fo we may find a like principle of a generous kind. When upon recollection we prefent to our minds the notion of the greateft poffible fyftem of fenfitive beings, and the higheft happinefs it can enjoy, there is alfo a calm determination to defire it, abftracting from any connection with or fubferviency to our private enjoyment. We fhall find thefe two grand determinations, one toward our own greateft happinefs, the other toward the greateft general good, each independent on the other, each capable of fuch ftrength as to reftrain all the particular affections of its kind, and keep them fubordinate to itfelf.

Whether fhould the felfifh yield to But here arifes a new perplexity in this complex

structure, where these two principles seem to draw dif- CHAP. 3.
ferent ways. Must the generous determination, and
all its particular affections, yield to the selfish one, and
be under its controll? must we indulge their kind motions so far as private interest admits and no further? or
must the selfish yield to the generous? or can we sup-
pose that in this complex system there are two ultimate
principles which may often oppose each other, without any umpire to reconcile their differences? or shall
we deny any original calm determination toward a
publick interest; allowing only a variety of particular
ultimate kind affections; not indeed arising from self-
love, or directly aiming at private good as their natural termination, and yet in all our deliberate counsels
about the general tenor of our conduct, subjected, in
common with all the particular appetites and passions
of the selfish kind, to the original impulse in each one
toward his own perfection and happiness? This last
seems to be the scheme of some excellent authors both
antient and modern.

    To alledge here that, by our reason and reflection, we
may see what was the intention of God the Author
of our Nature in this whole fabrick of our affections;
that he plainly intended the universal happiness, and
that of each individual, as far as it is consistent with
it; and that this intention should be our rule: that we
should therefore restrain and controll, not only all
selfish affections, but even all generous particular affections, within such bounds as the universal interest
requires: this is true in fact, but does not remove the

the benevolent principle or not.

This determined by the moral sense.

BOOK I. difficulty, unlefs we are firft told from what determination of foul, from what motive, are we to comply
with the divine intentions? if from a defire of reward,
then the felfifh calm determination is the fole ultimate
principle of all deliberate counfels in life: if from a
perception of his moral excellence, a defire of imitat-
ing him, and from love and gratitude, then the defire
of moral excellence muft be the fupreme original determination. But this defire of moral excellence, however an original principle, muft prefuppofe fome antecedent determinations of the will as its object. And
among thefe there muft be fome one in which the fupreme moral excellence confifts, otherways our very
fenfe and defire of moral excellence, fince it may recommend many particular affections, which may interfere with each other, will again lead us into a new
labyrinth of perplexity.   The folution of thefe difficulties muft be found by confidering fully that *moral faculty* above-mentioned, to which, in the next
place, we proceed; briefly touching at thofe reafons
which fhew this *moral faculty* to be *an original determination* or *fenfe* in our nature, not capable of being
referred to other powers of perception.

CHAP. IV.

Concerning the Moral Senfe, *or faculty of perceiving moral excellence, and its fupreme objects.*

I. ALTHO' we have kind affections ultimately aim-ing at the good of others, the fuccefs of which is joyful to us, yet our approbation of moral conduct is very different from liking it merely as the occafion of pleafure to ourfelves in gratifying thefe kind affec-tions. As we do not approve all conduct which gives us this pleafure, fo we approve fometimes fuch con-duct as does not give it; and our approbation of the good conduct which gives this pleafure is not propor-tioned to the pleafure it gives us. Thus many in-ventions, and much art and induftry which does good to the perfons or country we love; is not approved as virtuous: we approve generous attempts tho' unfuc-cefsful; we approve the virtues of enemies, which may hurt the chief objects of our love. We equally approve the virtues or generous defigns of good men in for-mer ages toward their contemporaries, or in the re-moteft nations, toward their countrymen, for whom our affections are very faint and weak, as if the like were done to our friends, or country, the objects of our ftrongeft affections.

The notion of moral goodnefs is not giving us pleafure by fym-pathy;

Again----Tho' the approbation of moral excellence is a grateful action or fenfation of the mind, 'tis plain the good approved is not this tendency to give us a

nor pleafing our moral fenfe.

grateful fenfation. As, in approving a beautiful form, we refer the beauty to the object; we do not fay that it is beautiful becaufe we reap fome little pleafure in viewing it, but we are pleafed in viewing it becaufe it is antecedently beautiful. Thus, when we admire the virtue of another, the whole excellence, or that quality which by nature we are determined to approve, is conceived to be in that other; we are pleafed in the contemplation becaufe the object is excellent, and the object is not judged to be therefore excellent becaufe it gives us pleafure.

nor that of ufe-fulnefs to the agent ; II. Much lefs is it the approved fpecies of virtue, that it is an affection or action which gives pleafure to the agent. It always may indeed give him pleafure upon reflection, by means of this moral faculty: but 'tis plainly *then* that we moft admire the virtue of another when we attend to its labours, dangers, difficulties, pains; and have no thought of any prefent or future pleafures of the agent.

or to the appro-ver; 'Tis ftrange that men fhould be at a lofs to difcern what form, or conception, or fpecies it is, under which they approve efteem or admire their own affections and conduct, or that of others; and difapprove and condemn the contrary. One would think it manifeft that the notion under which one approves virtue, is neither its tendency to obtain any benefit or reward to the agent or to the approver. The approver never expects a reward for the virtue of another; he approves where he fees no intereft of his own promoted: and he would lefs approve fuch actions as are

beneficent, the more he confidered them as advantageous to the agent, and imagined him influenced by
the views of his own advantage. Actions are conceived
rewardable becaufe they are good, not good becaufe
they are to be rewarded. Both the fpectator and the
agent value good actions the more in point of virtue,
the more expenfive or difadvantageous they are to the
agent; and both will difapprove as immoral fome actions which the one will allure to by bribes, and the
other undertake; both conceiving them in this manner advantageous.

Now, if direct explicite opinions of tendencies to *nor imaginations*
the advantage of the approver or agent do not raife *of advantage.*
moral approbation, much lefs can we fuppofe that any
confufed imaginations, or vague affociations of ideas,
about fuch advantages to the approver or the agent,
can be the form under which virtue is approved.

'Tis alfo obvious that the notion under which we
approve virtue is not its tendency to procure honour.
A profpect of honour may be a motive to the agent,
at leaft to external actions: but the tendency of an action to procure honour cannot make another approve
it, who derives no honour from it. Our very defire of
gaining honour, and the difpofition in fpectators to
confer it, muft prefuppofe a moral fenfe in both. And
any views an agent may have to obtain felf-approbation muft alfo prefuppofe a moral fenfe. We cannot
therefore fay an action is judged good becaufe it gains
to the agent the pleafure of felf-approbation; but it
gains to him this pleafure becaufe it was antecedent-

BOOK I. ly good, or had that quality which by the conftitution of this fenfe we muft approve. Our prefent queftion is, what is that quality, and how perceived?

Not conformity to laws;　III. The primary notion under which we approve
is not merely a *conformity to the divine will or laws.*
We ferioufly inquire about the moral goodnefs, juftice,
holinefs, rectitude, of the Divine Nature itfelf, and
likewife of his will or laws; thefe characters make up
our common praifes of them. They furely mean more
than that *his will or laws are conformable to themfelves.* This we might afcribe to an artful impure Demon. Conformity to his nature is not conformity to
immenfity, eternity, omnipotence. 'Tis conformity
to his goodnefs, holinefs, juftice. Thefe moral perfections then muft be previoufly known, or elfe the
definition by *conformity to them* is ufelefs.

nor conformity to truth.　Neither is the notion of moral goodnefs under
which we approve it well explained by conformity of
affections and actions to *truth, reafon, true propofitions, reafon of things;* as in the common acceptation
thefe characters agree to every object of the mind, a-
bout which it judges truly, animate or inanimate, virtuous or vicious. *Conformity to moral truth,* or true
propofitions about morals, equally belongs to virtue
and vice; as the mind difcerns truth about both;
and, as every true propofition is conformed to its object, fo is the object to the propofition. If 'tis faid
that thefe moral truths intended are only fuch as fhew
what actions are *good,* what we are *obliged to do,* what
ought to be done. Thefe words mean no more than the

word moral goodnefs; and then the definition is no better than this, " the moral goodnefs of an action is its
" conformity to fuch true propofitions as fhew the
" action to be good;" or, " good actions are fuch a-
" bout which 'tis true that *they are good.*"

In general, all defcriptions of moral goodnefs by
conformity to reafon if we examine them well, muft
lead us to fome immediate original fenfe or determination of our nature. All reafons exciting to an action will lead us to fome original affection or inftinct
of will; and all juftifying reafons, or fuch as fhew an
action to be good, will at laft lead us to fome original fenfe or power of perception.

In like manner all defcriptions of it by *fitnefs, con-* *or fitnefs, con-*
gruity, agreement, muft lead us to thefe original de- *gruity, &c.*
terminations. The fitnefs of means or fubordinate
ends, does not prove them to be good, unlefs the ultimate end be good. Now fitnefs of an end truly ultimate muft be an abfurd expreffion; as it is referred
to nothing, or is fit for nothing further. All ultimate
ends are fetled by fome of the original determinations of our nature.*

'Tis in vain here to alledge inftruction, education,
cuftom, or affociation of ideas as the original of moral
approbation. As thefe can give no new fenfes, let us examine what the opinion or what the notion is upon which
we approve, and to what fenfe it belongs, whatever
way the notion may have been conjoined, or whatever

---

* A compleat examination of thefe cha- | prefent defign; we muft therefore refer to
racters would call us off too much from the | *the illuftrations on the moral fenfe.*

Book I. have been the caufes of our getting this opinion that
ﬧﬧﬧﬧﬧ ſuch a quality is inherent in or connected with the
action? and this will lead us to an original principle.

There is a mo-
ral ſenſe.
 IV. There is therefore, as each one by cloſe attention and reflection may convince himſelf, a natural and immediate determination to approve certain
affections, and actions conſequent upon them; or a natural ſenſe of immediate excellence in them, not referred to any other quality perceivable by our other ſenſes or by reaſoning. When we call this determination
a *ſenſe* or *inſtinct*, we are not ſuppoſing it of that low
kind dependent on bodily organs, ſuch as even the
brutes have. It may be a conſtant ſetled determination in the ſoul itſelf, as much as our powers of judging
and reaſoning. And 'tis pretty plain that *reaſon* is only a ſubſervient power to our ultimate determinations
either of perception or will. The ultimate end is ſetled
by ſome ſenſe, and ſome determination of will: by ſome
ſenſe we enjoy happineſs, and ſelf-love determines to
it without reaſoning. Reaſon can only direct to the
means; or compare two ends previouſly conſtituted
by ſome other immediate powers.

This plainly a-
nalogous to other
parts of nature.
 In other animal-kinds each one has inſtincts toward its proper action, and has the higheſt enjoyment
in following them, even with toil and ſome pain. Can
we ſuppoſe mankind void of ſuch principles? as brutes
ſeem not to reflect on their own temper and actions,
or that of others, they may feel no more than preſent
delight in following their impulſes. But in men, who
can make their own tempers and conduct the ob-

jects of reflection, the analogy of nature would make
one expect a fenfe, a relifh about them, as well as a-
bout other objects. To each of our powers we feem to
have a correfponding tafte or fenfe, recommending
the proper ufe of it to the agent, and making him relifh or value the like exercife of it by another. This
we fee as to the powers of voice, of imitation, defigning, or machinery, motion, reafoning; there is a
fenfe difcerning and recommending the proper exercife of them. It would be anomalous in our ftructure if we had no relifh or tafte for powers and actions of yet greater importance; if a fpecies of which
each one is naturally capable of very contrary affections toward its fellows, and of confequent actions, each
one alfo requiring a conftant intercourfe of actions
with them, and dependant on them for his fubfiftence,
had not an immediate relifh for fuch affections and
actions as the intereft of the fyftem requires. Shall an
immediate fenfe recommend the proper ufe of the inferior powers, and yet fhall we allow no natural relifh for that of the fuperior?

V. As fome others of our immediate perceptive *This fenfe re-*
powers are capable of culture and improvement, fo is *quires culture and improve-*
this moral fenfe, without prefuppofing any reference *ment.*
to a fuperior power of reafon to which their perceptions are to be referred. We once had pleafure in the
fimple artlefs tunes of the vulgar. We indulge ourfelves in mufick; we meet with finer and more complex compofitions. In thefe we find a pleafure much
higher, and begin to defpife what formerly pleafed us.

Book I. A judge, from the motions of pity, gets many crimi-
nals acquitted: we approve this fweet tendernefs of
heart. But we find that violence and outrages abound;
the fober, juft, and induftrious are plagued, and have
no fecurity. A more extenfive view of a publick intereft fhews fome forts of pity to occafion more extenfive mifery, than arifes from a ftrict execution of juftice. Pity of itfelf never appears deformed; but a
more extenfive affection, a love to fociety, a zeal to
promote general happinefs, is a more lovely principle,
and the want of this renders a character deformed.
This only fhews, what we fhall prefently confirm, that
among the feveral affections approved there are many degrees: fome much more lovely than others. 'Tis
thus alone we correct any apparent diforders in this
moral faculty, even as we correct our reafon itfelf. As we
improve and correct a low tafte for harmony by enur-
ing the ear to finer compofitions; a low tafte for beauty, by prefenting the finer works, which yield an higher pleafure; fo we improve our *moral tafte* by prefenting larger fyftems to our mind, and more extenfive
affections toward them; and thus finer objects are exhibited to the moral faculty, which it will approve,
even when thefe affections oppofe the effect of fome
narrower affections, which confidered by themfelves
would be truly lovely. No need here of reference to
an higher power of perception, or to reafon.

Is not our reafon itfelf alfo often wrong, when we
rafhly conclude from imperfect or partial evidence?
muft there be an higher power too to correct our rea-

son? no; prefenting more fully all the evidence on
both fides, by ferious attention, or the beft exercife
of the reafoning power, corrects the hafty judgment.
Juft fo in the moral perceptions.

VI. This moral fenfe from its very nature appears *The moral fenfe*
to be defigned for regulating and controlling all our *deftined to go-*
vern our other
powers. This dignity and commanding nature we *powers.*
are immediatly confcious of, as we are confcious of
the power itfelf. Nor can fuch matters of immediate
feeling be otherways proved but by appeals to our
hearts. * It does not eftimate the good it recommends
as merely differing in degree, tho' of the fame kind
with other advantages recommended by other fenfes,
fo as to allow us to practife fmaller moral evils acknowledged to remain fuch, in order to obtain fome great
advantages of other forts; or to omit what we judge
in the prefent cafe to be our duty or morally good,
that we may decline great evils of another fort. But as
we immediatly perceive the difference in kind, and that
the dignity of enjoyment from fine poetry, painting,
or from knowledge is fuperior to the pleafures of the
palate, were they never fo delicate; fo we immediatly
difcern moral good to be fuperior in kind and dignity to all others which are perceived by the other perceptive powers.

In all other grateful perceptions, the lefs we fhall
relifh our ftate, the greater facrifice we have made of

* Thus the Stoick in *Cicero de Fin.* | *aeftimatio genere valet, non magnitudine.*
l. iii. c. 10. *Bonum hoc, de quo agimus, eft* | ——*Alia eft aeftimatio virtutis, quae gene-*
illud quidem plurimi aeftimandum, fed ea | *re, non crefcendo valet.*

inferior enjoyments to the superior; and our sense of the superior, after the first flutter of joy in our success is over, is not a whit increased by any sacrifice we have made to it: nay in the judgment of spectators, the superior enjoyment, or our state at least, is generally counted the worse on this account, and our conduct the less relished. Thus in sacrificing ease, or health, or pleasure, to wealth, power, or even to the ingenious arts; their pleasures gain no dignity by that means; and the conduct is not more alluring to others. But in moral good, the greater the necessary sacrifice was which was made to it, the moral excellence increases the more, and is the more approved by the agent, more admired by spectators, and the more they are roused to imitation. By this sense the heart can not only approve itself in sacrificing every other gratification to moral goodness, but have the highest self-enjoyment, and approbation of its own disposition in doing so: which plainly shews this moral sense to be naturally destined to command all the other powers.

The chief objects of approbation are kind affections.

VII. Let us next consider the several powers or dispositions approved or disapproved by this faculty. And here 'tis plain that the primary objects of this faculty are the affections of the will, and that the several affections which are approved, tho' in very different degrees, yet all agree in one general character, of tendency to the happiness of others, and to the moral perfection of the mind possessing them. No actions, however in fact beneficial to society, are approved as virtuous if they are imagined to flow from no inward

CHAP. 4.

good-will to any perſon, or from ſuch diſpoſitions as do not naturally ſuppoſe good-will in the agent, or at leaſt exclude the higheſt ſelfiſhneſs. The deſires of glory, or even of rewards in a future ſtate, were they ſuppoſed the ſole affections moving an agent in the moſt beneficial ſervices, without any love to God, eſteem of his moral excellencies, gratitude to him, or good-will to men, would not obtain our approbation as morally good diſpoſitions: and yet a firm belief of future happineſs to be obtained by Divine appointment, upon our doing beneficent actions, might be as ſteddy and effectual a cauſe of or motive to ſuch actions as any other. But mere deſire of one's own happineſs, without any love to God, or man, is never the object of approbation. This itſelf may ſhew us how diſtinct moral approbation is from a perſuaſion of the tendency of actions to the intereſt of the approver, ſince he might hope equally great advantages from ſuch a ſteddy intereſted diſpoſition to actions in fact beneficent, as from any kind affection.

That ſome ſort of benevolent affections, or ſome *This evident from experience.* diſpoſitions imagined to be connected with them, are the natural objects of approbation; and the oppoſite affections, or the want of the kind ones, the objects of condemnation, will be plain from almoſt all our reaſonings in praiſing or cenſuring, applauding or condemning the characters and actions of mankind. We point out ſome kind or beneficent intention, or ſome beneficent purpoſes propoſed by the agent in what we praiſe, or would vindicate from cenſure. We ſhew some detriment enfuing to others, either intended or known, or what eafily might have been known by one who had any tender regard for the interefts of others, as the evidence either of ill-nature in the agent, or fuch felfifhnefs, or fuch felfifh paffions as over-power all kindnefs and humanity.

A decency and a dignity diftinct from virtue. VIII. There is a plain gradation in the objects of our approbation and condemnation, from the indifferent fet of actions afcending to the higheft virtue, or defcending to the loweft vice. It is not eafy to fetle exactly the feveral intermediate fteps in due order, but the higheft and loweft are manifeft. The indifferent affections and actions are fuch as purfue the innocent advantages of the agent without any detriment to fociety, and yet without any reference made by the agent to any good of others. Such are the neceffary and moderate gratifications of appetite, and many trifling actions. To explain the different degrees, we muft obferve, what was hinted at formerly, that befide the moral approbation of virtue, there is alfo another relifh or fenfe of a certain dignity or decency in many difpofitions and actions not conceived as virtuous. Thus we value the purfuits of the ingenious arts, and of knowledge, nay even fome bodily perfections, fuch as ftrength and agility, more than mere brutal fenfuality. We in like manner value more in another activity, patience of labour, fagacity, and fpirit in bufinefs, provided they are not injurious, tho' we conceive them folely exercifed for his own promotion to wealth and honour, than a lazy inactive indolence.

The calm defire of private good, tho' it is not approved as virtue, yet it is far from being condemned
as vice. And none of the truly natural and felfifh appetites and paffions are of themfelves condemned as
evil, when they are within certain bounds, even tho'
they are not referred by the agent to any publick intereft. It was neceffary for the general good that all
fuch affections fhould be implanted in our fpecies; and
therefore it would have been utterly unnatural to
have made them matter of difapprobation even while
they were not hurtful. Nay, as thefe felfifh affections
are aiming at an end neceffary to the general good,
to wit the good of each individual, and as the abilities
of gratifying them are powers which may be very ufe-
fully employed in fubferviency to the moft generous
affections, it was highly proper and benign in the Author of Nature to invite us to the culture of thefe
powers by an immediate relifh for them wherever we
obferve them, in ourfelves or in others; tho this relifh is plainly different from moral approbation.

We all have by confcioufnefs and experience a notion of the human conftitution, and of a certain proportion of affections requifite to an innocent character. The felfifh affections are then only difap-
proved when we imagine them beyond that innocent proportion, fo as to exclude or over-power the
amiable affections, and engrofs the mind wholly to
the purpofes of felfifhnefs, or even to obftruct the proper degree of the generous affections in the ftation and
circumftances of the agent.

Degrees of virtue; first some abilities and dispositions different from kind affections.

IX. But there is another set of dispositions and abilities still of a finer nature, tho' distinct from both the calm universal benevolence and the particular kind affections; which however are naturally connected with such affections, natural evidences of them, and plainly inconsistent with the highest sorts of selfishness and sensuality; and these seem immediate objects of the *moral sense*, tho' perhaps not the highest. They seem to be approved immediatly, even before we think of this connexion with disinterested affections, or imagine directly that the agent is referring them to beneficent purposes. Of these moral dispositions there are several sorts, all immediatly approved, unless the mind directly discerns that they are employed in vicious purposes. Thus is fortitude approved, as it imports that something moral is more valued than life, and as plainly inconsistent with the highest selfishness: if indeed it be seen employed in rapine, and merely selfish purposes, such as those of lust or avarice, it becomes the object of horror. Candour, and openness of mind, and sincerity, can scarce ever be unattended with a kind honest heart; as 'tis virtue and innocence alone which need no disguise. And these dispositions too are immediatly approved, perhaps before we think of this connexion; so is also a stedfast principle of veracity whenever we speak.

When veracity is approved.

I know not if CICERO's account of this be exact; " that we naturally desire knowledge, and are averse " to ignorance, and error, and being deceived; and " thence relish these dispositions which are the natu-

" ral means of knowledge, and the prefervatives a-
" gainft deceptions." Veracity feems to be immediatly and ftrongly approved, and that from our infancy;
as we fee the firft natural impulfe of the young mind
is to fpeak truth, till by experiencing fome inconveniencies it is taught to counteract the natural impulfe. One
needs not mention here courtefy and good manners :
they are the very drefs of virtue, the direct profeffion
of kind affections, and are thus approved. As all thefe
abilities and difpofitions are of great importance in
life, highly beneficial to mankind when exerted in
confequence of kind affections, and are naturally connected with them, or exclude the oppofite extreme, 'tis
with the higheft goodnefs and wifdom that they are
immediatly recommended to our approbation by the
conftitution of our *moral faculty.*

But of all fuch difpofitions of our nature, different *The relifh and*
from all our kind affections, none is fo nearly connec- *defire of moral*
ted with them, none fo natural an evidence of them, *excellence.*
none fo immediatly and neceffarily fubfervient to them,
as an acute moral fenfe itfelf, a ftrong defire of moral excellence, with an high relifh of it wherever it is
obferved. We do not call the power or fenfe itfelf virtuous; but the having this fenfe in an high degree naturally raifes a ftrong defire of having all generous affections; it furmounts all the little obftacles to them,
and determines the mind to ufe all the natural means
of raifing them. Now, as the mind can make any of
its own powers the object of its reflex contemplation,
this high fenfe of moral excellence is approved above

all other abilities. And the confequent defire of moral excellence, the confequent ftrong love, efteem, and good-will to the perfons where it is found, are immediatly approved, as moft amiable affections, and the higheft virtues.

The degrees recited. X. Having premifed thefe confiderations, we may obferve the following degrees of approbation, as they arife above what is merely indifferent.

Certain abilities of dignity. 1. One may rank in the firft ftep, as the object of fome fort of efteem or good liking, the exercife even of thofe more manly powers, which have no neceffary or natural connexion with virtue, but fhew a tafte above fenfuality and the lower felfifhnefs: fuch as the purfuits of the ingenious arts, of the elegance of life, and fpeculative fciences. Every one fees a dignity in thefe pleafures, and muft relifh the defires of them; and indeed they are far lefs oppofite to virtue, or the publick intereft, than keen taftes or appetites of a lower kind.

2. 'Tis plain however, that our moral fenfe puts a much higher value upon abilities and difpofitions immediatly connected with virtuous affections, and which exclude the worft forts of felfifhnefs. Thus candour, veracity, fortitude, and a ftrong fenfe of honour, have a moral eftimation above other abilities.

Calm kind affections more approved than paffions. 3. But to come to the more immediate objects of moral approbation, the kind affections themfelves; 'tis certain that, among affections of equal extent, we more approve the calm ftable refolute purpofes of heart, than the turbulent and paffionate. And that,

of affections in this respect alike, we more approve CHAP. 4.
thofe which are more extenfive, and lefs approve
thofe which are more confined. Thus, the ftable conjugal and parental love, or the refolute calm purpofe
of promoting the true happinefs of perfons thus related to us, is preferable to the turbulent paffionate difpofitions of tendernefs. And the love of a fociety, a
country, is more excellent than domeftick affections.
We fee plainly the fuperior dignity in thefe cafes from
this, that, notwithftanding the ftruggle felt in our
breafts, and the oppofition made by the paffionate or
more limited affections, yet, when we refolutely follow the calm and extenfive notwithftanding of this
oppofition, the foul in its calmeft hours and moft deliberate reflections approves of its own conduct; and
fcarce ever fails to approve the like conduct in others
at once; as in the cafe of others its paffions are not
raifed to give oppofition. On the contrary, when we
have yielded to the paffion or the limited affection, in
oppofition to the calm or more extenfive principle,
the foul upon reflection is diffatisfied with itfelf, and
at firft view it condemns the like conduct in others.

Extenfive more approved than the narrow.

That difpofition therefore which is moft excellent,
and naturally gains the higheft moral approbation, is
the calm, ftable, univerfal good-will to all, or the moft
extenfive benevolence. And this feems the moft diftinct notion we can form of the moral excellency of
the Deity.

The chief moral excellence, univerfal good-will,

Another difpofition infeparable from this in men,
and probably in all beings who are capable of fuch ex-

and love of this affection.

tenfive affection, is the relifh or approbation of this affection, and a naturally confequent defire of this moral excellence, and an efteem and good-will of an higher kind to all in whom it is found. This love of moral excellence is alfo an high object of approbation, when we find it in ourfelves by reflection, or obferve it in another. It is a pretty different affection from benevolence or the defire of communicating happinefs; and is as it were in another order of affections; fo that one cannot well determine whether it can be compared with the other. It feems co-ordinate, and the higheft poffible of that kind; never in oppofition to benevolence, nay always confpiring with and affifting it. This defire of moral excellence, and love to the mind where it refides, with the confequent acts of efteem, veneration, truft, and refignation, are the effence of true piety toward God.

We never fpeak of benevolence toward God; as that word carries with it fome fuppofal of indigence, or want of fome good, in the object. And yet, as we have benevolence toward a friend when he may need our affiftance; fo, the fame emotion of foul, or the fame difpofition toward him, fhall remain when he is raifed to the beft ftate we can wifh; and it then exerts itfelf in congratulation, or rejoicing in his happinefs. In this manner may our fouls be affected toward the Deity, without any fuppofition of his indigence, by the higheft joy and complacence in his abfolute happinefs.

The degrees of vice.   XI. 'Tis eafy to obferve the like gradation from the

indifferent ftate of the foul through the feveral degrees of moral turpitude. The firft may be the want
of thefe more reputable abilities; which indeed implies
no evil affection, and yet plainly makes a character
defpicable, tho' not immoral. Thus we diflike the
imprudent conduct of any man with refpect to his
own intereft, without thinking of any detriment to
arife to fociety from it. Thus negligence, rafhnefs,
floth, indolence, are naturally difliked, abftracting
from their effects upon fociety. So is a mind infenfible to the more manly pleafures of arts and genius.
When indeed imprudent conduct, in point of private
intereft, is confidered alfo as affecting a publick, or
fome other perfons than the agent, whofe interefts he
ought to have regarded, as it generally does; then it
may be matter of high moral condemnation and remorfe: fo may the meannefs of our talents or abilities,
when occafioned by our immoderate floth and fenfuality, and a defect of generous affections.

1. The objects of the gentleft moral difapprobati- *Several degrees*
on or cenfure are thofe cafes " where one in gratify- *recited.*
" ing fome lovely narrower affection has inadvertent-
" ly omitted what would have moft tended to the
" publick good." Such is the promcting a good friend
or benefactor in oppofition to a competitor of fuperi-
or merit and abilities. The preferring, in fuch cafes, a
lefs worthy friend to one's felf, may be cenfured indeed as a want of due proportion among thefe lovely affections, when a more extenfive one yields to the more
limited; but the moral beauty of fome limited affecti-

ons is so great that we readily overlook some defects in the more extensive. The same is the case if one has served a friend at a trouble or expence to himself much above the value of the good he has done his friend; perhaps too incapacitating himself for some wiser services hereafter. Where indeed one preferred to himself a friend of equal merit, the publick interest is as well promoted this way, and a beautiful affection of friendship is displayed. And yet the contrary conduct, when there are no special circumstances pleading for a friend, could not be censured as immoral.

2. Other objects of lighter censure are those actions detrimental to the publick which a person is forced to do to avoid death torture or slavery; when yet the publick detriment is still greater than those evils he avoids. Here the agent may have no ill will; nay may have many generous affections, tho' not of that heroick strength which the moral sense would recommend. The guilt is exceedingly extenuated by the greatness of the temptation, which few have sufficient strength of soul to resist. In order to retain the character of innocence, we expect, not only the absence of all malicious dispositions, but many good affections, and those too of an extensive nature; with much caution about the interests of others. The precise degrees cannot well be determined; nor is it necessary. But the stronger and the more extensive the generous affections are, so much the better is the temper; the lower they are, and the more that any opposite or narrower ones prevail against them, so much the temper is the worse.

'Tis our bufinefs to aim at the higheft moral excellence, and not content ourfelves with merely avoiding
infamy or cenfure.

3. Another degree of vice are the fudden paffionate
motions of anger, refentment, and ill-will, upon provocation either falfely apprehended, or aggravated beyond any real ground. Such paffions when they lead
to injury are vicious, tho' not in the higheft degree.
When indeed by indulgence they turn into habitual
rancour and fettled malice or revenge, they form a
moft odious charaƈter.

4. A more deformed fort of vice is when the felfifh
paffions and fenfual appetites lead men into like injuries. Thefe are worfe excufes and weaker extenuati-
ons of guilt than the angry paffions.

5. A degree more deformed is when calm felfifhnefs raifes deliberate purpofes of injury known to be
fuch. In thefe cafes the moral faculty muft be quite
over-powered, and deprived of all its natural force in
the foul, and fo muft all humanity. The like is the cafe
when men from mere felfifhnefs, without any grievous
temptation, or without any motives of publick intereft, counteraƈt their moral fentiments by falfehood,
treachery, ingratitude, a negleƈt of honour, or low
cowardice dreading to lofe fome pofitive advantages,
even while there is no fuch evil impending as could
much affeƈt a brave and good man.

6. In this clafs, or rather in a worfe one, we muft
rank impiety, or the want of all due affeƈtions to the
Deity, when he is known and conceived to be good.

VOL. I.   K

Book I. Our moral faculty muſt be ſtrangely aſleep where the deſire of knowing the Supreme Excellence is a-wanting, or love to it when it is known: or where there is no care to cultivate devout affections of gratitude where there have been the greateſt benefits received, and where they are repeated every moment.

There is a diſpoſition ſtill worſe, conceivable in the abſtract, but ſcarce incident to mankind, or the creatures of a good Deity; a fixed unprovoked original malice, or a deſire of the miſery of others for itſelf, without any motives of intereſt.

The moral ſenſe reduces all our powers into order. XII. Without a diſtinct conſideration of this moral faculty, a ſpecies endued with ſuch a variety of ſenſes, and of deſires frequently interfering, muſt appear a complex confuſed fabrick, without any order or regular conſiſtent deſign. By means of it, all is capable of harmony, and all its powers may conſpire in one direction, and be conſiſtent with each other. 'Tis already proved that we are capable of many generous affections ultimately terminating on the good of others, neither ariſing from any ſelfiſh view, nor terminating on private good. This moral faculty plainly ſhews that we are alſo capable of a calm ſettled univerſal benevolence, and that this is deſtined, as the ſupreme determination of the generous kind, to govern and controll our particular generous as well as ſelfiſh affections; as the heart muſt entirely approve its doing thus in its calmeſt reflections: even as in the order of ſelfiſh affections, our ſelf-love, or our calm regard to the greateſt private intereſt controlls our particu-

lar felfifh paffions; and the heart is fatisfied in its doing fo.

To acknowledge the feveral generous ultimate af- *Calm felf-love*
fections of a limited kind to be natural, and yet main- *not the fupreme*
tain that we have no general controlling principle *principle.*
but felf-love, which indulges or checks the generous
affections as they conduce to, or oppofe, our own nobleft intereft; fometimes allowing thefe kind affections their full exercife, becaufe of that high enjoyment
we expect to ourfelves in gratifying them; at other
times checking them, when their gratification does
not over-ballance the lofs we may fuftain by it; is a
fcheme which brings indeed all the powers of the
mind into one direction by means of the reference
made of them all to the calm defire of our own happinefs, in our previous deliberations about our conduct: and it may be juftly alledged that the Author
of Nature has made a connexion in the event at laft
between our gratifying our generous affections, and
our own higheft intereft. But the feelings of our heart,
reafon, and hiftory, revolt againft this account: which
feems however to have been maintained by excellent
authors and ftrenuous defenders of the caufe of virtue.

This connexion of our own higheft interefts with
the gratifying our generous affections, in many cafes
is imperceptible to the mind; and the kind heart acts
from its generous impulfe, not thinking of its own intereft. Nay all its own interefts have fometimes appeared to it as oppofite to, and inconfiftent with the
generous part, in which it perfifted. Now were there

no other calm original determination of soul but that toward one's own intereſt, that man muſt be approved intirely who ſteadily purſues his own happineſs, in oppoſition to all kind affections and all publick intereſt. That which is the ſole calm determination, muſt juſtify every action in conſequence of it, however oppoſite to particular kind affections. If it be ſaid "that 'tis a miſtake to imagine our intereſt oppoſite "to them while there is a good providence:" grant it to be a miſtake; this is only a defect of reaſoning: but that diſpoſition of mind muſt upon this ſcheme be approved which coolly ſacrifices the intereſt of the univerſe to its own intereſt. This is plainly contrary to the feelings of our hearts.

Another ulti-
mate determina-
tion of will to-
ward publick
good.

　　Can that be deemed the ſole ultimate determination, the ſole ultimate end, which the mind in the exerciſe of its nobleſt powers can calmly reſolve, with inward approbation, deliberately to counteract? are there not inſtances of men who have voluntarily ſacrificed their lives, without thinking of any other ſtate of exiſtence, for the ſake of their friends or their country? does not every heart approve this temper and conduct, and admire it the more, the leſs preſumption there is of the love of glory and poſtumous fame, or of any ſublimer private intereſt mixing itſelf with the generous affection? does not the admiration riſe higher, the more deliberately ſuch reſolutions are formed and executed? all this is unqueſtionably true, and yet would be abſurd and impoſſible if ſelf-intereſt of any kind is the ſole ultimate termination of all

calm defire. There is therefore another ultimate determination which our fouls are capable of, deftined to
be alfo an original fpring of the calmeft and moft deliberate purpofes of action; a defire of communicating
happinefs, an ultimate good-will, not referred to any
private intereft, and often operating without fuch reference.

In thofe cafes where fome inconfiftency appears between thefe two determinations, the moral faculty at
once points out and recommends the glorious the a-
miable part; not by fuggefting profpects of future interefts of a fublime fort by pleafures of felf-approbation, or of praife. It recommends the generous part
by an immediate undefinable perception; it approves
the kind ardour of the heart in the facrificing even
life itfelf, and that even in thofe who have no hopes
of furviving, or no attention to a future life in another world. And thus, where the moral fenfe is in its
full vigour, it makes the generous determination to
publick happinefs the fupreme one in the foul, with
that commanding power which it is naturally deftined to exercife.

*Which the mo-
ral faculty fhews
deftined to con-
troll all others.*

It muft be obvious we are not fpeaking here of the
ordinary condition of mankind, as if thefe calm determinations were generally exercifed, and habitually controlled the particular paffions; but of the condition our nature can be raifed to by due culture; and
of the principles which may and ought to operate,
when by attention we prefent to our minds the objects or reprefentations fit to excite them. Doubtlefs

ſome good men have exerciſed in life only the particular kind affections, and found a conſtant approbation of them, without either the moſt extenſive views
of the whole ſyſtem, or the moſt univerſal benevolence.
Scarce any of the vicious have ever conſidered wherein it is that their higheſt private happineſs conſiſts,
and in conſequence of it exerted the calm rational
ſelf-love; but merely follow inconſiderately the ſelfiſh
appetites and affections. Much leſs have all good
men made actual references of all private or generous
affections to the extenſive benevolence, tho' the mind
can make them; or bad men made references of all
their affections to calm ſelf-love.

Comparing, rea-
ſoning, laws, re-
ligion, ſtill ne-
ceſſary.   XIII. But as the ſelfiſh principles are very ſtrong,
and by cuſtom, by early and frequent indulgences, and
other cauſes, are raiſed in the greateſt part of men
above their due proportion, while the generous principles are little cultivated, and the moral ſenſe often
aſleep; our powers of reaſoning and comparing the ſeveral enjoyments which our nature is capable of, that we
may diſcover which of them are of greateſt conſequence
to our happineſs; our capacity, by reaſoning, of arri-
ving to the knowledge of a *Governing Mind* preſiding
in this world, and of a moral adminiſtration, are of
the higheſt conſequence and neceſſity to preſerve our
affections in a juſt order, and to corroborate our *moral*
faculty: as by ſuch reaſoning and reflection we may diſcover a perfect conſiſtency of all the generous motions
of the ſoul with private intereſt, and find out a certain tenor of life and action the moſt effectually ſub-

fervient to both thefe determinations. This fhall be the fubject of fome following chapters, after we fhall have fubjoined fome further confirmation of thefe moral principles, from the fenfe of honour; and obferved the univerfality of both, and how far they feem uniform principles in our fpecies.

CHAP. V.

The Senfe of Honour and Shame explained. The univerfal influence of the Moral Senfe, and that of Honour, and their uniformity.

I. IF we confult our own feelings we muft acknowledge that as there are certain affections and actions which we naturally approve, and efteem, and praife, fo there is an immediate grateful fenfation felt when we are approved and praifed by others, and generally a moft uneafy one when we are cenfured; without the expectation of any other advantages or difadvantages which may thence accrue to us. A more diftinct confideration of this fenfe of honour and fhame will much confirm the preceding account of our *moral faculty*.

Senfe of honour an immediate principle.

They who refer all the motions of the heart to private intereft, and would reduce all our perceptive powers to a very fmall number, by one artful reference or another, depart exceedingly from nature in their accounts of thofe determinations about honour and fhame, which are acknowledged to appear univerfally among men.

Abftracted from private intereft.

They tell us "our honouring a man is merely reput-
"ing him useful to us either explicitely, and thus we
"honour the generous and beneficent, with whom we
"have intercourse, and by whose offices we are profi-
"ted; or implicitely, and by some confused imagina-
"tions, and thus we honour *heroes* who lived in prior
"ages, or remote nations, imagining they are our
"contemporaries or countrymen ; or thinking that
"they would be very useful to us if we had intercourse
"with them. And thus our esteem is only an opini-
"on of a character or conduct as useful to us, and a
"liking it on this account." And, say they, " we de-
"sire to be honoured, or reputed useful to others, not
"from an immediate sensation, but because we know
"that men are studious of serving such as they ho-
"nour and repute useful to them; not indeed from
"ultimate love to them, but as a further allurement
"to continue thus useful; and we, in hopes of such
"services from those to whom we are reputed use-
"ful, desire to obtain this reputation of being useful
"to others." 'Tis a pain to dwell upon such schemes
as contradict the immediate feelings of the heart so
manifestly.

This proved by several reasons.   Upon this scheme, the man who honours an agent,
and the agent himself who approves his own conduct,
must have notions of the same honoured action the
most different imaginable. The honourer must only
value it as tending to his ease, wealth, pleasure, safety;
and the agent values it as the artful, and necessary, but
disagreeable means of obtaining some remote advan-

tages from others, who will probably invite him to CHAP. 5.
continue fuch conduct by making him fome returns
of ufeful fervices. But 'tis plain there are many tempers and actions ufeful to us, nay to a whole community, which we don't honour; fuch as ufeful treachery,
a felfifh inventive induftry in improving manufactures;
a promifcuous profufenefs. Nay we honour fometimes what we conceive directly to be detrimental; as
patriotifm or courage, in a foreigner, or an enemy.
Shall confufed imaginations of ufefulnefs be regarded
here, againft the moft direct opinions of detriment to
ourfelves? Who finds thefe imaginations refpecting
his own interefts, in reading antient hiftories, or dra-
matick writers, when the foul is fo ftrongly moved
with the feveral *moral forms?*

And then, furely, this notion of my own temper and
conduct as beneficial to others can upon their fcheme
have nothing immediately grateful to me. Thefe cool
uncertain profpects of returns of advantage from the
felfifh arts of others can have nothing alluring amidft
certain expences, labours, wounds, and death? whence
the ardour for a furviving fame? this is all monftrous
and unnatural. Is all our admiration, our high zeal
for the brave, and merciful, and generous, and mag-
nanimous, all our ambition and ardour for glory, this
cool traffick, this artful barter of advantageous fervices without an exprefs bargain? We appeal to every human heart in this matter; to the hearts of the
young, who are moft ardent in praifing, and moft delighted with praife; and have little felt thofe artful

VOL. I. L

Book I. mean defigns of intereſt. Is all eſteem and honour a mere cool opinion that from ſome actions and affections we ſhall reap ſome advantage? Is all the confounding ſenſe of ſhame, and bluſhing, only a fear of ſome future uncertain loſſes, which we know not well what they ſhall be, or how they will befal us? Are not men conſcious of their own defigns in the purſuits of honour; of their own apprehenſions in their avoiding of what is ſhameful; and of the occaſion of their ſorrow when they are aſhamed? ſurely theſe artful views of our own intereſt could not be unknown to us.

This ſenſe appears very early. II. There is therefore an immediate ſenſe of honour and ſhame; often operating where there are no ſuch views of intereſt, and plainly preſuppoſing a *moral ſenſe*. It generally appears very early in life, before any conſiderable reaſoning or reflection can ſettle well the notions of morality; and thus before we can judge for ourſelves we are wiſely and benignly ſubjected to the direction of others, are rewarded for our compliance by a moſt grateful ſenſation, and by a moſt uneaſy one deterred from frowardneſs and obſtinacy. The ſelfiſh accounts of this principle make all the ardour for glory the ſame baſe temper with that of a traitor or informer, who deſires to appear uſeful to others in hopes of a reward. No better notion can they give of modeſty, the ſenſe of ſhame, the abhorrence of any imputation of moral turpitude, that *pudor* of the R O M A N S, the fineſt ſtroke in a character.

We fee this fenfe of *honour* admits feveral degrees in conformity to the *moral fenfe* on which it is
founded. But firft, in confequence of that natural de- *There are feve-*
fire or impulfe toward the perfection of all our powers, *ral degrees of the honourable and fhameful.*
and a fenfe of dignity and decency in fome of them
above others, we find a natural pleafure in difcovering
to others the perfection of any manly powers, and in
being valued in that refpect. Hence a tafte for the
ingenious arts of mufick, fculpture, painting, and
even for the manly diverfions, is reputable. The grandeur and elegance of living, in drefs, architecture,
furniture, gardens, are in certain circumftances matter of glorying and of praife: much more fo are the
abilities yet higher, a ftrong genius in acquiring knowledge, the high lively imagination of the poet or orator. This laft indeed plainly includes an high moral
fenfe. ~

But to come directly to our fenfe of pleafure in obtaining moral approbation. All actions which proceed
from any friendly or kind affection, and are not oppofite to fome more extenfive one, are attended with
affurance, and opennefs of behaviour, and we glory
in them. The fenfual paffions, and ill-natured affections of anger, malice, envy, and even cool felfifhnefs,
we naturally conceal; and are afhamed of them.

III. One cannot well pafs by that peculiar branch *The modefty of*
of modefty fo confpicuous in all ages and nations, a- *the fexes natu ral.*
bout venereal enjoyments. As there is a very violent
appetite implanted for the moft neceffary purpofes of
the fyftem, requiring however, in order to anfwer thefe

ends more effectually, a great deal of nice regulation, by our reason and confideration of the common intereft of fociety. 'Tis with great wifdom and goodnefs that fuch an early check is provided for this appetite by a natural principle of modefty. Children uninftructed would not foon difcover to us this modefty, nor have they for fome years a notion of the object or defign of it, as the appetite does not arife in our firft years. Should we whimfically fuppofe favages come to maturity in folitude, without thefe objects occurring to them which could excite focial affections or moral notions; in this unnatural ftate fome natural principles might not appear. But were they brought into fociety, and had the actions and fentiments of others prefented to them, their moral faculty, and their fenfe of honour and fhame, would foon difcover themfelves; and particularly their natural modefty of this peculiar kind would quickly appear. As they would approve all humanity and kindnefs, even when practifed toward others, and abhor the contrary difpofitions, they would foon defpife fenfuality and felfifhnefs. As foon as they knew how the race of mankind is preferved, they would defire marriage and offspring; and when the occafion of this natural modefty was felt, and the intention of the appetite known, this natural check of fhame would difcover itfelf.

When the neceffity of ftrict marriage-laws for the afcertaining to the fathers their own offspring was once obferved, new reafons would appear for modeft behaviour, and for creating an early habit of it in the

education of both sexes. But, besides, there seem to be
several natural dispositions and senses peculiarly relative to this affair, distinct from the general shame of
all immoderate selfishness, particularly that of mo-
desty, which begins at that period when the appetite
which needs its controll arises, and seems to abate in
old age along with the appetite.

IV. Having a natural capacity for moral notions, *This sense how*
we may be ashamed of actions without knowing the *affected by educa-*
true reasons why they are immoral. By education we *tion.*
may contract groundless prejudices, or opinions about
the qualities perceivable by any of our senses, as if
they were inherent in objects where they are not. Thus
we are prejudiced against meats we never tasted: but
we could not be prejudiced on account of savour, or
under that notion, if we had not the natural sense.
Thus it is always under some species recommended
by the *moral faculty* that we praise or desire to be prai-
sed, tho' we frequently have very imperfect views of
the tendencies of actions, and of the affections from
which they proceeded.

What we observed about the *moral faculty*, holds
also in our sense of honour, that we are highly delighted with the approbation of others, not only for the
good affections themselves, but for all those abilities
and dispositions which are their natural concomitants;
or which exclude the contrary affections. Thus we
glory in fortitude, veracity, candour, openness of mind,
and the desire of honour itself; tho' the pleasure of
receiving praise is known to be so strong, and there are

Book I. fuch fufpicions of our being envied for it, that men are averfe to let any impatience for this pleafure appear, or to difcover their high delight in it, leaft it fhould argue too much felfifhnefs.

The moral fenfe and that of honour affect all parts of life.   V. The force of the *moral fenfe*, and that of *honour*, is diffufed through all parts of life. The very luxury of the table derives its main charms from fome mixture of moral enjoyments, from communicating pleafures, and notions of fomething honourable as well as elegant. How univerfally defpicable is the character of one who in folitude purfues eagerly the pleafures of the palate without fociety or hofpitality.

·The chief pleafures of hiftory and poetry, and the powers of eloquence are derived from the fame fources. Hiftory, as it reprefents the moral characters and fortunes of the great and of nations, is always exercifing our *moral faculty*, and our focial feelings of the fortunes of others. Poetry entertains us in a way yet more affecting, by more ftriking reprefentations of the fame objects in fictitious characters, and moving our terror, and compaffion, and moral admiration. The power of the orator confifts in moving our approbation or condemnation, and the enfuing affections of efteem or indignation, by prefenting fully all the moral qualities of actions and characters, all the pityable circumftances which may extenuate or excufe, to engage our favour; or all the aggravating ones, to encreafe our indignation; difplaying all the high colours on both fides, as he is either praifing or making invectives.

The very arts of mufick, ftatuary, and painting, befide Chap. 5. the natural pleafures they convey by exact imitations, may receive an higher power and a ftronger charm from fomething *moral* infinuated into the performances.

The chief beauties of countenance, and even of behaviour, arife * from indications of fome fweet affections, or morally efteemable abilities, as it appears by almoft all the epithets of commendation. 'Tis always fome real or imagined indications of fomething vicious which chiefly caufes our diflike, as we fee from the qualities cenfured and condemned. Hence it is that fuch deformity is † obferved in the countenances of the angry, the envious, the proud, and the felfifh; and fo much alluring fweetnefs in thofe which difplay the tender gentle and friendly affections.

We fee how thefe moral indications affect the natural defires between the fexes. Could one attain to maturity without having any moral notions, which however fcarce ever happened in one inftance, except in ideots; he might be moved by this inftinct as the brutes are. But we find that beauty raifes firft fome favourable notions of an inward temper; and, if acquaintance confirms them, we feel an high efteem and a defire of mutual friendfhip. Thus we are admiring wit, good-nature, prudence, kindnefs, chaftity, a command over the lower appetites, while the inftinct is

---

* See *Inquiry* into *Beauty* &c. § vi.

† See *Cicero de Offic.* l. i. c. 29. *Appetitus qui longius evagantur — a quibus non modo animi perturbantur, verum etiam cor-* pora. *Licet ora ipfa cernere iratorum, aut eorum qui libidine aliqua, aut metu commoti funt, aut voluptate nimia geftiunt* &c. and often in his other works.

Book I. alſo exciting to its natural purpóſe. Hence it is that this paſſion is often obſerved to make conſiderable improvements of the temper in ſeveral amiable virtues.

'Tis in like manner ſome *moral worth* apprehended, ſome juſtice or goodneſs of intention in perſons and cauſes, which occaſions moſt of that keen zeal for certain parties and factions, and thoſe ſtrong attachments to them, in people who have no hopes of thoſe advantages which the leaders of them may have in view.

Our intimacies not from intereſt. To alledge that our * chuſing perſons of knowledge, courteſy, and good-nature for our intimates, and our avoiding the ignorant, the moroſe, or ſelfiſh, argues all our intimacies to ariſe from ſelfiſh views, is plainly unjuſt. 'Tis true the one ſort of companions are improving, pleaſant, obliging, ſafe; and the other uſeleſs, unpleaſant, dangerous. But are all friendſhips and intimacies mere grimace and hypocriſy? does one feel no inward eſteem of certain characters, and good-will to the perſons? does one only deſire his own improvement or pleaſure or gain, as when he hires a maſter to teach him a mechanick art, or a muſician to entertain him, or a labourer to do a piece of common work? do we only intend a fair outward appearance with our beſt friends, that we may not loſe theſe advantages? On the contrary does not every one feel an inward eſteem and good-will toward any virtuous acquaintances, which ſhall remain when we are ſeparated, and hope not to meet them again?

Were there no ſuch *moral ſenſe* and ſenſe of *honour*

* See *Hobbes, Bayle, Mandevil,* in many places, after *Rochefocault.*

in our conftitution, were we as entirely *felfifh* as fome CHAP. 5.
refiners alledge, human life would be quite different〜〜〜
from what we feel every day, *a joylefs, lovelefs, cold,*
fullen ftate of cunning and fufpicion.

'Tis worth our notice here that however by the *Things infenfible*
early prejudices of the external fenfes we are apt to *are moft real.*
imagine little reality in any thing which is not the object of one or other of them, and to conceive what is
not thus fenfible to be fictitious and imaginary; yet if
we attend to the inward feelings of our hearts, the
greateft realities, our very happinefs and mifery, that
dignity or worth in which alone we can have the moft
entire fatisfaction with ourfelves, or for which we love,
efteem, and admire another, and count him excellent
or happy, or chufe him for a friend, are qualities entirely infenfible, too noble and excellent to fall under
the cognizance of thefe powers which are chiefly deftined for the fupport of the body.

VI. Many fufpect that no fuch fenfes can be natu- *Thefe fenfes uni-*
ral, becaufe there are fuch different and oppofite no- *form.*
tions of morality, among different nations. But granting that their relifhes were different, that different
men and nations approved and condemned actions
upon different accounts, or under different notions;
this only proves that their fenfes are not uniform;
and not that no fuch principles are natural. Men's
palates differ as much; but who thence denies a fenfe
of tafting to be natural?

But the uniformity is much greater in our *moral*
faculty than in our palates. The different reafons gi-

BOOK I. ven by different perfons for their approving or condemning will all lead us at laft, when we examine
them, into the fame original fpecies or notions of moral good and evil.

In approving or vindicating of actions, in all nations, men generally alledge fome tendency to the happinefs of others, fome kind intention more or lefs extenfive, fome generous affections, or fome difpofitions naturally connected with them. When we alleviate any imprudent conduct, we fay, the agent intended well; did not forefee the bad confequence; or
had fuch provocation as might have tranfported even
a kind temper, or a man of juftice. When we inveigh
againft bad conduct, we fhew that all the contrary affections or difpofitions were evidenced by it, fuch as
cruelty, wrath, immoderate felfifhnefs, or a want of
fuch kind affections as we generally expect in our fpecies. If we blame imprudent conduct, without this reference to evil affections, or to the want of the good
ones, 'tis fometimes from our good-will and pity toward the agent, with fome contempt of his mean abilities, his floth, ftupidity, or indolence. And yet how
are we foftened by the thought that " the poor creature
" intended no harm, or occafioned none to others."
This is often indeed a falfe excufe, as the publick fuffers by any one's making himfelf lefs capable of fer-
ving it, as well as his more peculiar friends.

The immediate
objeƈ approved
is generally the
fame.
Nay we fhall find that men always approve upon
fome opinion, true or falfe, that an action has fome of
thofe qualities or tendencies, which are the natural

objects of approbation. We may indeed often imagine without ground, that actions have good effects
upon the publick, or that they flowed from good affections, or that they are required by the Deity and
acceptable to him; and then under thefe appearances
we approve them. 'Tis our reafon which prefents a
falfe notion or fpecies to the *moral faculty.* The fault
or error is in the opinion or underftanding, and not
in the *moral fenfe:* what it approves is truly good; tho'
the action may have no fuch quality. We fometimes
chufe and like, in point of intereft, what is in event
detrimental to ourfelves. No man thence concludes
that we are not uniform in felf-love or liking of our
own intereft. Nor do like miftakes about the moral
qualities of actions prove either that we have no *moral
fenfe,* or that it is not uniformly conftituted. The paffions of fpectators, as well as thofe of agents, prevent
a ma ure examination of the moral natures of thofe
actions which are fubfervient to the defigns of the paffions; as luft, rage, revenge, will hurry men into what a
calm man would difcern to be ruinous. But thefe
things do not prove that men are diffimilar to each
other, either in their *moral faculty,* or their *felf-love.*

To prove that men have no *moral faculty,* or very
diffimilar ones; we muft fhew either that nations or
great numbers of men hold all actions to be indifferent which don't appear to them to affect their own
private intereft; or that they are pleafed with cruelty,
treachery, ingratitude, unprovoked murders, and tortures, when not practifed toward themfelves, juft as

much as with their contraries: they fhould in fome nations be deemed as reputable and lovely as humanity, compaffion, liberality, faith: the action of Sextus Tarquin, or Claudius the decemvir, fhould be approved as much as that of Scipio with his Spanifh captive. But fuch nations have not yet been difcovered to us, not even by the invention of the boldeft traveller.

The caufes of different appro-bations and cen-fures, different notions of happi-nefs.

VII. The chief caufes of different approbations are thefe three. 1. Different notions of happinefs and the means of promoting it. Nations unacquainted with the improvements which life receives from art and induftry, may fee no occafion for incouraging them by fecuring to each man a property in the fruits of his labours, while the bare neceffaries of life are eafily obtained. Nay they can fee no harm in depriving men of their artificial acquifitions, and ftores beyond their prefent ufe, or of fuperfluities tending to diffolve them in pleafure and floth: hence no evil may appear in theft. If any nation faw no ufe in the afcertaining of their offspring to the fathers, or had no defire of it; they might difcern no moral evil in practices which more civilized nations fee to be deftructive to fociety. But no nation has yet been found infenfible to thefe matters.

The caufes of barbarous laws

In fome civilized ftates laws have obtained which we repute barbarous and impious. But look into the reafons for them, or the notions under which they were approved, and we generally find fome alledged tendency to fome publick good There may no doubt

be found fome few inftances where immoderate zeal
for their own grandeur, or that of their nation, has
made legiflators enact unjuft laws, without any moral fpecies recommending them.   This only proves
that fometimes a different principle may over-power
our fenfe of juftice.   But what foolifh opinions have
been received! what fantaftick errors and diffimili-
tudes have been obferved in the admired power of reafoning, allowed to be the characteriftick of our fpecies!   Now-almoft all our diverfities in moral fentiments, and oppofite approbations, and condemnations,
arife from oppofite conclufions of reafon about the
effects of actions upon the publick, or the affections
from which they flowed.   The *moral fenfe* feems ever
to approve and condemn uniformly the fame immediate objects, the fame affections and difpofitions; tho'
we reafon very differently about the actions which evidence certain difpofitions or their contraries. And yet
reafon, in which all thefe errors happen is allowed to
be the natural principle; and the *moral faculty* is not,
becaufe of the diverfities of approbation; which yet
arife chiefly from the diverfity of reafonings.

2. A fecond caufe of different approbations are the *Different fyftems*
regarded.
larger or more confined fyftems which men regard in
confidering the tendencies of actions; fome regarding
only their own country and its intereft, while the reft
of mankind are overlooked; and others, having yet
narrower fyftems, only a party, fect, or cabal.   But if
we enlarge our views with truth and juftice, and obferve the ftructure of the human foul, pretty much

BOOK I. the fame in all nations; none of which wants multitudes of good men, endued with the fame tender affections to kindred, friends, benefactors; with the fame compaſſion for the diſtreſſed, the fame admiration and love of eminent virtue, the fame zealous concerns for their countries which we think ſo lovely among ourſelves; we muſt find a ſacred tye of nature binding us even to foreigners, and a ſenſe of that juſtice, mercy and good-will * which is due to all. To men of ſmall attention their own countrymen or partiſans are the only valuable part of mankind: every thing is juſt which advances their power, tho' it may hurt others. The different approbations here ariſe again from different opinions about a matter of fact. Were certain nations or ſects entirely impious, cruel, and fixed upon ſuch meaſures as would involve all men in eternal as well as temporal miſery, and poſſeſſed of ſuch arts of faſcination as no reaſonings could effectually withſtand; one could ſcarce blame any violent deſtruction made of ſuch monſters by fire or ſword. Under this very notion all perſecutors out of principle behold ſuch as they call hereticks; under it they raiſe a general abhorrence of them. The like notions many little ſects form of each other ; and hence loſe the ſenſe of moral evil in their mutual hatreds and perſecution.

Different opini-
ons about God's
commands. 3. A third cauſe of different ſentiments about actions, as frequently occurring as any one, are the different opinions about what God has commanded.

* See this often inculcated in *Marc. Antonin.*

Men fometimes from defire of rewards, and fear of Chap. 5. punifhments, counteract their *moral fenfe,* in obedi- ence to what they conceive to be divine commands; as they may alfo from other felfifh paffions: they may have fome confufed notions of matters of duty and obligation, diftinct from what their hearts would approve were the notions of divine commands removed. Habits and affociations of ideas affect men's minds in this matter. But where there are different opinions in different nations about the objects of the divine command, there are fuch ftrong *moral colours* or *forms* in obedience and difobedience to God, that they muft neceffarily caufe very different approbations and cenfures, even from the moft uniformly conftituted *moral faculties.* *God* is generally conceived to be good and wife, to be the author of our lives, and of all the good we enjoy. Obedience muft be recommended to our approbation generally under the high fpecies of gratitude, and love of moral excellence, as well as under the notion of advantageous to the publick: and difobedience muft appear cenfurable, under the contrary notions. Difobedience therefore to what one believes *God* has commanded, from any views of fecular advantages or fenfual pleafure, or the inveigling others into fuch difobedience, muft appear grofsly ungrateful, fenfual, felfifh or cruel. Where different opinions about God's commands prevail, 'tis unavoidable that different approbations and cenfures muft be obferved in confequence of thefe opinions, tho' the natural immediate objects of praife and cenfure were the

Book I. fame to all men. This accounts for the different rites of worfhip, different notions of fanctity and prophanity, and for the great abhorrence fome nations may have of fome practices in which others can difcern no pernicious tendency, and repute indifferent, having no opinion of their being prohibited.

Different rites of religion and notions of impiety. Thefe confiderations account fufficiently for the approbation of human facrifices and other monftrous rites: tho' 'tis probable they have been often practifed merely from fear, without moral approbation, by fuch as fcarce were perfuaded of the goodnefs of their gods: they likeways fhew how inceft and polygamy may be generally abhorred in fome nations, where a few only can fhow their pernicious confequences; and yet be deemed lawful in other nations.

Errors often criminal. Let no man hence imagine that fuch actions flowing from falfe opinions about matters of fact, or about divine commands, are light matters, or fmall blemifhes in a character. Where the error arifes from no evil affection, or no confiderable defect of the good ones, the action may be very excufable. But many of thofe errors in opinion which affect our devotion toward the Deity, or our humanity toward our fellows, evidence very great defects in that love of moral excellence, in that juft and amiable defire of knowing, reverencing, and confiding in it, which is requifite to a good character; or evidence great defects in humanity, at leaft in the more extenfive and noble kinds of it. Where thefe principles are lively, they muft excite men to great diligence and caution about their

duty and their practical conclusions: and consequent-
ly must lead them to just sentiments in the more important points, since sufficient evidence is afforded in
nature to the sincere and attentive. No man can have
sufficient humanity of soul, and candour, who can
believe that human sacrifices, or the persecution of
his fellow-creatures about religious tenets which hurt
not society, can be duties acceptable to *God*.

VIII. Our having a *moral sense* does not infer that we *No innate ide-*
have innate complex ideas of the several actions; or *as supposed.*
innate opinions of their consequences or effects upon
society: these we discover by observation and reasoning, and we often make very opposite conclusions a-
bout them. The object of this sense is not any external motion or action, but the inward affections and
difpositions, which by reasoning we infer from the
actions observed. These immediate objects may be
apprehended to be the same, where the external actions are very opposite. As incisions and amputations.
may be made either from hatred, or from love; so love
sometimes moves to inflict painful chaftisements, and
sometimes to confer pleasures, upon its object. And
when men form different opinions of these affections in
judging about the same actions, one shall praise what
another censures. They shall form these different opinions about the affections from which actions proceeded, when they judge differently about their tendency to
the good or the hurt of society or of individuals. One
whose attention is wholly or chiefly employed about
some good tendencies of the actions, while he over-

BOOK I. looks their pernicious effects, fhall imagine that they flowed from virtuous affections, and thus approve them: while a mind more attentive to their pernicious effects, infers the contrary affections to have been their fpring, and condemns them.

Why it is ne-ceſſary to confi-der the connexion of virtue with intereſt. Were nothing more requifite in laying the foundation of *morals,* but the difcovering in theory what affections and conduct are virtuous, and the objects of approbation, and what are vicious, the account now given of the conftitution of our *moral faculty* would be fufficient for that purpofe; as it points out not only what is virtuous and vicious, but alfo fhews the feveral degrees of thefe qualities in the feveral forts of affections and actions; and thus we might proceed to confider more particularly the feveral offices of life, and to apply our power of reafon to difcover what partial affections, and actions confequent upon them, are to be entirely approved, as beneficial to fome parts of the fyftem, and perfectly confiftent with the general good; and what affections and actions, even of the beneficent kind, tho' they may be ufeful to a part, are pernicious to the general fyftem; and thus deduce the fpecial laws of nature, from this *moral faculty* and the generous determination of foul. But as we have alfo a ftrong determination toward private happinefs, with many particular felfifh appetites and affections, and thefe often fo violent as not immediately to fubmit to the *moral power,* however we may be confcious of its dignity, and of fome confiderable effect it has upon our happinefs or mifery; as ftrong fufpici-

ons may often arife attended with great uneafinefs, CHAP. 5.
that in following the impulfe of our kind affections
and the *moral faculty* we are counteracting our intereft, and abandoning what may be of more confequence to our happinefs than either this felf-approbation or the applaufes of others; to eftablifh well the foundations of morality, and to remove, as much as may
be, all oppofition arifing from the felfifh principles,
that the mind may refolutely perfift in the courfe
which the *moral faculty* recommends, 'tis neceffary to
make a full comparifon of all human enjoyments with
each other, and thence difcover in which of them our
greateft happinefs confifts.

N 2

BOOK I.   PART II.

An Inquiry into the SUPREME HAPPINESS of MANKIND.

CHAP. VI.

How far the several Sensations, Appetites, Passions and Affections are in our power.

I. THE chief happiness of any being must consist in the full enjoyment of all the gratifications *Wherein hap-* its nature desires and is capable of; or if its nature ad-
pinefs consists. mits of a great variety of pleasures of different and sometimes inconsistent kinds, some of them also higher and more durable than others, its supreme happiness must consist in the most constant enjoyment of the more intense and durable pleasures, with as much of the lower gratifications as consists with the full enjoyment of the higher. In like manner; if we cannot ward off all pain, and there be different kinds and degrees of it, we must secure ourselves against the more intense and durable kinds, and the higher degrees of them; and that sometimes by bearing the lower kinds or degrees, or by sacrificing some smaller pleasures, when 'tis necessary for this end.

To direct us in this conduct 'tis necessary to premise some distinct account in what manner we have power over our several affections and desires, and how far any meditations or self-discipline may affect our

very perceptions of good and evil, of happiness or misery, in the several objects.

1. As the calm desires and aversions of the soul
naturally arise from our opinions of good or evil in
their objects, so they are proportioned to the degrees
of good or evil apprehended. We have power over the
selfish desires of any particular good only by means of
the calm original determination toward the greatest
happiness; and by the power of reasoning and comparing, which may discover what are the values of the
several objects of desire. 'Tis by the correcting our
opinions of their values that the several desires are
kept in their due proportion. 'Tis also by means of
the other original determination toward publick happiness of the most extensive kind, and by a like exercise of reason in comparing the values of the objects
desired for others, that we can regulate the several kind
affections and desires: since where a greater good is
discerned, the calm desire of it is stronger than that
toward a smaller inconsistent good, whether pursued
for ourselves or others.

Here too the *moral faculty* displays much of its
power. As the several narrower affections may often
interfere and oppose each other, or some of them be
inconsistent with more extensive affections to whole
societies, or to mankind; our *moral sense* by its stronger and warmer approbation of the more extensive,
both points out the affection which should prevail,
and confirms this nobler affection by our natural desire of *moral excellence.*

The turbulent appetites and particular paſſions whether of the ſelfiſh or generous kind, are governed by the ſame means. They naturally ariſe on certain occaſions, and that often with great vehemence. To govern and reſtrain them an habit is neceſſary, which muſt be acquired by frequent recollection and diſcipline. While we are calm we muſt frequently attend to the danger of following precipitantly the firſt appearances of good or evil; we muſt recollect our former experiences in ourſelves, and our obſervations about others, how ſuperior and more laſting enjoyments have been loſt by our haſty indulgence of ſome preſſing appetite, or paſſion: how laſting miſery and remorſe has enſued upon ſome tranſient gratification: what ſhame, diſtreſs, and ſorrow have been the effects of ungoverned anger: what infamy and contempt men have incurred by exceſſive fear, or by their averſion to labour and painful application. We may thus raiſe an habitual ſuſpicion of unexamined appearances, and an habitual caution when we feel any turbulent paſſion ariſing. When the calm principles are thus confirmed by frequent meditation, and the force of the paſſions abated, then it is we obtain the true liberty and ſelf-command: the calm powers will retain and exerciſe that authority for which their natural dignity has fitted them, and our reaſon will be exerciſed in correcting all appearances of good and evil, and examining the true importance of the ſeveral objects of our appetites or paſſions.

II. To this purpoſe 'tis neceſſary to obſerve the or-

dinary caufes of our deception, and of our unjuft eftimation of objects: fuch as, 1. The ftrength of the
impreffions and keennefs of the defires raifed by things *Prefence to the senfes.*
prefent and fenfible, beyond what the infenfible or fu-
ture objects prefented by the underftanding and reflection can raife. Frequent meditation alone can remedy this evil. Our younger years are almoft totally
employed about the objects of fenfe: few can bear
the pains and energy of mind requifite to fix the attention upon intellectual objects, and examine the
feelings of the heart. Strength is acquired by thofe
powers which are moft exercifed. The recurring motions of the appetites annex confufed notions of high
felicity to their objects, which is confirmed by the intenfenefs of fome fenfations while the appetite is keen.
Few deliberately compare thefe enjoyments with o-
thers, or attend to the confequences, to the fhort duration of thefe fenfations, and the enfuing fatiety,
fhame and remorfe. And yet 'tis evident to our reafon that the duration of any enjoyment is as much to
be regarded as the intenfenefs of the fenfation; and
that the enfuing ftate of the mind when the brutal impulfe is fated, is to be brought into the account as
well as the tranfient gratification.

2. Again----Allowing the imagination to dwell *Indulging the imagination.*
much upon fome objects prefenting hopes of high
pleafure inflames our paffions and byaffes our judgments. Little indeed is hereby added to the enjoyment when we obtain it: nay our pleafure is rather
diminifhed, as it feldom anfwers the previous expecta-

tion, and brings with it the air of difappointment. But by roving over all the pleafures and advantages of certain ftations, certain pitches of wealth or power, our defires of them are made more violent, and our notions reprefent an happinefs in them, much higher than we fhall find it to be when we attain to them. And this uncorrected imagination never fails to increafe the torment we fhall find upon a difappointment.

Affociations of ideas.　　3. But no caufe of immoderate defires, or unfair eftimates is more frequent than fome groundlefs affociations of ideas, formed by inftruction, or our ufual converfation, annexing confufed notions of happinefs, and even of virtue, and moral perfection, or their contraries, to what has little affinity to them. Seldom are objects of defire prefented to the mind as they are, without fome difguife. Wealth and power are truly ufeful not only for the natural conveniencies or pleafures of life, but as a fund for good offices. But how many notions are there often likewife annexed of great abilities, wifdom, moral excellence, and of much higher joys than they can afford; which fo intoxicate fome men that they forget their natural purpofes, begin to love them for themfelves, affect the oftentation of them; and dread the lower ftations as abject, miferable, and inconfiftent with moral worth or honour. Some natural pleafures too by like affociations are eftimated far above their worth, and immoderate defires of them torment the foul.

Superftitious o- pinions.　　4. Some perverfe fuperftitions alfo, inftilled bye-

ducation, cause groundlefs averfions to tenets and
practices of the moft innocent nature, by annexing to
them notions of impiety, enmity to God, and obftinate wickednefs of heart; while contrary tenets or
practices, not a whit better, are made indications of
piety, charity, holinefs and zeal for the fouls of men.
Hence arifes that rancour in the hearts of unwary
zealots of all forts againft thofe who differ from them;
and that perfecuting fpirit, with all the wrathful paffions, which have been fo long a reproach to human
nature, and even to that religion which fhould infpire
all love and meeknefs.

III. It is the more neceffary to obferve thefe feve- *All men feel the*
ral caufes of the wrong eftimations made of the ob- *feveral original*
desires pleafures
jects of our defire, and of the feveral enjoyments of *and pains.*
life, becaufe fcarce any of mankind can live without
fome folicitation or other from every one of thefe feveral forts of enjoyments; nor can one hope to be
wholly unexperienced in contrary evils. The pleafures and pains of the external fenfes are in fome degree felt by all who have the natural powers, and muft
raife defires and averfions. The impulfes of the appetites too are unavoidable: they recur after certain
intervals, nor can their uneafy fenfations be otherways prevented altogether, than by gratifying them
with their natural objects. But, according to the benign order of nature, fuch gratifications as may prevent the pain of the appetites may very generally be
obtained; and where fome moral reafon prevents the
gratification, there are higher moral joys accompany-

ing this abſtinence, which fully make up the loſs. Bodily pain ſeldom employs a great part of life; wiſe men find out many preſervatives, which are generally effectual; and when they are not, may obtain ſtrong conſolations and ſupports under it.

Other deſires more difficultly gratified than the appetites. ’Tis more difficult to gratify other moſt uneaſy deſires, ariſing from ſome opinions of great happineſs in certain enjoyments. Had we formed no ſuch opinions or confuſed notions, we had felt no miſery in the want of theſe enjoyments; which is not the caſe with the appetites. But when we can change theſe opinions, and rectify our confuſed imaginations, the deſires and their attendant uneaſineſſes ceaſe or abate. A greater ſhare of the miſery of life is chargeable on theſe deſires than upon the appetites. Of this kind are the deſires of wealth, power, the grandeur and elegance of living, and of fame; and our averſions to their oppoſites are of the ſame nature. Our affections to others, and our kind deſires, are affected by opinions in the ſame manner with our ſelfiſh ones. What we conceive as a great good we muſt warmly deſire for thoſe we love; we muſt be uneaſy upon any diſappointment.

The neceſſity of correcting our opinions and imagination. Now when theſe opinions are true and natural, we cannot alter them, nor would it be deſirable. Reaſon and reflection will confirm them. But many opinions and confuſed notions which raiſe our deſires are falſe and phantaſtick; and when they are corrected we are freed from much pain and anxiety. Some enjoyments are ſtill in our power, which too may be found to be

the higheſt. If this be true, it is our higheſt intereſt CHAP. 6.
to be fully perſuaded of it; that our ſtrongeſt deſires
may be raiſed toward ſuch things as may certainly be
obtained, and can yield us the nobleſt enjoyments.

In general, the greater any good or evil is imagined, the ſtronger are our deſires and fears, the greater
is our anxiety while the event is in ſuſpence, and the
higher ſhall our ſorrows be upon diſappointment and
our firſt tranſports upon ſucceſs: but where the previous imagination was falſe, this joy ſoon vaniſhes, and
is ſucceeded by uneaſineſs: on the other hand, the
ſorrow upon diſappointment may remain long and very intenſe, as the falſe imagination is not corrected
by experience of the enjoyment. This ſhews the great
importance of examining well all our notions about
the objects of deſire or averſion. Thus we ſhould break
off from ſenſual enjoyments, in our eſtimation of
them, all theſe foreign notions of moral dignity, liberality, elegance, and good-nature, which diſpoſitions we may diſplay in a much wiſer and more virtuous manner, without expenſive luxurious tables or
ſumptuous living. Theſe additional notions inflame
the deſires of ſplendid opulence, and are a fund of
perpetual anxiety.

IV. Ideas once firmly aſſociated in this manner *Aſſociated ideas not eaſily ſeparated.*
give laſting uneaſineſs to the mind; and a full conviction of the underſtanding will not break the aſſociation, without long meditation and diſcipline. There
are only confuſed imaginations, and not ſettled concluſions, or direct opinions, in the minds of the luxu

rious, the mifer, the ambitious, the lover, reprefen-ting fome wonderful excellence in their favourite ob-jects proportioned to their eager defires. But long in-dulgence and repeated acts of defire, in a mind called off from other objects, the ftrain of converfation, and the airs of countenance, and the very tone of voice of the men of the fame turn with whom they have haunted, affociate high notions of felicity to the fa-vourite gratification fo firmly, that a long attention and reflection is neceffary to rectify the confufed ima-gination.

Juft notions of virtue neceffary to happinefs. A full perfuafion of the excellence and importance of virtue above all other enjoyments, provided we have juft notions of it, muft always be for our intereft. The opinion will ftand the teft of the ftricteft inqui-ry, as we fhall fhew hereafter; and the enjoyment is in our power. But difproportioned admirations of fome forts of virtue of a limited nature, and of fome inferior moral forms, fuch as mere fortitude, zeal for truth, and for a particular fyftem of religious tenets, while the nobler forms of goodnefs of more extenfive good influence are overlooked, may lead men into very bad affections, and into horrid actions. No na-tural fenfe or defire is without its ufe, while our opi-nions are true: but when they are falfe, fome of the beft affections or fenfes may be pernicious. Our *moral fenfe* and kind affections lead us to condemn the evil, to oppofe their defigns; nay to wifh their deftruction when they are conceived to be unalterably fet upon the ruin of others better than themfelves. Thefe ve-

ry principles, along with the anger and indignation CHAP. 6.
naturally ariſing againſt what appears evil, may lead
us into a ſettled rancour and hatred againſt great bo
dies of mankind thus falſely repreſented as wicked;
and make us appear to them, as they appear to us,
maliciouſly ſet upon the deſtruction of others.

When our opinions and imagination are corrected, *Correcting our opinions abates many deſires.*
the natural appetites and deſires will remain, and may
be attended with ſome uneaſineſs; but the ſtrength of
many will be abated and others will acquire more.
The ſimpler gratifications of appetite, theſe of the
eaſieſt purchaſe, may by good management be as ſatisfying, nay almoſt as joyful and exhilarating as any.
The pleaſures of the imagination may be highly reliſh-
ed, and yet no diſtreſs ariſe from the want of them.
Much of this pleaſure is expoſed to all, and requires no
property, ſuch as that ariſing from the exquiſite beauties of nature, and ſome of the beauties of art. Nor are
even theſe either the ſole or the higheſt enjoyments.

V. The ſympathetick pleaſures and pains in ſome *The ſympathetick feelings unavoidable.*
degree or other muſt affect us; no management can
prevent it. We muſt live in ſociety, and by the aid
of others, whoſe happineſs, or miſery, whoſe pleaſures,
or pains, we cannot avoid obſerving. Nay mankind
univerſally feel the conjugal and parental affections;
eminent goodneſs too, when it occurs, muſt excite
ſtrong love and friendſhip. Thus we muſt experience
the ſympathetick joys and ſorrows of the higher kinds.
In this matter too we muſt watch carefully over our
opinions and imagination, that our minds be not in-

Book I. flamed with vain defires about mean tranfitory or unneceffary goods for others, or oppreffed with forrow
upon fuch evils befalling them as are fmall and tolerable. But unlefs we get the imaginations of our
friends corrected, we fhall ftill have occafion for fympathy. All mifery is real to the fufferer while it lafts.
Whoever imagines himfelf miferable, he is fo in fact,
while this imagination continues.

Where choice binds the tye of love, the previoufly
examining well the character of the perfon, his opinions and notions of life, is of the higheft confequence.
In the ftronger bonds of love with perfons of juft fentiments and corrected imaginations, we have a fair
hazard for a large fhare of thefe higher focial joys,
with fewer intenfe pains; as the happinefs of fuch perfons is lefs uncertain or dependent on external accidents.

No neceffary As there are not in human nature any neceffary
caufes of ill-will. caufes of ultimate ill-will or malice, a calm mind confidering well the tempers, fentiments, and real fprings
of action in others, will indeed find much matter of
pity and regret, but little of anger, indignation or envy, and of fettled ill-will none at all. And thus we
may be pretty free from the uneafineffes and mifery
of the unkind affections and paffions. Human nature
is indeed chargeable with many weakneffes, rafh opinions, immoderate defires of private intereft, ftrong
fenfual appetites, keen attachments to narrow fyftems
beyond their merit; and very fubject to anger upon appearance of injury to themfelves, or thofe they

love: but 'tis free from all ultimate unprovoked malice; much influenced by some moral species or o-
ther; and abounding with some sorts of kind affections. Many of their most censurable actions flow from
some mistaken notion of duty, or are conceived by the
agent to be innocent, and are the effects of some partial and naturally lovely affection, but raised above its
proportion, while more extensive ones are asleep.

VI. As soon as one observes the affections of others *Moral forms universally affect*
or reflects on his own, the moral qualities must affect *mankind.*
the mind. No education, habit, false opinions, or even
affectation itself can prevent it. A Lucretius, an
Hobbes, a Bayle, cannot shake off sentiments of gratitude, praise, and admiration of some moral forms;
and of censure and detestation of others. This sense
may be a sure fund of inward enjoyment to those who
obey its suggestions. Our own temper and actions
may be constant sources of joy upon reflection. But
where partial notions of virtue and justice are rashly entertained, without extensive views and true opinions
of the merit of persons and causes, the pursuit of
some moral forms may occasion grievous distaste and
remorse. False notions of virtue may be less lasting
than other mistakes. Persons injured by them seldom
fail to remonstrate; spectators not blinded by our passions and interest will shew their disgust. And thus
our ill-grounded joy and self-approbation may soon
give place to shame and remorse.

The sense of honour too must occasion pleasure or *The sense of honour affects all.*
pain, as the world about us happen to disclose their

fentiments of our conduct: and as we have not the opinions of others in our power, we cannot be fure of efcaping all cenfure. But we can make a juft eftimate of men and of the value of their praifes or cenfures, in proportion to their qualifications as judges of merit; and thus we may turn our ambition upon the praifes of the wife and good. The approbation of our own hearts, and the approbation of *God*, give fatisfactions of an higher nature than the praifes of men can give. We can reprefs the defire of this lower enjoyment, when it proves inconfiftent with the higher.

The defires of wealth and pow-er univerfal. VII. The defires alfo of wealth and power muft affect the mind when it difcerns their obvious ufefulnefs to gratify every original defire. Thefe purfuits in men of corrected minds may be eafy and moderate, fo that difappointment will not give great pain. But when the notions not only of external convenience and pleafure, and of a fund for good offices, but of all valuable ability, and moral dignity, and happinefs are joined to wealth or power, and of all bafenefs and mifery joined to poverty and the lower ftations; when the natural ufe of thefe things is overlooked, and the mind is conftantly intent upon further advancement, anxiety and impatience muft imbitter and poifon every enjoyment of life.

How fantaftick defires arife. When the mind has been diverted from its natural purfuits and enjoyments, fantaftick ones muft fucceed. When through indolence and averfion to application men defpair of fuccefs in matters naturally honourable; when any accidents have called off their

minds from the affections natural to our kind, toward Chap. 6.
offspring, kindred, and a country; the defires of fome
fort of eminence, and of amufement and pleafure, in
an incapacity for all valuable bufinefs, muft fet them
upon any purfuits, which have got reputation among
their fellows of like floth, incapacity, or depravation,
under fome confufed notions of genteelity, liberality, fociablenefs, or elegance. How elfe fhall one account for years fpent by young people of eafy fortunes
in hunting, gaming, drinking, fauntering, and the fil-
ly chat and ceremonies of the places of rendezvous
for gayety and amufement.

VIII. Now it is obvious our nature is incapable *Many enjoy-ments oppofite and inconfiftent.*
of the higheft pleafures of all kinds at once, or of
purfuing them together. There are manifeft incon-
fiftencies among them, and the means of obtaining
them. An high relifh for one kind is inconfiftent with
a tafte for fome others. Senfuality and indolence are
plainly oppofite to all the higher active enjoyments.
The purfuits of knowledge and the ingenious arts are
oppofite to avarice, fenfuality, and to fome forts of
ambition: fo are the purfuits of virtue. Nay the higheft enjoyments of fome kinds are much increafed by
confcioufnefs of our having facrificed other inferior
purfuits and enjoyments to them, as thofe of virtue
and honour.

'Tis equally manifeft that in our prefent ftate, one *Few enjoyments are certain.*
cannot conftantly fecure to himfelf any one enjoyment
dependent on external things, which are all fubject
to innumerable accidents. The noble enjoyments of

piety, of which hereafter, and thofe of virtue, may be ſtable and independent on fortune. But a virtuous temper, whatever ſure enjoyment it may afford upon reflection, ever carries a man forth beyond himſelf, toward a publick good, or ſome intereſts of others; and theſe depend not on our power. There's great pain in the diſappointment of virtuous deſigns, tho' the temper be ever approved. In this, as in all other things, we depend on providence, which, as it gave us at firſt all our perceptive powers, and their objects, ſo it diſpoſes of them, and particularly of the happineſs or miſery of others, the object on which the virtuous affections terminate. This ſufficiently ſhews that the Deity muſt, for this reaſon, as well as many others, be the ſupreme object of our higheſt happineſs: ſince we can never be ſecure, nor can we enjoy true ſerenity and tranquillity of mind, without a firm perſuaſion that his goodneſs, wiſdom, and omnipotence are continually employed in ſecuring the felicity of the objects of our nobleſt affections.

No ſolid tranquillity without religion. It would not be improper to conſider here the plain evidence for the exiſtence of God and his moral perfections; not only as a firm perſuaſion of theſe points is an high matter of duty, but as the Deity and his providence are the foundations of our tranquillity and higheſt happineſs. But as the moſt perſuaſive arguments on ſome of theſe points are derived from the very conſtitution of human nature, and that *moral adminiſtration* we feel within ourſelves, that ſtructure of our ſouls deſtined to recommend all thoſe kind and

generous affections which refemble the moral perfec- CHAP. 6.
tions of God; we fhall poftpone the fentiments and
duties of piety to be confidered afterwards as the
higheft perfection of happinefs, as well as of moral excellence.

IX. As to other enjoyments which are uncertain; *How our endea-*
tho' pure unmixed happinefs is not attainable, yet *vours have fome effect.*
our endeavours are not ufelefs. We hinted alrea-
dy that having had high previous expectations, tho' it
may increafe the firft tranfports of fuccefs, when the
preceeding anxiety is removed; yet rather leffens the
fubfequent enjoyment, and ftill embitters difappointments, and makes misfortunes, in their own nature
light, become unfupportable: fo having our notions
lower about thefe uncertain objects, and our defires
moderate, rather encreafes our ftable fenfe of pleafure
in the object obtained, and abates the fenfe of difappointment.

Thus the temperate, the fober, the chafte, the
humble, have fenfes as acute at leaft as others, and
enjoy all the good in fenfual objects, and in honour.
Abftinence and reftraint, when virtue requires, viti-
ates no fenfe or appetite. Moderation in profperity,
temperance, humility, and modefty, low notions of
happinefs in fenfual objects, prevent no fenfe of pleafure in advantages obtained. Men of this turn have
their reafon calm and active to procure the gratifications they defire, and to find out other preferable enjoyments when they are difappointed. In this uncertain world their profperity and fuccefs is as joyful as

that of others. And then under misfortunes,

Si quis, quae multa vides discrimine tali,

A lively sense of the instability of human affairs very useful. *Si quis in adversum rapiat casusve, deusve,** (And sure such disappointments are as incident to the inflamed admirers of external things as to others) the difference is manifest. The one had other funds of happiness: he foresaw such accidents; the loss to him is tolerable. To the other; *he is deprived of his gods; and do you ask what aileth him?* So necessary is frequent consideration of the uncertainty of human affairs; the accidents we are subject to; and the proper resorts, and springs of relief, and the other enjoyments which may still be in our power. This abates no solid joy in prosperity, but breaks vain associations, and corrects the imagination; gives strength of mind, and freedom from that terror and consternation which distracts the unprepared mind, and deprives it of the good remaining in its power.

C H A P. VII.

A Comparison of the several Sorts of Enjoyment, *and the opposite Sorts of* Uneasiness, *to find their Importance to* Happiness.

TO discover wherein our true happiness consists we must compare the several enjoyments of life, and the several kinds of misery, that we may discern what enjoyments are to be parted with, or what uneasiness

* *Virg. Aeneid.* ix. vers. 210.

to be endured, in order to obtain the higheſt and CHAP. 7.
moſt beatifick ſatisfactions, and to avoid the moſt diſtreſſing ſufferings.

As to pleaſures of the ſame kind, 'tis manifeſt their *Enjoyments va-luable by their dignity and du-ration.*
values are in a joint proportion of their intenſeneſs
and duration. In eſtimating the duration, we not only regard the conſtancy of the object, or its remaining
in our power, and the duration of the ſenſations it
affords, but the conſtancy of our fancy or reliſh: for
when this changes it puts an end to the enjoyment.

In comparing pleaſures of different kinds, the value
is as the duration and dignity of the kind jointly. We
have an immediate ſenſe of a * dignity, a perfection,
or beatifick quality in ſome kinds, which no intenſeneſs of the lower kinds can equal, were they alſo as
laſting as we could wiſh. No intenſeneſs or duration
of any external ſenſation gives it a dignity or worth e-
qual to that of the improvement of the ſoul by knowledge, or the ingenious arts; and much leſs is it equal
to that of virtuous affections and actions. We never
heſitate in judging thus about the happineſs or perfection of others, where the impetuous cravings of appetites and paſſions do not corrupt our judgments, as
they do often in our own caſe. By this intimate feeling of dignity, enjoyments and exerciſes of ſome kinds,
tho' not of the higheſt degree of thoſe kinds, are incomparably more excellent and beatifick than the
moſt intenſe and laſting enjoyments of the lower kinds.
Nor is duration of ſuch importance to ſome higher

* See above chap. iv. § 10.

kinds, as it is to the lower. The exercise of virtue for a short period, provided it be not succeeded by something vicious, is of incomparably greater value than the most lasting sensual pleasures. Nothing destroys the excellence and perfection of the state but a contrary quality of the same kind defacing the former character. The peculiar happiness of the virtuous man is not so much abated by pain, or an early death, as that of the sensualist; tho' his complex state which is made up of all his enjoyments and sufferings of every kind is in some degree affected by them*. Nor is it a view of private sublime pleasures in frequent future reflections which recommends virtue to the soul. We feel an impulse, an ardour toward perfection, toward affections and actions of dignity, and feel their immediate excellence, abstracting from such views of future pleasures of long duration. Tho' no doubt these pleasures, which are as sure as our existence, are to be regarded in our estimation of the importance of virtue to our happiness.

Now if we denote by intenseness, in a more general meaning, the degree in which any perceptions or enjoyments are beatifick, then their comparative values are in a compound proportion of their intenseness and duration. But to retain always in view the grand differences of the kinds, and to prevent any imaginations, that the intenser sensations of the lower kinds

---

* The Stoicks have run into extravagance on this head. See *Cicero de Fin.* l. iii. c. 10. *Haec de quibus dixi non fiunt tempo-* | *ris productione majora.——non intelligunt valetudinis aestimationem spatio indicari; virtutis, opportunitate.*

with sufficient duration may compleat our happiness; CHAP. 7.
it may be more convenient to estimate enjoyments by
their dignity and duration: dignity denoting the excellence of the kind, when those of different kinds are
compared; and the intensenefs of the sensations, when
we compare those of the same kind.

II. Tho' the several original powers above-mention- *The different*
ed are natural to all men, yet through habit, associated *tastes of men.*
ideas, education, or opinion, some generally pursue enjoyments of one kind; and shew a disregard of others,
which are highly valued by men of a different turn.
Some are much given to sensuality; others to more ingenious pleasures; others pursue wealth and power;
others moral and social enjoyments, and honour.
Wealth and power have some few faithful votaries a-
doring them for themselves: but the more numerous
worshipers adore them only as ministring spirits, or
mediators with some superior divinities, as *pleasure,
honour, beneficence.*

Thus different men have different tastes. What *These must be*
one admires as the supreme enjoyments, another may *examined.*
despise. Must we not examine these tastes? Are all
persons, all orders of beings equally happy if each obtains the enjoyments respectively most relished? At
this rate the meanest brute or insect may be as happy
as the wisest hero, patriot, or friend can be. What
may make a brute as happy as that low order is capable of being, may be but despicable to an order endued with finer perceptive powers, and a nobler sort
of desires. Beings of these higher orders are immedi-

ately confcious of the fuperior dignity and importance to happinefs in their peculiar enjoyments, of which lower orders are incapable. Nature has thus diftinguifhed the different orders by different perceptive powers, fo that the fame objects will not be fufficient for happinefs to all; nor have all equal happinefs when each can gratify all the defires and fenfes he has.

The fuperior orders in this world probably experience all the fenfations of the lower orders, and can judge of them. But the inferior do not experience the enjoyments of the fuperior. Nay in the feveral ftages of life each one finds different taftes and defires. We are confcious in our ftate of mature years that the happinefs of our friends, our families, or our country are incomparably nobler objects of our purfuit, and adminifter proportionably a nobler pleafure than the toys which once abundantly entertained us when we had experienced nothing better. God has affigned to each order, and to the feveral ftages of life in the fame perfon, their peculiar powers and taftes. Each one is as happy when its tafte is gratified as it can then be. But we are immediately confcious that one gratification is more excellent than another, when we have experienced both. And then our reafon and obfervation enables us to compare the effects, and confequences, and duration. One may be tranfitory, and the occafion of great fubfequent mifery, tho' for the prefent the enjoyment be intenfe: another may be lafting, fafe, and fucceeded by no fatiety, fhame, difguft, or remorfe.

Superior beings by diviner faculties and fuller knowledge may, without experience of all forts, immedi- ∿∿∿
ately difcern what are the nobleft. They may have *What men are the beft judges.*
fome intuitive knowledge of perfection, and fome ftan-
dard of it, which may make the experience of fome
lower forts ufelefs to them. But of mankind thefe
certainly are the beft judges who have full experience,
with their taftes or fenfes and appetites in a natural
vigorous ftate. Now it never was alledged that focial
affections, the admiration of moral excellence, the defire of efteem, with their attendant and guardian temperance, the purfuits of knowledge, or a natural activity, impaired any fenfe or appetite. This is often
charged with great juftice upon luxury, and furfeit-
ing, and indolence. The higheft fenfual enjoyments
may be experienced by thofe who employ both mind
and body vigoroufly in focial virtuous offices, and allow all the natural appetites to recur in their due fea-
fons. Such certainly are the beft judges of all enjoyments. Thus according to the maxim often inculcated by Ariftotle, " The good man is the true judge
" and ftandard of every thing."

But it may juftly be queftioned, whether men much *The vicious fel-*
devoted to fenfual pleafures, to thofe of the imagina- *dom can judge well.*
tion, or to wealth and power, are fufficiently prepa-
red to judge in this queftion. Such purfuits indeed
are feldom continued long without fome notion of
their innocence, nay of fome duty or moral obligation. Habits fometimes deface natural characters and
powers. Men of vicious habits have fmall experience

Book I. of the generous affections, social joys, and the delights of true impartial uniform goodness. Bad habits weaken social feelings, and the relish of virtue. And yet even such men on some occasions give a strong testimony to the cause of virtue.

III. Having premised these things we may first compare the several sorts of enjoyment in point of dignity and duration; and in like manner their opposites, sufferings. And then compare a little the several tempers or characters in point of inward satisfaction.

Sensual plea-
sures are the
meanest.

The pleasures of the external senses, are of two classes; those of the palate, and those betwixt the sexes. Both these we call sensual.

Those of the pa-
late.

The pleasures of the palate how grateful soever they may be to children, must appear the meanest and most despicable enjoyments to all men of reflection who have experienced any others. The uneasiness felt when the body needs support may be pretty intense; as 'tis wisely contrived, to engage us to take necessary care of the body. The allaying this pain may give a strong sensation of pleasure at first. But the proper pleasure of taste, the positive enjoyment, must be despicable to all who are above the order of brutes. The differences in point of pleasure among the several kinds of food is so small, that the keenness of appetite is allowed to make a much greater. The most exquisite cookery can scarce give such high sensation of this kind to a satisfied appetite, tho it be not surfeited; as the plainest fare will give to a brisk appetite after abstinence and exercise; even altho'

there was no pain, inconſiſtent with mirth and gayety, to be allayed. When therefore the allaying ſo
gentle an uneaſineſs cauſes more pleaſure than any exquiſite favours without it, the poſitive pleaſure muſt
be very inconſiderable. The preventing of appetite,
or the increaſing or prolonging it by incentives of any
kind, are vain efforts for pleaſure; ſo are all arts, except exerciſe and abſtinence, till the natural appetite
returns. The greateſt Epicures have acknowledged
this when buſineſs or diverſions have caſually led them
to make the experiment.

Men would univerſally agree in this point, were not *Reaſons of miſ*
theſe pleaſures generally blended with others of very *takes, a miſtur*
different natures. Not only nice oeconomy, art, and *of moral plea*
elegance in fine ſervices and grandeur of apartments, *ſures.*
but even moral qualities, liberality, communication
of pleaſure, friendſhip, and meriting well from others,
are joined in our imaginations. Strip ſenſuality of all
theſe borrowed charms, and view it naked and alone
as mere pleaſing the palate in ſolitude, and it is ſhameful and deſpicable to all.

Imagine a life ſpent in this enjoyment without in-
terruption, and that, contrary to the preſent order of
nature, the appetite ſtill remained; but that there was
no ſocial enjoyment or affection, no finer perceptions,
or exerciſe of the intellectual powers; this ſtate is below that of many brutes. Their appetites allow intervals for ſome pleaſures of a ſocial nature, and for
action; and when thus employed, they ſhew an higher
joy than in feeding.

The duration too of thefe fenfations is inconfide-
rable. Such indeed is the bounty of *God*, that the

The duration
fmall. means of allaying the cravings of appetite may be eafily procured; and thus by good management we may
all frequently enjoy almoft the higheft pleafures of
this kind. But the appetite is foon fatisfied, and re-
curs not till after long intervals. Artificial incentives
may raife an unnatural craving, but the allaying of
this gives little pleafure. 'Tis a real depravation and
ficknefs; and, when long continued, turns to fuch bodily indifpofition as muft ftop all enjoyments. Where
grandeur and variety are affected, the fancy grows capricious and inconftant, and the objects uncertain.
The humour may grow too expenfive for our fortunes,
and increafe, while the means of gratification are diminifhed.

The fame true   Many of the fame confiderations depretiate the o-
of amorous en- ther fpecies of fenfual pleafure, which much depends
joyments.
upon the allaying the uneafy craving of a brutal impulfe, as the pofitive good is of itfelf mean and incon-
fiderable. Conceive the fenfation alone, without love
or efteem of any moral qualities, or the thought of
communicating pleafure, and of being beloved; it
would not equal the delights which fome of the finer
brute beafts feem plainly confcious of. And then this
enjoyment is the moft tranfitory of all. Indulgence,
and variety, and incentives, bring upon the mind a
miferable craving; an impatient ardour; an incapacity of felf-government, and of all valuable improvement; a wretched flavery, which ftrips the mind of all

candour, integrity, and sense of honour. Add to this
the capriciousness of fancy, the torments of disappointment, which such wandering dissolute desires must
be exposed to; and that after the transient sensation,
there can scarce remain any thing agreeable, to one
who has not lost all manly sense of good. The reflection on any past sensual enjoyments gives no sense of
any merit or worth, no ground of self-esteem, or scarce
any sort of joy except from the low hopes of repeat-
ing the same, which may a little revive the appetite
after intervals. The remembrance is no support under any calamity, chagrin, pain, provocation or sorrow, or any inward disturbance of mind, or outward
misfortune. The very nature of these sensations we
call sensual, and the inward sentiments of our hearts
about them, abundantly declare that the supreme happiness of human nature must consist in very different
enjoyments of a more noble and durable nature.

IV. 'Tis often occurring, on the other hand, that *Objections removed from the
practice of the
dissolute.* we see multitudes who prefer such pleasures to all o-
thers, and make the pursuits of sensuality the business of their lives; and that therefore the bent of the
mind is naturally toward them; and their power superior to our *moral sense*, and to the generous affections.

To remove this cause of suspicion; let us recollect
that the constant pursuits of sensuality are seldom e-
ver observed without an opinion of their innocence.
Our *moral faculty*, our sympathetick sense, and our
kind affections are seldom set in opposition to them,
or combat with them, in the minds of men much de-

voted to fenfuality. Where without this notion of in-nocence men are hurried into fenfual enjoyments by impetuous appetites, the ftate is miferable and full of abject remorfe after the tranfient gratifications. The profeffedly diffolute have fome fpecious reafons by which they are deluded into a perfuafion of the inno-cence of their purfuits.

Nay fome moral notions, fuch as communication of pleafure, love, friendfhip, meriting well, and being beloved, make the main charm even in fenfual enjoy-ments. This is manifeft in the luxury and intempe-rance of fuch as are not funk below the beafts, and u-niverfally defpifed. It holds too in the unchafte paffi-ons: and hence fome notions of moral excellencies, good nature, friendlinefs, fweetnefs of temper, wit, and obligingnefs recommend their objects. But on the other hand; fuch as by generous affections, and love of moral excellence and honour, are led into a virtuous courfe, avowedly defpife fenfual enjoyments; nor does any confufed imaginations of them, or hopes even of immunity from labour and pain recommend it to their choice. The external evils, toil, expence, and hardfhips are known and defpifed as well as the allurements of eafe and pleafure: the moral forms by their own proper power are fuperior to them. In the voluptuous, the *moral fenfe* is feldom conquered; the enjoyments feem innocent, or at leaft the guilt is fo diminifhed by the fophiftry of the paffions, that 'tis only the fmalleft moral evil which feems to be incur-red for the higheft fenfual good; and the weakeft ef-

forts of the moral kind overcome by the ftrongeft of CHAP. 7.
fenfuality; and often, even by the affiftance of fome
miftaken moral fpecies.

It is here likewife proper to obferve that all fenfu- *The fenfual en-*
al gratifications are not oppofite to moral enjoyments. *joyments confi-*
ftent with virtue
There is a moderate indulgence perfectly innocent, *as high as any.*
fufficient to allay the uneafinefs of appetite; which too
by wife oeconomy may frequently be as high as any
fort of fenfual enjoyments, and even fubfervient to the
moral. The temperate, and fuch as, after proper felf-
government in coelibacy, have made a wife choice in
marriage, may have as high fenfual enjoyments as
any. In recommending of virtue we need not fuppofe
it oppofite to all gratifications of fenfe; tho its power
in our hearts fhould be maintained fo high that it may
be able to controll all the appetites which by accident
may oppofe it. Its gentle fway generally allows fuch
gratifications as may be the higheft of the kind; or
where it does not, it makes abundant compenfation
for the lofs, by the joyful approbation of fuch abftinence and felf-government. What rich compenfation
is made by the joyful approbation one muft feel of fidelity, friendfhip, and meriting well, and by the returns of a conftant affection from a worthy heart, for
the want of the irregular, fhameful, perplexing, joylefs paffions and indulgences, with perfons of no moral worth or ftedfaftnefs of affection.

V. We come next to confider the pleafures of the *The pleafures*
of knowledge and
imagination in the grandeur and elegance of living, and *the ingenious arts*
fuperior to the
the perceptions of beauty and harmony, to which we *fenfual in digni-*
ty.

Book I. may add thofe of the ingenious arts, and knowledge. Here there is no brutal uneafy previous appetite, the fating of which might enhance the pleafure; and yet one may immediately find that thefe are enjoyments fuperior to the fenfual, and more recommended by the conftitution of our nature. When the cravings of appetite are grown painful, one will readily quit thefe pleafures till the pain is removed; efpecially when there are no apprehenfions of our not being at liberty of fpeedily returning to them. But the beholding beautiful forms, the curious works of art, or the more exquifite works of nature; the entertainments of harmony, of imitation in the ingenious arts; the difcovering of the immutable relations and proportions of the objects of the pure intellect and reafon, give enjoyments in dignity far fuperior to any thing fenfual, where the fenfual are confidered alone without borrowed charms of an higher nature. Thefe more manly pleafures are more fuited to our nature; and are always more efteemed and approved when we are judging of the purfuits of others.

They are alfo fuperior in duration. Thefe pleafures too far furpafs the fenfual likewife in duration. They can employ a great part of life without fatiety or cloying, as their pleafure is fo much pofitive enjoyment independent upon the allaying of any previous uneafy fenfations. They are the proper exercifes of the foul, where none of the higher focial offices, or thofe of rational piety claim its activity. They partake of its lafting nature, and are not tranfitory, as all enjoyments are which are merely fubfervi-

CHAP. 7.

ent to the perifhing body. Thus, as often as the more important offices of virtue allow any intervals, our time is agreeably and honourably employed in hiftory natural or civil, in geometry, aftronomy, poetry, painting, and mufick, or fuch entertainments as ingenious arts afford. And fome of the fweeteft enjoyments of this fort require no property, nor need we ever want the objects. If familiarity abates the pleafure of the more obvious beauties of nature, their more exquifite inward ftructures may give new delights, and the ftores of nature are inexhauftible.

Such objects of thefe taftes as require property are more uncertain, and the purfuit of them more folicitous and anxious, and the fancy more inconftant, as long poffeffion abates the relifh. The imagination here needs ftrict reins, that it may not run out into exceffive admiration by affociated notions of moral dignity, and liberality; and thus involve us in innumerable vexatious purfuits of what is not effential to happinefs.

VI. Pleafures of the fympathetick kind arifing from the fortunes of others are proportioned to the ftrength of the kind affections we have for them. Our nature is exceedingly fufceptible of thefe affections; efpecially the ftronger forts of them toward offspring, parents, kinfmen, benefactors, or eminently worthy characters; toward fects, parties, countries. They furnifh the far greater part of the bufinefs, and of the happinefs or mifery of life.

Sympathetick feelings very intenfe.

Compare thefe with others: Confider the joy of

VOL. I.   R

Book I. heart upon any confiderable profperity, or any eminent virtue of one whom we heartily love, of a child,
a brother, a friend: upon any glory or advantage to
our party, or country; to any honourable caufe we
have efpoufed, or any admired character; or upon their
efcaping any imminent danger. Where there is an
hearty affection thefe joys are incomparably fuperior
to any of the former. What pleafure of fenfe or imagination would we not forego to obtain thefe events?
Some ecftacies of joy upon the efcaping of great imminent perfonal dangers have been too violent for nature, and have proved fatal: we have more*inftances
of fympathetick joys which proved alfo unfupportable and fatal. And if fome tempers cannot bear life
after fome misfortunes befallen themfelves; more inftances are found of fuch as throw it away upon the
misfortunes of others. The enjoyments muft be very
high which can fweeten all the toil and labour about
offspring and friends, even in common characters. Having affluence of all things defired for one's felf, abates
very little of the diligence of mankind.

And may be of
long duration.   Thefe pleafures endure as long as the perfon continues to be beloved and to be profperous. New fuc-
ceffes of our own, or of our friend, raife greater commotions at firft than advantages long poffeffed. But
while the affection continues, the fenfe remains; and
the fympathetick pleafure never cloys. Where indeed
affections are founded upon wrong fentiments of the

---

* See two inftances in Livy upon the defeat at Thrafymen, l. xxii. c. 7. See on
this fubject *Cicero de Fin.* l. v. c. 24.

merit of perfons, or caufes, they can have no ftability, and the fympathetick joy may be loft, and fucceeded by difguft and indignation. But the chief caufe of
inftability in this branch of happinefs is the uncertainty of the fortunes of thofe we love; for their mifery
muft occafion the moft fevere diftrefs. In this we
wholly depend on providence.

All that we can do to fecure any fund of joys of *Belief of provi-*
this kind is to examine well the merit of perfons, and *dence the fole fe-*
caufes, and by thefe means to turn our ftronger affec- *curity.*
tions toward the fuperior merit of men of true goodnefs and correct imaginations, whofe happinefs is lefs
inconftant than that of others; to have a firm perfuafion of the wifdom and goodnefs of providence, and
to cultivate the moft extenfive affections. The ftronger our univerfal good-will is, if our joys be fo much
the higher upon the general profperity, the greater
alfo fhall our regret be upon apprehended general mifery. But what makes this affection ever fafe in all
events, and a fund of fuperior joy, is a firm perfuafion of a good Providence governing the univerfe for
the beft, amidft all the apparent evils and diforders.
Of this more hereafter.

VII. The fourth clafs of enjoyments are the *moral,* *Moral enjoy-*
arifing from the confcioufnefs of good affections and *ments are among*
actions. Thefe joys are different from the fympathe- *the higheft in our*
tick, which may arife from that happinefs of others *nature.*
to which our affections and actions contributed nothing. But our affections and actions themfelves, abftracting from the ftate of others, cannot be indiffe-

rent to us when we attend to them. When we find our whole soul kind and benign, we muſt have a joyful approbation; and a further and higher joy ariſes from exerting theſe affections in wiſe beneficent offices. Theſe joys we find the higheſt and moſt important both in reſpect of dignity and duration.

In reſpect of dignity.   How much inferior are the higheſt ſenſual pleaſures, or even thoſe of the imagination, or ſpeculative knowledge, to the ſtable joy of conſcious goodneſs of heart; and to that high approbation one feels of himſelf in any important offices for the good of his country, or his friend; and to the joyful thought of meriting well of mankind, and deſerving their applauſes? The kind affections alone ſit eaſy in the heart; there is an inward complacence in them, and we joyfully entertain them for life.* But our nature is fitted for more than unactive affection. An high happineſs ariſes from the exerting our powers; and the nobler the power is, the more beatifick is its exerciſe: when the virtuous efforts are ſucceſsful, there is ſuch an aſſemblage of pure joys from conſcious goodneſs, ſympathy with others, and the expected love and approbation of all, eſpecially the complacency of our Maker, as far ſurpaſſes all other enjoyments. If we ſhould fail of ſucceſs, we may want the ſympathetick joy, and may be touched with compaſſion; but the other ſources of joy remain: the moral enjoyments can ſweeten theſe diſtreſſes from the misfortunes of the perſon or cauſe eſpouſed; which without the conſciouſneſs of our hav-

---

* This is often juſtly obſerved by Ariſtotle and Cicero.

ing acted our part well, muft have been much more CHAP. 7.
intolerable.

The fancy here is not inconfiftent. Our tafte for *Thefe pleafures are moft durable.*
virtue increafes by exercife; and habits make it ftill
more pleafant. The remembrance is ever delightful, and makes the enjoyment lafting, where there
have been juft notions of virtue, and of the merit of
perfons and caufes. One end propofed in the creating
different orders of beings, and ordaining the different
ftates of thofe of the fame fpecies, fome more, fome
lefs perfect, is probably this, that the nobler minds
fhould never want opportunities for the joyful exercife of their good difpofitions toward the inferior either in perfection or in fortune. Thefe joys too are
feated above the power of fortune while men retain
foundnefs of mind. A low ftation, and a hard condition of life, or external difadvantages may prevent our
doing the moft important fervices to others in external things; but can neither hinder the found inward
affections of heart, nor a courfe of action fuited to
our abilities; and this is the higheft virtue.

Unexamined admirations of fome partial moral *Juft notions of virtue neceffary.*
forms, and fome narrow affections, without true no-
tions of merit in perfons and caufes, may lead us into
fuch conduct as upon better information may be matter of fhame and remorfe. But where by clofe reflection we have attained juft notions of virtue and merit,
and of the effectual means of doing good, virtuous
action, as it is the natural purpofe of a rational and

focial fpecies, fo it is their higheft happinefs, and always in their power.

Among thefe moral enjoyments, the joys of religion and devotion toward God well deferve to be particularly remarked, which in the clafs of moral enjoyments are the higheft of all. But as thefe enjoyments are of a pretty different nature from the reft of the moral ones, they fhall be confidered apart hereafter, for reafons above-mentioned; and we fhall fhew their high importance to a ftable and fublime happinefs above all others.

Pleafures of lo-nour very in-tenfe. IX. The pleafures of honour from the approbation, efteem, and gratitude of others as they naturally enfue upon virtue, fo when they are founded on it, are among the moft grateful feelings of the foul. Thefe joys of honour and virtue and the fympathetick joys are naturally connected, nor need we minutely compare them; as the fame conduct is naturally fubfervient to them all: and where they concur, no words can exprefs the happinefs enjoyed. The fympathetick feelings may be more intenfe in fome tender affectionate hearts: active fpirits in publick ftations may be more affected with confcious virtue and merited glory. But where the three are united, with a firm perfuafion of a good *God* approving our temper, and enfuring the univerfal order and happinefs, our ftate muft come neareft to *that joy unfpeakable and full of glory*, which we hope for as the perfect confummation of the rational nature.

True glory is also durable, not like the sensual en- CHAP. 7.
joyments, which pass like the shadow of a cloud leaving ∿∿∿
no trace behind them. The approbation and esteem *And of great duration.*
of others, when founded on virtue, may probably con-
tinue during life, and survive us: and the approbation of God shall be everlasting. The pursuits of extensive fame for eminent abilities and virtues may indeed
be subject to disappointment, and be full of labour
and liable to excess. Ordinary virtues, or even the
highest virtues in the low stations will not obtain the
extensive applauses of nations. But a wise and virtuous man may generally obtain such honour either in
a narrower or larger sphere as may give great joy And
a good heart, persuaded of a good providence observing all things, is sure of the approbation of the best
judge, and that to eternity.

X. Among such solemn subjects the pleasures of *The pleasures*
mirth and gayety must be of small account. And yet *of mirth are on the side of virtue.*
even children despise sensuality in comparison of them:
and sensual enjoyments borrow from them many of
their charms, without which they would be despicable
and shameful. They are an agreeable seasoning to o-
ther enjoyments, and some relief from the fatigues of
serious business. The nobler joys are grave, severe,
and solemn. But human life must have relaxations.
Now whatever value we put upon mirth and gayety
it must be cast into the side of virtue: since that mind
is always best disposed for the reception of all chear-
fulness and pleasantry where all is kind and easy; free
from anger, ill-will, envy, or remorse. These pleasures

are always social, and fly solitude. They are best che-rished amidst love, good-nature, and mutual esteem.

Wealth and power are more beatifick to the virtuous than others. As wealth and power are not immediately pleasant, but the means of obtaining pleasures; their importance to happiness must be in proportion to that of the enjoyments to which they are referred by the possessor. The virtuous man therefore who refers them to generous and virtuous purposes, has a much nobler enjoyment of them than those who refer them to the pleasures of the imagination, or the elegance of life; and yet this is a finer reference than that to sensuality. Where through confused imaginations they are not directly referred to their natural purposes, but pursued for themselves, avarice and ambition become wretched insatiable cravings, hateful to all mankind; and the possessions become joyless to the person who obtains them.

Ill-natured gratifications mean, and not durable. XI. As to some other pretended enjoyments in gratifying the passions of anger, malice, envy, revenge: 'tis certain there is no small sense of joy in these gratifications, where the passions were intense. But then 'tis obvious, that as good-will, love, esteem, gratitude, and every kind affection are natural and original pleasures sitting easy in the mind; so the happiness of any innocent person observed is the occasion of pure unmixed joy, not arising from the allaying any previous pain. If the person has been in misery, and thus has raised our compassion: his being relieved adds also another joy from stopping our sympathetick pain. But the misery of another is naturally uneasy to the ob-

ferver: it muſt then be by ſome accident that it ever CHAP. 7.
becomes grateful: by ſome previous anger, or envy;
ſome injury apprehended, or ſome oppoſition to the
intereſts of ſome perſon beloved.

    Theſe paſſions of the unkind ſort are not uſeleſs *Such paſſions not uſeleſs in our* parts in our conſtitution. Upon apprehenſion of inju- *conſtitution.* ry or damage done to us, or to thoſe we love, anger naturally ariſes to rouſe us for defence. When per- ſons we do not eſteem are preferred to thoſe of higher merit, an honeſt concern and indignation ariſes. A like indignation ariſes againſt all ſuch as appear groſs- ly immoral. Indulgence may make theſe paſſions ſtrong and habitual. The feelings attending them are original uneaſineſs and torment; to which however it was reaſonable for the general good that we ſhould be in ſome degree ſubjected on certain occaſions, as we are to bodily pain. The ſweeteſt tempers have expe- rienced ſome ſhort fits of them, and have felt how un- eaſy theſe moments paſs. Where ſuch paſſions are high and laſting, degenerating into rancour and ſtated malice and envy, the miſery muſt be very great: no wonder then that the removal of it ſhould give at firſt a conſiderable pleaſure. The miſery is removed by the ſufferings of the perſon hated or envied. But this tur- bulent joy, even while it laſts, is not to be compared with the ſweet ſympathetick joys, the ſenſe of merited love and eſteem, or the ſelf-approbation of forgiving, where no publick intereſt requires puniſhing. And then this ill-natured joy ſoon ceaſes after the paſſion is ſated, as the miſery of the moſt hated object cannot pleafe us long; nor is it ever the object of approbation, either in ourfelves or others, upon reflection; nay 'tis generally fucceeded by remorfe, regret, and forrow. The calm mind can have no pleafure in the mifery of another, tho it may acquiefce in fuch fufferings as a publick intereft requires. We cannot wifh to prolong vengeance but upon fome notion of repeated acts of unrelenting wickednefs; or from fome remains of the preceeding fear with which we were tormented. And this fhews one reafon why " the brave are not " cruel." The pleafures then of this ill-natured kind are to the calm joys of humanity, as the flaking the burning thirft of a fever, or the fating a gnawing difeafed ftomach, to the enjoyment of grateful food with an healthy and vigorous appetite.

Our moral fenfe values affections and enjoyments in proportion to their tendency to the general good

XII. We may obferve concerning thefe feveral enjoyments, that with the moft benign counfel our minds are fo conftituted that we value them upon calm reflection in proportion to their importance to the happinefs of the whole fyftem. Thefe which only regard the fafety and animal gratifications of the individual are felt to be the meaneft; fuch as may be of more extenfive ufe, and incite men to be ferviceable to others, are naturally more efteemed, and that in different degrees according to their extent. Thus we value more the pleafures of the ingenious arts, and fuch exercifes of body or mind as may naturally be ufeful to many. The partial narrow affections are lovely and joyful; but ftill the more ftable and calm and extenfive, as they are more ufeful, are alfo more

joyful both in the exercife, and in the remembrance, CHAP. 7.
where there has been any tolerable attention and reflection. We fee then that the *moral faculty* moft approves and recommends fuch difpofitions as tend
moft to the general good, and at the fame time fuch
as may give the nobleft enjoyments to the agent upon
reflection. And thus the two *grand determinations* of
our nature, by a thorough confideration of our conftitution, may appear perfectly confiftent, and be generally gratified by the fame means. The fame conclufion will be confirmed by a comparifon of the feveral forts of pain.

XIII. We come next to compare the feveral forts *The feveral*
of uneafinefs, or pain. And firft it immediately oc- *forts of pain com-*
pared.
curs, that the feveral forts of pain are not in the exact
proportion of the pleafures of thefe fenfes. Mere bo- *Bodily pain not*
the higheft.
dily pleafure is the loweft and leaft intenfe, and yet
bodily pain may be very violent. But we cannot thence
conclude that it may be the greateft poffible mifery, as fome have maintained. In pain, as in pleafure, the kind is to be regarded as well as the intenfenefs. The prefervation of the body required this
ftrong connection with the foul, and that the fenfations indicating its fufferings fhould be very ftrong;
fuch as fometimes wholly to occupy the weaker minds,
making them incapable of any attention to other
things. But the foul finds that it cannot approve the
facrificing its duty to the avoiding of any bodily pain;
and that moral evil is ftill fomething worfe. Some
kinds of pain have a quality contrary to that dignity

we mentioned, which makes them the caufes of greater mifery than any bodily pain, how intenfe foever it
may be. This debafes not the worth of the perfon;
nor caufes fuch an abject ftate of mifery, as the confcioufnefs of the more odious moral evils, which occafion remorfe, and felf-abhorrence. We rafhly conclude otherways from feeing perfons of ordinary virtue breaking all tyes of affection, duty, and honour,
to avoid tortures ; and betraying their friends and
country under fuch temptations.

The caufes of But in fuch cafes the higheft bodily pain is com-
miftake in this pared with fome lower fympathetick pain, in fome
matter. weaker bonds of affection, or with fome lower moral
fpecies; whereas the higheft of both forts fhould be
compared to find their importance. One who has no
high fenfe of virtue betrays his friend, or country, in
fome point not conceived abfolutely neceffary to their
fafety, nor certainly involving them in ruin by the
difcovery of it; whereas his tortures are prefent and
unavoidable any other way. The cafes fhould be put
of men of high virtue, where the point to be extorted
would be certain unavoidable ruin to their friends,
or country. Brave men in fuch cafes have endured all
tortures; and fuch as cannot, yet feel they have acted
wrong, and difapprove their own choice of incurring
moral evil rather than the higheft pain. There is a
fine machinery of nature here; that men of fmall reflection who may conceive tortures as the greateft e-
vil, yet fome way expect it as natural conduct, and
highly approve it, that men fhould facrifice what they

take to be their higheſt private intereſt, by ſuffering CHAP. 7. the greateſt miſery, for a publick good. This con- firms what we ſaid above of a calm determination to- ward a publick good without any reference to the pri- vate intereſt of the agent, how ſublime ſoever; and that this determination ſhould controll all others in our nature.

In the more common caſes, how often do parents, friends, patriots, endure the higheſt ſufferings to free others from the like? The direct ſenſe of hunger, toils, wounds, and bodily pain, is lighter than the ſympa- thetick with the like ſufferings of others. And in parental affection there is ſeldom any view to duty, honour, or compenſation. Some crimes are ſo horrid that many ordinary characters would endure tortures rather than commit them; and freely expoſe their lives to avoid the imputation of them.

In the caſes where duty yields to torture; the pri- vate evil is preſent, certain and ſenſible: the publick *What caſes are proper and what not.* detriment abſent, uncertain, and otherways perhaps avoidable. The moral turpitude is extenuated by the greatneſs of the temptation, and the effort of the *mo- ral faculty* is thus made more languid. Where virtue conquers pain, the pain appears in its full ſtrength; but is over-powered, by the generous affection, or the abhorrence of what is baſe. Put both ſenſations in their full ſtrength without alleviation. Whether would one chuſe to commit the worſt crimes without ſuch extenuating neceſſity, or to be in the condition of on

tortured with the gout or ſtone, as ſeverely as any ty-
rant could torture him?

Put caſes, as in ſome antient fables; that, upon
ſuch falſe information as nothing but a faulty, paſſionate, impetuous, and cruel temper could have entertained, one had tortured to death a perſon unknown,
who is afterwards found to have been his tender parent, his dutiful ſon, or his generous friend, or affectionate brother; what bodily pain could equal the remorſe and ſympathetick ſorrow which muſt ariſe? and
yet here the guilt is alleviated by ignorance. When
men have thrown away their own lives from remorſe,
the crimes have generally flowed from ignorance, inadvertence, or ſome furious paſſion; all which are ſome
alleviation of guilt. What muſt the torment have
been had men knowingly, and unprovoked, committed the like crimes, and ſoon after recovered a ſenſe
of virtue? But tis hard to find inſtances of ſuch guilt;
as our nature is ſcarce capable of it, or if it is, the
moral ſenſe is irrecoverable.

Take the ſympathetick ſenſe alone. Where is the
great difference, in point of miſery, between enduring
tortures, and beholding the tortures of a beloved or
only child, or of a tender parent; or beholding them
ſubjected to ſomething more ignominious? *Would to
God I had dyed for thee,* is no feigned wiſh on ſuch
occaſions.

In conſidering the ſtate of ſuch as are dear to us,
moral evil appears always ſuperior to bodily pain.

Who could wifh a fon or friend to be rather funk irre- CHAP. 7.
coverably in all vice and bafenefs of foul, but free from
pain, and abounding with fenfual pleafures; than expofed to the greateft tortures in fome act of heroifm,
with a lively fenfe of integrity and felf-efteem, and the
fympathetick joys in the profperity of every intereft
that is dear to him?

The natural ftrength of the human mind in refifting pain would appear much greater, were it not for
the terrors of death which generally attend the feverer kinds of it. Remove this fear, and the foul can
bear it much eafier. In fome diverfions, and in the accidents which attend them, where there is no fear of
any thing fatal, men without dejection of mind, nay
fometimes with gayety, can bear very acute pain, and
defpife it.*

Pain in the extremities of the body may be very *Bodily pain may*
lafting. But all bodily pain differs in this from moral *be very lafting.*
feelings, that it leaves no fenfe of evil when the un-
eafy fenfation ceafes. The reflection on it is rather
pleafant than uneafy, when there is no fear of its returning. The foul is often bettered by it, as experience gives it more ftrength and fortitude. Where
pain was endured in any honourable caufe, it always
remains matter of joy and glorying.

XIV. Our higher fenfes by which we receive the *By the imagi-*
pleafures of the imagination, admit far lefs pain than *nation we receive*
pleafure, if the mind is under good difcipline. Bodily *than pain.*
deformity or diftortion may be very uneafy to the per-

* On this fubject many noble fentiments are to be found in *Cicero's Tufculan.* l. ii.

son who is fo unfortunate; and fo may meannefs, or the want of the decencies and elegancies of life, to fuch as have high defires and notions of happinefs in fuch things. But there is no uneafy craving, as in the appetites, previous to thefe imaginations of great good in the objects; and the correcting of thefe imaginations may remove all the pain, efpecially where nobler enjoyments compenfate the want of thefe pleafures. And then beauty, harmony, and ingenious works of art, and true imitation of every kind, without any property in the external objects, give pretty high pofitive pleafures; whereas the deformity of external objects, diffonance, bad imitations, or rude works of art, give no other pain than that trifling fort from a difappointment of expectation in a matter of no neceffity in life. Knowledge is attended with exquifite pleafure; but the want of it only occafions pain where there is an high defire and admiration of it, or a fear of fhame for the want of it. The uneafinefs even to an inflamed imagination from the want of the grandeur and elegance of life is generally lighter than bodily pain, or the fympathetick, or the fenfe of moral turpitude and infamy; and 'tis wife and juft that it fhould be fo, as thefe other fenfes are intended to guard mankind againft evils more pernicious to the fyftem. If men expofe fometimes their friends, families, and country, to many evils by immoderate expences on grandeur and elegance; the diftant miferies of others are unexpected, or not attended to: there are hopes of new friends, of fupport, of profitable employments by the

friendſhip of the great, the approaching evils are not C͟ʜ͟ᴀ͟ᴘ͟. 7.
apprehended, and the guilt is unobſerved.

XV. The ſympathetick, and moral pain of remorſe, *The ſympathe-*
and infamy, are the higheſt our nature admits, as *tick and moral pains the higheſt*
their oppoſite joys are the higheſt: they can make life *of all.*
quite intolerable. The miſery of one beloved, while
it continues and is attended to, is inceſſant pain to
the obſerver. When it ceaſes by death, the painful
remembrance long ſurvives in an affectionate heart;
till buſineſs diverts the thoughts, or deep reflection
ſuggeſts conſolations. The ſure refuge in ſuch caſes
is to a good providence, and that future happineſs provided for all worthy objects of kind affections.

'Tis vain to alledge that all ſympathy carries with
it pleaſure ſuperior to the pain. We ſhould not then *Why we are prone to tragical*
incline to change the ſtate of the object. 'Tis true we *ſights.*
are prone to run to ſpectacles of miſery, and are fond
of tragedies: and yet miſery alone obſerved is the
cauſe of miſery only. But there is a natural impulſe,
implanted for the kindeſt reaſons, forcing us to ſuch
ſpectacles of miſery, which generally brings relief to
the ſufferers. And we can reſtrain this impulſe where
we foreſee that it can do no good. Let none be ſur-
priſed at ſuch impulſes where no pleaſure is in view, or
any removal of our own pain: do not we obſerve after the death of a dear friend, when we can ſerve him
no more, nor enjoy any ſympathetick pleaſures with
him, the tormenting thoughts of his dying agonies
and groans are for many weeks, and months, and
years recurring to our minds. Our many efforts to

banifh the painful ufelefs thoughts are long ineffectual. When thefe efforts are repeated frequently and
vigoroufly, they may at laft banifh them; but when
we intermit our watch they return again and torment
us. Can that fenfation have fuperior pleafure which
upon reflection we fhun to retain and guard againft
as a torment; which in tenderer conftitutions turns
into bodily ficknefs?

The delights in
tragedy.
In tragedy there is a lively imitation of manners,
of heroick virtues, ftruggling againft fortune ; and
noble fentiments and affections are expreffed. Our
fympathetick feelings indeed of every kind are exercifed; and compaffion and terror are gently raifed upon diftreffes which we know are feigned. Can one fay
that terror has fuperior pleafure in it ; and yet we
fometimes court fuch ftories as terrify ourfelves. But
when the imitations by fculpture, painting, and mufick, pleafe us fo much that we can bear toil and hunger, in prolonging the entertainment; what wonder
is it that fuch noble imitations of manners delight
us, notwithftanding the gentle uneafinefs of fympathy with imaginary fufferings? what pleafure is there
in an infirmary or lazar-houfe, and in hearing real
groans, where there is abundant matter of compaffion, but without fuch virtues difcovered? fhould one
forget that the diftreffes in tragedy are feigned, his
pain will increafe; but the lovely virtues and noble
fentiments affect the mind with the higher pleafure.

Remorfe the
greateft and moft
lafting torment.
Remorfe may be the higheft torment, and make
life and all its enjoyments hateful. 'Tis not like ex-

ternal fenfations referred to a body, a material fyftem, indicating its diforders, but not abating that
inward worth for which a man efteems himfelf or
his friend. We feem confcious that the body is not
the *perfon*, the *felf* we efteem; and that its diforders
or decays of any kind do not abate the excellence or
worth of a rational active being. Moral evil we feel
to be the immediate bafenefs of this *felf*. It makes
our inmoft nature odious and diftafteful to ourfelves,
and to all who know it.

Thefe feelings are not tranfitory; the remembrance
is always tormenting. They * are lefs acute while the
unfated paffion continues impetuous: their violence
appears when the crime is committed. They gnaw
the foul a long time, nor ceafe unlefs habit brings on
a ftupor on this power, and men become abandoned
to every thing that is bad. And even here any confiderable adverfity or danger, which checks a while the
vicious paffions, may revive the *moral principle*, and
renew the torment.

XVI. Infamy and reproach when they juftly befal us, are a great mifery. But when we unjuftly fuffer this way, while our own hearts approve our conduct, the fuffering is much lighter, and we may have
many ftrong fupports under it. The evil in this latter
cafe is lefs durable; as the truth often breaks out beyond
expectation. The omnifcient God knows we are in-

Infamy a great mifery.

---

* *Quum fcelus admittunt fupereft conftantia. Quid fas*
Atque nefas, tandem incipiunt fentire, peractis
Criminibus.   Juv. Sat. 13.

jured, and the wifer part of men with whom we have to do will fooner or later difcern our innocenec, and we are fure of their compaffionate regards. Reproach however is generally a greater evil and more afflicting than moft of the bodily pains, and may be pretty lafting. It over-balances all fenfual pleafures with fuch as are not abandoned: to repel it many would facrifice their all, and many have hazarded even life itfelf.

After this impartial enquiry into our feveral forts of pleafures and pains, how unnatural muft that account of the fupreme good and evil given by the old Cyrenaicks and Epicureans, and by fome moderns likewife, appear, which places the origin of both in the bodily fenfations, and refers both ultimately to them.

C H A P. VIII.

A Comparifon of the feveral TEMPERS *and* CHARACTERS, *in point of* HAPPINESS, *or* MISERY.

THE grounds of fufpecting a great oppofition between one s private intereft and the indulging of the focial affections in all generous offices of virtue, may be pretty well removed by what is already faid of the high enjoyments of the fympathetick and moral kinds. But the unreafonablenefs of all fuch fufpicions will further appear by confidering which of the feveral fets of affections conftituting the various characters of men, are of themfelves the fweeteft enjoyment, the moft eafy and ferene ftate of mind.

As all the senses and affections above-mentioned are parts of our inward fabrick, so each of them have their natural use either to the animal itself, or to the system of which it is a part. Moral goodness indeed consists principally in the social and kind affections carrying us out beyond ourselves. But there is a natural subserviency of the private or selfish affections, while they are kept within certain bounds, not only to the good of the individual, but to that of the system ; nor is any one compleat in his kind without them. And as the happiness of a system results from that of the individuals, 'tis necessary to it, that each one have the selfish affections in that degree which his best state requires, consistently with his most effectual services to the publick.

The most benign and wise constitution of a ratio- nal system is that in which the degree of selfish affection most useful to the individual is consistent with the interest of the system; and where the degree of generous affections most useful to the system is ordinarily consistent with or subservient to the greatest happiness of the individual. A mean low species may indeed be wholly subjected to the interests of a superior species, and have affections solely calculated for these higher interests. But in the more noble systems it would be a blemish if in fact there was an established inconsistence between the two grand ends to each rational being, personal enjoyment and publick happiness, and in consequence, an irreconcilable variance between the affections destined for the pursuit of them.

*No natural af-
fection abfolute-
ly evil.*

None of our affections can be called abfolutely evil, in every degree; and yet a certain high degree, beyond the proportion of the reft, even in fome of our generous affections, may be vicious, or at leaft a great imperfection, detrimental both to the individual and the fyftem. At the fame time the greateft ftrength of any one kind is not of itfelf necessarily evil: nay it may be innocent, if the other affections have a ftrength proportioned to this kind, and to the dignity of their feveral natures, and of the purpofes for which they were implanted. But where the mind is not capacious enough to contain this high degree of other affections, any one of the felfifh, and many of the generous, may be excessive. The calm extensive good-will, the defire of moral excellence, the love of God, and refignation to his will, can never exceed: as they exclude not any partial good affection as far as it is ufeful, nor any juft regard to private good. But the more confined affections even of the generous fort may exceed their due proportion, and exclude or over-power other affections of a better fort: as we often fee in parental love, pity, party-zeal, &c. The moral turpitude confifts, not in the ftrength of thefe affections, but in the weaknefs of the more extensive ones in proportion to their dignity and fuperior ufe.

*The evil confifts
in want of pro-
portion.*

'Tis ftill more evident that the felfifh affections may be excessive and vicious. But it ought alfo to be obferved that there may be a degree of them too low and defective with refpect to the intention of nature. If a creature expofed to dangers, and yet neither ar-

med by nature or art, were fearless, and had no concern for its own safety in its services to others ; we
do not count this temper vicious, but 'tis manifestly
imperfect, hurtful to the individual, and useless to the
system. In the lower orders we discern the wise oeconomy of nature giving courage to the males along
with their superior strength or armour, and denying it
to the females, unless where the defence of their young
requires it. Strong social passions, little self-regard,
with ardent desires of honour, in men of very small
abilities, would be an excess on one hand, or a defect
on the other. The same generous ardours in men of
great abilities, with proportional caution, would be
useful and well proportioned: such social affections
and relishes for some fine enjoyments of the imagination, as sit easy in some characters, and exclude no duties of life, might to others occasion useless misery,
and starve all their other parts or faculties.

II. Now as we shewed the social and moral enjoy- *Affections to-*
ward social and
ments, with those of honour, to be the highest; we *moral enjoyments*
are the most ad-
shall briefly shew that the affections pursuing those ob- *vantageous;*
jects with which these enjoyments are connected, when
they are all kept in due proportion to their dignity
and use in the system, are the most advantageous and
easy to the individual; and that the selfish affections
when they are too strong and inconsistent with the
generous, are hurtful to the individual.

Our nature is susceptible of such ardour toward
they are capable
moral and social enjoyments as generally to be able to *of the greatest*
strength.
surmount all other desires, and make men despise all

Book I. bodily pleasure or pain. We see instances not only among the civilized, or where notions of virtue are strengthened by a finer education, but even among rude barbarians and robbers. From a point of honour, from gratitude, from zeal to a clan, or resentment of wrongs done to it, they can joyfully embrace all hardships, and defy death and torments.

Moral disturbance destroys all pleasure.   On the other hand, place one amidst the greatest affluence of sensual enjoyments, but let him feel some social or moral disturbance from some distress of his friend, some danger to his party, or to his character from the imputation of cowardice, or treachery; sensual pleasures become nauseous, and wounds, and death appear little to him. He scorns one who tells him, " that befall his party, his friend, his character, " what will, he may still enjoy his sensual affluence." He finds within himself superior springs of action, which are likewise superior sources of happiness, or misery.

Since then these social and moral enjoyments are the highest; that taste, those affections, and that course of action which tends to procure a constant train of such enjoyments, and secure us from their contraries, must be the natural means of the chief happiness, and preservatives from the deepest misery. Now these highest enjoyments are either these very affections and suitable actions, or the natural concomitants or consequences of them.

Social affections the most joyful.   Have we felt the state of mind under lively affections of love, good-will, bounty, gratitude, congratula-

tion? What when we have acted vigorously and suc- CHAP. 8.
cefsfully from such affections; served a friend, relieved the diftrefled, turned forrows into joy and gratitude, preferved a country, and made multitudes safe
and happy? The fenfe of every man tells him this
ftate is preferable to all others. The vicious themfelves, who feem wholly devoted to fenfuality, yet are
not void of such affections and fentiments. They have
their friendfhips, their points of honour, and engagements to parties, how rafh or capricious foever. Some
delights of this kind, fome focial affections, and imperfect virtues are their higheft enjoyments: 'tis * the
general voice of nature that where thefe pleafures are
excluded there is no happinefs. And as fenfuality cannot fufficiently employ or gratify human nature, affections of a contrary fort, fullennefs, morofenefs, fufpicion, and envy muft arife, which are both immediate
mifery, and the fruitful fources of it, wherever the focial affections are fupprefled.

Tho' the tendency of the focial affections is to pre- *But require re-*
vent mifery, and thus prevent fympathetick forrows; *lief and truft in*
yet when this cannot be effected we muft neceffarily *Providence.*
feel fome degree of uneafinefs of this generous fort.
Here we fhould have recourfe to fome higher confiderations, of the wifdom and goodnefs of the Divine
Providence, of the duty and the moral excellence of an
entire refignation to the fupreme wifdom and goodnefs, and of the firm grounds of hope thence arifing,
that fuch evils as our beft efforts cannot prevent, are

* *Cicero de Amicit.* l. 23. and often elfewhere.

deſtined by our univerſal Parent for the beſt purpoſes. Upon leſs preſumptions than theſe our ſympathetick ſufferings are often alleviated; when we have probable hopes that what at preſent moves our compaſſion is ſubſervient to ſome ſuperior future intereſt of thoſe we love. This truſt and reſignation, with hope, upon a firm perſuaſion of the divine goodneſs, ſhould be maintained by frequent meditation in ſuch ſtrength and vigour as to controll all narrower affections, and ſupport the ſoul under the ſocial diſtreſſes occaſioned by them. Of this hereafter.

Reſtraining the ſocial affections immoral and hurtful. To root out or abate the ſocial affections, if it would prevent or abate our ſocial ſorrows, muſt alſo deſtroy or abate proportionably all our ſocial and moſt of our moral joys. The abatement of even the narrower affections is rather a detriment to the human character. The moſt natural and perfect ſtate which our minds at preſent ſeem capable of, is that where all the natural affections, deſires and ſenſes are preſerved vigorous, in proportion to the dignity of the object they purſue; ſo that the inferior are ſtill kept under the reſtraint of the ſuperior, and never allowed to defeat the end for which God intended them; or to controll either of the two grand determinations of our ſouls toward the happineſs and perfection of the individual, and that of the ſyſtem.

All the unkind affections uneaſy. III. The ſeveral unkind affections and paſſions, 'tis plain, are originally uneaſy. Nature clearly ſhows that they ſhould not be the ordinary ſtate of the mind. The very degrees of them which are innocent, nay neceſ-

fary to the fyftem, are attended with uneafy fenfations, and little approbation can for any length of time
accompany them. Such is anger, even in that degree
which is neceffary for defending ourfelves or our
friends, and repelling injuries: fuch is that deliberate
refentment againft the infolent and injurious, which
aims at no more punifhment than the fafety of fociety requires: fuch that honeft indignation againft men
advanced far above their merit. Thefe all are uneafy
affections; and there is little lovely in them. The fame
is true of that felfifh defire of being fuperior to o-
thers, or the emulation or ftrong defire of eminence
in fome valuable qualities. This affection may be innocent, and is an ufeful fpur to fome tempers; but
'tis generally uneafy; and there is no moral beauty
which the heart can calmly approve of this fondnefs
of furpaffing upon comparifon.

Befide the uneafinefs which attends thefe paffions, *And only tran-*
fient emotions.
'tis plain they naturally tend to make fuch changes
upon their objects, as fhall put an end to themfelves,
and raife contrary motions of regret and pity; when
the objects are fo depreffed that we ceafe to fear evil
from them, or are brought into an hearty repentance
for any thing in them vicious or injurious: whereas the
kind affections which we conftantly approve, aim at
fuch ends as remain delightful, and prolong and
ftrengthen the affections. Good-will, and pity, aim at
the happinefs of their objects, and this, when obtained, is matter of permanent delight to the agent: and
fuch offices done to worthy objects increafe our love

to them. This shews that the former set of affections are destined by nature to be only transient occasional emotions; but the latter to be the stable permanent dispositions of soul.

These not abso-lutely evil in all degrees.

We have stated names for the excesses of these unkind passions, or when they arise without just or proportional causes, and are habitual; to wit, *malice, revenge, envy, ambition* or *pride*. But we have no such settled names for the innocent degrees. Hence some have too rashly imagined that some of our natural passions are absolutely evil in all degrees.

But these unkind passions, thus uneasy even while innocent, were implanted partly for the interest of the individual, and partly for that of the system. As the external senses by grateful perceptions point out the safe state of the body, and the ordinary enjoyments, to the individual; and rouse him on the other hand by uneasy sensations occasionally, to ward off what is destructive: so the *moral faculty* in a like subserviency to the publick, recommends to the agent, and to every observer too, by a grateful approbation, all kind affections and actions; and on the other hand by an uneasy reluctance and remorse deters the agent from such affections as are pernicious to the system; and by the uneasy impulses of anger and indignation rouses every observer to oppose his designs.

Not intended by nature as perma-nent dispositions.

These passions of anger, resentment and indignation even while they are innocent, or useful, are uneasy: and this, as well as the foregoing observation, shews that they never were destined to be the ordinary permanent difpofitions of the foul: they fhould Chap. 8. only arife occafionally, when fomething pernicious to the individual or the fyftem muft be repelled. They are a fort of ungrateful medicines for diforders, and not the natural food : they were implanted to repell injuries, and fo far only as they are thus employed can they be deemed innocent. Now as a fenfe or appetite is depraved in an individual, which loaths its natural food, or craves what is not nourifhing; as the organs of feeling muft be difordered and fickly when they are pained with the falutary air, or neceffary cloath-ing; furely that temper of mind muft be as much de-praved, where anger arifes without hurt or injury re-ceived; or averfion and hatred, where there is no mo-ral evil in the object; or envy upon the fuccefs of me-rit; or ill-will toward any innocent part of a fyftem formed for, and preferved by, a focial life, and an in-tercourfe of good offices.

'Tis therefore our intereft to examine well the me-rit of perfons and caufes, and to keep a ftrict rein over the unkind paffions, which are uneafy while innocent; and fo apt to exceed, that even in their moderate de-grees they look fo like fomething evil that they are little approved. The calmer affections of the foul to-ward the good either of the individual or the fyftem, are more generally effectual than the turbulent paffi-ons, whatever ufe thefe paffions may have in minds not enured to reflection. 'Tis defireable therefore to have our lives committed to thefe fafer conductors, and to have an habitual caution againft all violent commotions of the unkind fort, as what are frequent-ly dangerous.

Imperfections incident to our kind affections of two forts;

IV. If the focial affections are in themfelves and their confequents the nobleft enjoyments, 'tis plain the calm and extenfive are the beft of that kind, when they are in their full vigour, and enjoy their natural authority to direct or reftrain the feveral narrower af-fections.

Two imperfections are incident to our kind affec-tions; one when they extend only to a part, and yet without any bad difpofitions toward any other part; the other is, where in the courfe of the operation of ftrong kind partial affections towards fome, unkind and mifchievous affections are apt to be excited to-wards others.

1ct of full ex-tent,

In the firft cafe, Men of fmaller reflection may ne-ver form that moft diffufed calm purpofe or defire of good to all, which is the higheft moral excellence; and yet have friendly difpofitions as far as their views and fphere of action extend, without ill-will to any. This temper is very excellent, nor can more be expec-ted from the generality of mankind: nor is more need-ful; as very few can have power to do the moft exten-five fervices. 'Tis no unjuft partiality, when men ge-nerally follow the ftronger tyes of nature, or bonds of gratitude, or the motions of hearty efteem toward their worthy friends; provided they neglect no fuch of-fices as occur toward others, and can reftrain thefe narrower affections when oppofite to any more exten-five intereft which they difcover.

The dangerous partiality is when there are ftrong CHAP. 8. affections to a few, without any regards to other parts of the fyftem equally valuable which are within the *or unjuftly partial.* compafs of our knowledge and fphere of action; or, perhaps, malicious difpofitions toward them without natural caufes, or quite beyond the proportion of them, or any fubferviency to a publick intereft. Thefe focial tho' partial affections are often occafions of pleafure; but the averfions may create as great uneafinefs. When the kind affections are thus capricioufly placed, there is little merit in them; they muft be inconftant, and the felf-approbation muft vanifh upon reflection. The object now admired may prefently be difliked, and abhorred, by the fame capricioufnefs which made it agreeable. In thefe partial affections there is lefs participation of joy; and what merit is in love without a proportioned caufe? what fatisfaction in returns of love from favourites injudicioufly chofen? whereas the univerfal good-will, and even the limited affections upon natural caufes, which exclude no juft affection toward others, muft be full of joy, and give the confcioufnefs of meriting well from all; as fuch affections are fubfervient to the good of all.

The unjuft averfions from an erroneous confcience *Danger of ill-grounded averfions.* and falfe notions of religion and virtue formed by fuperftition and wrong education, muft lead into innumerable inconfiftences. If men do not banifh all reflection there muft be grievous remorfe and inward difpleafure : a bigot, a perfecutor, a robber, with a fort of confcience of duty to his party or his fyftem of opinions, oppoſing natural compaſſion and the plaineſt dictates of juſtice, can have but poor narrow ſatisfactions.   What are ſervices to a party or cauſe where we have no juſt perſuaſion of its worth, and in oppoſition to the intereſt of many others? What in pleaſing a Demon of whoſe moral perfections we can have no juſt or conſiſtent notion? The ſtruggles muſt be terrible between all the principles of humanity and this falſe conſcience.   Reflection muſt ever raiſe torturing ſuſpicions that all is wrong.   All ſtable ſatisfaction muſt be loſt; or they muſt baniſh reaſon and inquiry.

Upon a falſe point of honour one kills a friend. Compaſſion and remorſe immediately ſucceed. In perſecution too, or cruelty from any party-zeal, may not the remonſtrances of the ſufferers, the talk of the world, or of the perſecuted party, raiſe inward horrors and remorſe, where they are often boldly denied? What is it to offend multitudes, and to be abhorred by them? How hard is it to juſtify any conduct oppoſite to humanity? What may our condition be in cooler years, when our preſent ambition and party-ſpirit may abate, and we ſhall ſee our conduct to have been full of guilt and cruelty toward the innocent; and offenſive to God and all wiſe men? A good mind will never think it can be too cautious againſt any ſuch ſuperſtitions, or party-prejudices, as may imbitter it againſt any of its fellow creatures.

The ſelfiſh paſſions when too ſtrong are miſerable. V. We next conſider the temper where any or all the ſelfiſh paſſions are too violent.   They are chiefly

thefe, the *love* of *life*, and of *fenfual pleafure*, the de- CHAP. 8.
fire of *intereft*, or of the means of pleafure and the
conveniencies of life, *defire* of *power*, of *glory*, and *eafe*.

Of all thefe there is a moderate degree, confiftent
with focial affections in their full ftrength. But, as
we fhewed above, that the good, the happinefs aimed
at by them, is inferior to that arifing from the focial
affections; they ought therefore to yield to them and
to the purfuits of virtue. When they are beyond their
proportion they are called *cowardice* or pufilanimity,
luxury or voluptuoufnefs, *avarice, ambition, vanity,
floth.*

Love of life beyond a certain degree is a great un- *Thus love of*
happinefs. Life in many cafes is not worth retaining; *life.*
and to preferve it on certain terms may be too dear
a purchafe. Death doubtlefs in many circumftances
becomes an event earneftly to be longed for by the
perfon himfelf; and others may wifh for it as a joyful
releafe to their deareft friends, whilft they ftudioufly
decline what others fee is eligible. The love of life
makes fome act againft their own intereft as enemies
to themfelves. The dread of death often defeats its
own end, betraying to dangers inftead of repelling
them, and taking away that prefence of mind which
in the courageous finds out the means of fafety.

The very paffion itfelf is mifery; to feel cowardice
and to be haunted with perpetual horrors. None live
free from danger. The moft athletick conftitutions
are not fecured againft acute diftempers. The dread of
death will poifon all parts of life and all enjoyments,

even in the moſt fortunate circumſtances: it will force men on ſome occaſions into the meaneſt conduct, and make the heart ſuch a wretched ſight that we ſhall never endure to look into it; when for life, which is an uncertain enjoyment at beſt, and muſt be parted with at laſt, we have loſt every thing generous and a-miable which could make it worth retaining.

High ſenſuality is miſerable.   VI. The paſſions of ſenſuality, as we ſhewed above, purſue the meaneſt enjoyments, and where they en-groſs the man they make the moſt deſpicable charac-ter. There is nothing in the enjoyments which we can like upon reflection. Nay it requires a long habit to re-ſtrain a natural ſenſe of ſhame when we are keenly ſet upon ſuch gratifications. Moral ideas muſt be joined in our imaginations to make the indulgence appear reputable, and to avoid the uneaſy checks of that * *na-tural modeſty* which is deſigned to reſtrain theſe mean deſires.

Where paſſions of this ſort are immoderate, the ef-fects are moſt pernicious. They impair the health of body and mind; and exclude all manly improvement: the waſte of time, the effeminacy, and ſloth, and a thouſand diſorderly paſſions, break the natural ſtrength of the ſoul, and the reins of ſelf-government. The de-triment to ſociety from the extravagancies of the a-morous kind ; the bitter miſeries occaſioned in the deareſt relations of life; the diſtreſs and infamy this

---

* *Humiliorum appetituum moderator pu-dor*, is the pretty expreſſion of Cicero. The word is indeed often taken more exten- ſively for our *moral ſenſe*; and αἰδώς is uſed in the ſame extent by the Greeks.

treacherous love expofes its object to, muft be obvi- CHAP. 8.
ous to the flighteft attention; and muft give the moft
bitter remorfe, where any fenfe of virtue or humanity
remains; not to mention the wafte this paffion makes
in the honefty, ingenuity, and modefty of our nature.
Muft it not then be contrary to our intereft to have
fuch paffions violent?

VII. As wealth may be ufeful in gratifying any of *Avarice a*
our defires, may promote the good of the individual, *wretched paffion.*
or be a fund for offices of humanity, 'tis no wonder
that it is very generally purfued by fuch as extend their
views beyond the prefent moment. A moderate defire of it is innocent, and wife, and fubfervient to the
beft purpofes: and the poffeffion is moft joyful to fuch
as refer it to the purpofes of humanity and virtue. But
when the defire is violent, and referred only to felfifh
purpofes; or, by fome confufed notions of dignity and
power, terminating almoft only upon mere increafe of
poffeffions; the temper is as wretched as it is unreafonable, more oppreffive to the heart where it refides
than it can be to its neighbours. The natural defires
are eafily fatisfied. Frugality and temperance with
fmall expence may equal in pleafure the higheft luxury. The thirft for wealth without reference to pleafure or offices of liberality, is an eager, infatiable, reft-
lefs, joylefs craving. Such as entertain high profpects
of dignity and happinefs fecured to their pofterity by
their acquifitions, frequently by their example and
inftruction root out as far as they can every joyful and
honourable difpofition out of their minds; and when

Book I. the ungainly leſſon has not its effect, the deformed example preſented to their poſterity tempts them into the oppoſite extreme: and the hope of lazy opulence and luxury quenches all ardour for improvement in the honourable arts of life, and encourages every diſſolute inclination.

Ambition is miſerable. The ſame things may be ſaid of the deſires of power and of glory. A moderate degree is innocent and uſeful; but when they grow too violent they are reſtleſs and uneaſy to the individual, and often pernicious to ſociety, and generally break through the moſt ſacred tyes of duty and humanity, and ruin every good diſpoſition of heart. To deſire reputation for integrity and moral worth is natural to every good temper; and it excites men to be what they deſire to be reputed, which is the ſhorteſt way to true glory. Nay the deſire of eminence in valuable abilities, while it is moderate, is uſeful in our conſtitution and innocent. But it may grow ſo violent as to be a perpetual torment, and the ſource of the vileſt and moſt wretched paſſions. All ſuperior merit will then raiſe envy, and ill-will, and an humour of detraction. The mind will grow reſtleſs, violent, jealous, captious, eaſily provoked, incapable of bearing the leaſt neglect, uneaſy to all, and diſliked by all. No paſſion can more defeat its end than vanity; as nothing is more odious and contemptible than arrogance, nothing more lovely than its oppoſite, modeſty and humility.

Sloth and indolence miſerable. VIII. The moſt oppoſite temper to ambition is the love of eaſe. This too while moderate is innocent and

useful, as the desire of sleep when one is weary. But CHAP. 8.
when it turns to habitual sloth, not yielding to the social affections, and declining all laborious offices, it
must destroy all true worth, all social enjoyment, sense
of merit, and hopes of esteem. The languid sickly
state of a body uncapable of exercise appears in the
complexion and weak appetites; a worse disorder sei-
zes the mind that wants its natural exercise in the social offices of life. It must have tedious hours, be sus-
picious of contempt, jealous, and impotent in every
passion. The effects upon interest are obvious. The
indolent are exposed to all inconvenience and perplexity in their business; wanting to themselves in every
thing, and deprived of the aid of others, as they have
merited none from them, and discourage all assistance
by their own inactivity.

Thus the excesses of the selfish passions are certain
misery. They make up the character called *selfish*,
which is despicable and deprived of all the nobler joys
of life. The temper as it is shameful runs into sub-
tilty of conduct, and a feigned behaviour; loses its natural ingenuity and candour, and contracts distrust,
suspicion and envy. An interest separate from our fellows is more and more formed every day, and the social motions suppressed. At last the temper becomes
compleatly wretched and hateful.

IX. Some extraordinary and rare instances of most *Monstrous pas-*
immoderate excesses of these selfish passions are in *sions whence a*
common speech properly enough termed monstrous *rising.*
and unnatural, but seem to have these epithets given

Book I. them by fome authors, as if they were of a diftinct kind; fuch as when men feem to delight in torments, or to have an unprovoked defire of infulting, or petulancy, unnatural lufts, enormous pride, tyranny and mifanthropy. Thefe are only exceffes of fome paffions naturally implanted, but raifed to a prodigious degree without a juft caufe, upon fome falfe opinions or confufed imaginations, and by long indulgence and frequent irritation. Every one fees this to be the cafe in monftrous lufts, where the natural paffion is grown ungovernable; and caprice and curiofity oft make men try all kinds of indulgences.

Tyranny.   In the fame manner, when the temper from natural conftitution and other caufes happens to be favage and morofe, and where the mind has been long irritated and galled by oppofition or fome apprehended injuries, and no thorough reflection intervenes to ftop the growth of the paffion, furprizing rancour and cruelty may appear. One may eafily fuggeft to himfelf, how long continued felf-flattery and ambition, without any check from reflection, and the frequent anger arifing from the oppofitions which ambitious fpirits generally meet with; and the conftant caufes of fufpicion which their own conduct muft afford, may make that horrid temper of jealoufy, rage, cruelty, and oppreffion of every thing free and virtuous, which reigns in tyrants.

Petulancy and infolence.   Confider the affectation of liberty, the anger at thofe reftraints which the diffolute meet with from the laws of civilized focieties, the abhorrence they ex-

pect from their foberer fellow-citizens, and the often- CHAP. 8.
tation of fortitude; and they will account for that furprizing petulancy we meet with in fome characters.

Civilized nations of great humanity, from falfe con- *Savage cruelty.*
ceptions of the fpirit and tempers of the reft of mankind, and from fome abfurd notions of dignity and
pre-eminence in themfelves, have thought them fit
only to be flaves: fome have found fuch entertainment
from the furprizing efforts of art and courage, that infenfible to the mifery which was every moment obvious to their fight, they accounted it a fpectacle of high
delight, to behold gladiators putting each other to
death. We all know the notions entertained by the
vulgar concerning all hereticks; we know the pride of
fchoolmen and many ecclefiafticks; how it galls their
infolent vanity that any man fhould affume to himfelf
to be wifer than they in tenets of religion by differing
from them. When this infolent pride is long indulged by the enjoyment of power and popular veneration, it grows prodigious ; and, it may explain how
fuch men, and their implicite votaries, can behold with
joy the moft horrid tortures of men truly innocent,
but dreffed up in all the forms of impiety, and wickednefs. 'Tis needlefs to explain the original of other
monftrous difpofitions.

As we fhewed already the mifery which attends the
fmaller exceffes of thefe felfifh and ill-natured paffions; 'tis plain the more monftrous exceffes muft be
ftill greater mifery.

We have hitherto confidered what affections of

Book I. mind and what temper toward the enjoyments of this world, or toward our fellow-creatures, are the natural fources of the higheft enjoyment. There remains another object of affection to every rational mind to be fully confidered, and which, from what already hath often occurred in our former inquiry, muft be of the greateft importance to our happinefs, viz. the *Deity*, the *Mind* which prefides in the univerfe: and then we fhall have in view the fources of all the enjoyments our nature is capable of. Our *moral faculty* too finds here its fupreme object; as it naturally determines the mind to efteem and reverence all moral excellence, and perceives a duty and moral excellence in fuch veneration, and in the affections which enfue upon it.

C H A P. IX.

The D u t i e s *toward* G O D; *and firft, of juft Sentiments concerning his* N a t u r e.

OUR inquiries on this fubject are reduced to two heads; firft, What are the fentiments concerning the *Divine Nature?* And then, what are the affections and worfhip fuited to thefe fentiments, and what enjoyment or happinefs they afford to the human mind?

Juft fentiments, and firft that there is a Deity. Previous to our forming juft fentiments concerning the Deity there muft be a perfuafion of his exiftence. The world has ever agreed that there muft

be some superior *Mind*, or *Minds*, endued with knowledge and great power, presiding over human affairs. Tradition no doubt from race to race has contributed something to diffuse this persuasion. The
experience of evil from unknown causes, the fear of
them, and the desire of some further aids against them
when all visible powers have failed, may have excited
some to this enquiry: the natural enthusiasm and admiration arising when we behold the great and beautiful works of nature has raised the curiosity of others
to inquire into the cause: and this probably has been
the most general motive: but the certainty of any tenet depends not on the motives of inquiry into it,
but on the validity of the proofs; and its dignity depends upon its importance to happiness. Vanity or
avarice may have excited some to the study of Geometry; no man on this account will despise the science,
or count it less certain or useful in life. We shall
only point out briefly the heads of argument on this
subject. The whole of natural knowledge or natural
history, is a collection of evidence on this affair.

II. Whithersoever we turn our eyes or our thoughts, *Proofs from the*
there occur as great evidences of design, intention, *structure of the*
art, and power, as our imagination can conceive. The *world.*
most stupendous orbs, the greatest masses, moving
in constant order, with great rapidity : forces and
powers exerted every where, in worlds as large as this
habitation of men: an universe large beyond imagination and all our powers of observation. But as far
as we can make observations, manifest footsteps of

Vol. I.　　　　　　　Y

BOOK I. contrivance and regular defign appear in the moft exquifite fitnefs of parts for their feveral ufes, and in
mutual connexions and dependances of things very diftant in place. The earth, were it alone, would be a
ftupid mafs, inactive and ufelefs; but it is enlivened by
the fun: and tis impregnated with innumerable feeds,
which by warmth and moifture, and the other nutri-
tive principles in the earth and air, extend and unfold their wondrous beautiful parts, and break forth
in innumerable regular forms of different orders,
from the loweft mofs, to the ftately oak: and thefe
generally fitted for the nourifhment or other conveniences of fuperior orders of beings, endued with
powers of motion, of fenfe, of reafon.

From the ftruc-
tures of animal
bodies ; The animal bodies again difplay new wonders of
art, in their innumerable kinds, by the curious ftructures of their numerous parts, bones, mufcles, mem-
branes, nerves, veins, arteries. This wondrous ftructure appearing, not in a few inftances, but in every
one of the innumerable individuals of each fpecies;
fimilar to each other in their ftructures, and endued
with the feveral powers and inftincts of the kind, for
their prefervation and the continuance of the fpecies.
What nice organs to diftinguifh, receive, grind, fwallow, and digeft their food; and to diffufe the nourifhment to all their parts! what a variety and nice ftructure of organs for fpontaneous motions, fubfervient
to their pleafure, fupport, or defence!

And their pro-
pagation. As all plants produce their curious feeds, many of
them with proper mechanifm to be difperfed by the

winds into their proper places: fo animals are endued
with inftincts for the fame purpofe, a new form arifes
of the fame kind with the parent-animal; and, where
'tis neceffary, a falutary juice is prepared in the breafts
or teats of the parent for its nourifhment: the young
has an inftinct to apply to the proper fource of its
fupport, and nourifhment: and the parent by a like
inftinct is prone to fupply it. A fond care continues
in the parent while the young needs protection, and
the parent can be of ufe to it; and ceafes when it is of
no further ufe. And, that nothing may appear fuperfluous or ill defigned, where the young of certain kinds
needs no fuch food or protection from the parent, no
fuch juices are prepared, no fuch inftinct is implanted; as is the cafe with fome kinds of *fifh*, and *infects*.

III. The earth and all its beauties depend on the
fun. 'Tis placed at the moft convenient diftance: a *Connexion of the fun and atmo-*
confiderably nearer, or more diftant fituation, would *fphere with the earth and ani-*
make it a lefs convenient habitation. The eyes of a- *mal bodies.*
nimals are fitted to the degree of light, and to their
proper occupations, with the moft admirable art;
ftronger light would be painful and pernicious, and
fainter would be inconvenient. Their lungs, their
ears, their blood, are fuited to the furrounding air, its
weight, and ordinary motions. This yielding, pref-
fing, falutary fluid, is the means of life, of breathing,
of circulation of blood, of voice to communicate defires and fentiments, and of gratifying their tafte for
harmony.

Land animals continually need frefh water. Such

Book I. is the extent of the ocean, itself also full of inhabitants suited to that element, such the heat of the sun, that vaft quantities of vapours difencumbered of their falts are daily raifed, and float in the air, till grown too denfe they defcend in fructifying fhowers; or, meeting with hills or mountains in their motion, are condenfed and fupply fountains and rivers, which after carrying water to great tracts of land, are again difcharged into the ocean. Thus all is full of power, activity and regular motion, wifely and exquifitely adapted to the ufes of the living and fenfible parts of the creation.

No art of men or other vifible agents the caufe of thefe things. IV. The feveral claffes of plants, and animals, owe nothing of this wondrous ftructure to any wifdom of their own or their parents; no art of theirs contrived the material frame, or the inward fabrick of their powers and inftincts, or the conveniencies of their habitation. This immenfe power and wifdom muft refide fomewhere elfe; in fome other being Were the world fuppofed eternal, the argument is the fame. The effects, the evidences of wifdom, were upon that fuppofition in all times. In all times therefore wifdom and power fuperior to human exifted in fome other being. If this admirable frame had a beginning, the evidence is more manifeft.

Two forts of action, with, or without defign. Men have fome power, and make fome changes: we can exert our force in making them two ways; one in which we have no intention of any particular form or effect; as when we throw carelefly any materials out of our hands; another, when we defign fome end, intend

fome form, and direct motions for that purpofe. By CHAP. 9.
the former manner of action fcarce ever arifes any
thing regular, uniform, or wifely adapted to any purpofe: by the other it is that we produce things regu-
lar and well adapted. Now the forms of nature in ge- *All nature fhews*
neral, the changes and fucceffive appearances in the *defign.*
new plants and animals, are manifeftly of this later
fort, regular, uniform, curioufly adapted, and fimilar;
and hence we juftly conclude an original defigning
wifdom and power.

　　Had we any evidence that the power or art which
modified thefe materials refided in themfelves, we
fhould not perhaps recur to a prior caufe. But
whence that correfpondence, connexion, and fimilari-
ty? whence the mutual dependences of the feveral
fpecies, and of their individuals, on each other, and of
all of them upon the earth, the atmofphere, and the
fun? whence this adapted habitation? There muft
have preceded a concert among the feveral intelligences of the parts, or there muft have been one prefiding Intelligence. We have no evidence for fuch
wifdom in the parts themfelves as could have contrived their conftitutions: and therefore muft conclude
that there is a fuperior *all-ruling Mind.*

　　This *Mind* muft itfelf be *firft* and *original* in na- *This not refi-*
ture; nor is there any room for the queftion, from *dent in the mate-*
what caufe did it proceed? The order of nature fhews *rial world.*
that wifdom and power have always exifted fomewhere;
unlefs at fome period exiftence could commence without a prior caufe; or a being void of all power, thought,

and wifdom, could at a certain period, without the aid of any powerful or wife being, ftart into power or wifdom; or a being void of all power or wifdom could convey thefe perfections to others; all which fuppofitions are abfurd. Since then there is evidence for original intelligence and power, as high as we could have upon a fuppofition that it exifted, where fhall we conclude it refides? Whether in this vaft material fyftem is there one intelligence or counfel enlivening and moving the whole, and modifying fome parts of itfelf into particular intelligences for certain ends, and ftill governing them from certain affections toward them, and toward the whole; which was the notion of fome Stoicks, who zealoufly taught many duties of piety and humanity? or does it refide in a fpirit, a being fimple and uncompounded, diftinct from all divifible, changeable, or moveable fubftance; which was the notion of the Platonifts? The grand duties of piety, the foundations of our hopes, and the motives to virtue, fubfift on either fcheme; but that of the Stoicks is loaded with unfurmountable objections of a metaphyfieal kind.

The moral difpofitions of the original Mind.

V. When the exiftence of original boundlefs art and power is afcertained, the next point is the moral character, or the difpofitions of will toward other beings capable of happinefs or mifery; which muft be the foundation of all piety, and all joy in religion.

That it is benevolent, as this imports pure perfection.

Here firft, if we can any way reafon concerning the *original Nature* from what we feel in our own, or from any of our notions of excellency or perfection, we

muſt conceive in a *Deity* ſome *perceptive power* ana-
logous to our *moral ſenſe,* by which he may have ſelf-
approbation in certain affections and actions rather
than the contrary. Such a *power* muſt bring a large
addition of happineſs, and that of the nobleſt ſort, a-
long with it; and, in an omnipotent Mind, cannot be
inconſiſtent with any other perfection or ſource of enjoyment. The ultimate determinations or affections of
the *Divine Being,* which can be approved by himſelf,
muſt either be *that* toward his own happineſs; or a deſire of the greateſt univerſal happineſs; or a deſire of u-
niverſal miſery. The deſire of his own happineſs cannot
be the ſole ultimate deſire or determination; becauſe
the deſire of the happineſs of other beings diſtinct from
himſelf would be another ſource of ſublime pure happineſs, diſtinct from the former, but perfectly conſiſtent
with it, in a mind which always has it in its power to
gratify this deſire to the utmoſt, without obſtructing
any other ſource of happineſs. The approbation and
delight in this kind determination muſt be quite excluded from the *Divine Mind,* if there is no ſuch original determination in it. And 'tis inconceivable that
the *original Mind* can want any ſource of pure enjoyment or happineſs, conſiſtent with every other ſort of
excellence, while yet in other beings formed by the
counſels of that which is original we experience ſuch
ſources of happineſs.

The ultimate deſire of univerſal miſery cannot be *No ultimate deſire of the mi-*
ſuppoſed the determination approved in the Divine *ſery of others.*
Mind, nor can any ſuch affection be conceived as ori-

ginal and effential; fince there can be no original fenfe or power of perception correfponding to it in the *Divine Mind*. The *Deity* muft have powers perceptive of happinefs immediately. But in *that* which is *original* and *omnipotent* there can be no fenfe of mifery, nor any idea of it, but what is fuggefted by his knowledge of the perceptive powers he has granted to his limited creatures, and the laws of fenfation to which he has fubjected them. *That* cannot be fuppofed the object of an original defire, the idea of which is not perceived by fome original faculty of perception immediately fuggefting it.

Befides, all malevolent difpofitions of will, as they feem to carry along with them fome uneafinefs and mifery to the mind where they refide, fo they naturally tend to deftroy their objects, and thus to deftroy themfelves. A refolute malice muft ever be uneafy while its object fubfifts; and can only find reft by an entire removal of it, upon which the affection alfo ceafes. Anger tends to inflict fuch mifery on its object as muft at laft produce entire repentance, and thus remove the moral evil or turpitude which raifed the wrathful indignation; or to bring the object fo low that all oppofition of intereft muft ceafe, and, along with it, the paffion raifed by it. Envy has the fame tendency, and when its purpofe is accomplifhed muft in like manner ceafe. Whereas all the benevolent difpofitions are in their own nature everlafting, producing happinefs, and delighted with its continuance. Pity tends to remove the mifery of its object; and thus its own attendant pain is removed; but the love and good-will remain unabated by this change. 'Tis evi- dent therefore that malevolent difpofitions cannot be conceived as *original* in that *Mind* which is omnipo- tent, the fource of all, and the fovereign difpofer of all: but original good-will, and propenfity to commu- nicate happinefs muft be its effential permanent im- mutable difpofition.

To fuppofe a determination toward the univerfal mifery of others to be *original* in the Divine *Mind* is alfo entirely inconfiftent with the conftitution of all his rational creatures, in whom no fuch determination is found; and with that great degree of happinefs we experience in life. *Omnipotence* fure would have ef- fectually gratified its defires, by the higheft univerfal mifery.

We find in ourfelves that all the ill-will we are ca- pable of arifes from our weaknefs, when we apprehend fome damage or injury received, or dread it for the future; or find fome oppofition to our intereft, or to the interefts of thofe we wifh well to: in that which is *original, omnipotent*, and the *caufe* of all exiftence, there can neither be weaknefs, nor indigence, nor an oppofition of its interefts to thofe of its workmanfhip. If thefe more abftract reafonings do not fatisfy, let us confider others more obvious from the effects of the Divine counfel and power.

VI. In judging of the defign of any mechanifm, *Proofs of good-* where we tolerably underftand it, we can always difcern *nefs from the ef-* the *natural intention*, the *proper end* or *effect* of the *fects of Divine Power.*

Book I. contrivance; and diftinguifh it from events which may cafually enfue, or be the neceffary attendants or confequents of it, tho' they are no part of the end aimed at by the contriver. The fineft ftatue may hurt one, by falling on him: the moft regular and convenient houfe, muft obftruct the inhabitant's profpect of the heavens and the earth, more than a field does; and muft put him to fome trouble and expence in fupporting it. By the moft benign and wifely contrived courfe of the fun fome fevere weather muft happen in fome places. Some evils may be fo effentially connected with the means of the fupreme good, that *Omnipotence* cannot make it attainable to fome beings, without them. Such evils therefore muft exift in a

If the defign appears good and the effect a fuperiority of happinefs. world contrived by perfect Goodnefs. The goodnefs therefore of the author of a fyftem, in which fome evils appear, may be fufficiently proved, if the natural defign of the ftructure appears to be good and benign, and the evils only fuch as muft enfue upon laws well calculated for fuperior good. This reafoning will be exceedingly confirmed if we find a great fuperiority of pleafure, of happinefs, actually enjoyed by means of the conftitution and laws eftablifhed in nature. Creatures who have no immediate intuition of the Creator, nor a compleat knowledge of the whole plan and all its parts, can expect no better evidence; nor fhould they defire it.

The whole contrivance good. Now all the curious mechanifm obferved, has confervation of life, pleafure, happinefs, in fome fpecies or other, for its natural end. The external fenfes of

animals recommend things falutary, and reject what CHAP. 9.
is deftructive: and the fii er powers of perception in
like manner recommend t) every one what is beneficial to the fyftem, as well as to the individual; and
naturally raife averfion to what is pernicious. The
whole inward conftitution of the affections and *moral
faculty* above explained, is obvioufly contrived for the
univerfal good, and therefore we only hint at it in this
place. Some kinds of animals are plainly fubordinated to fome others, and the powers and inftincts of the
fuperior fpecies may be deftructive to the inferior; but
they are the means of good to the fpecies in which they
refide. The effects of them on the inferior is indeed
the depriving fome of them fooner of their exiftence;
but not in a worfe manner than they muft have loft
it however in a natural death : nay the fuddennefs of
the violent death, to a creature of no fore-thought,
makes it preferable to the tedious fort we call natural. And many of fuch low kinds muft have perifhed
as early by want of fuftenance, had not nature provided other caufes more gentle than famine. An *original malicious being* would have exercifed its art in
proper engines of torture, in parts formed for no other
purpofes, in appetites and fenfes leading ordinarily to
what would be ufelefs or pernicious, even in a moderate degree; in impatient ardours for what gave no
pleafure or ufe; in excrefcences ufelefs for life or action, but burdenfome and tormenting; and in affections pernicious to fociety, approved by a perverfe
tafte.

Observe all nature as far as our knowledge extends; we find the contrivance good. The objections of the *Epicureans*, and of fome *moderns*, arofe from their ignorance. The alledged blemifhes are now known to be either the unavoidable attendants or confequents of a ftructure and of laws fubfervient to advantages which quite over-ballance thefe inconveniences; or fometimes the direct and natural means of obtaining thefe advantages. The vaft ocean, often reputed barren, we find is a neceffary refervoir of water for the ufe of all land animals; itfelf alfo peopled with its own tribes, and richly furnifhed for their fubfiftence, from which too men derive a great fupport. The mountains are partly ufeful for pafture, for fruits, and grain; and partly for procuring rain, fountains, rivers. Storms arife from fuch caufes as are moft neceffary for life, the exhalation of vapours by the fun, and their motion in the air. The care, attention, and labour, incumbent on men for their fupport, invigorate both the foul and the body: without them the earth becomes a barren forreft, but by them becomes a joyful copious habitation: and they are the natural caufes of health and fagacity. 'Tis every way our advantage that we have no fuch flothful paradife as the poets feigned in the golden age.*

Contrary appearances are from ignorance.

VI. But tho' it be granted that the contrivance naturally tends to good, yet if God be omnipotent, fay

Why an omnipotent God permits any evil.

---

* Compare the cenfures of Lucretius on the ftructure of the earth lib. v. from line 195 to 236, with our prefent difcoveries in Natural Philofophy upon thefe fubjects. His brother-poet Virgil, beautifully defends Providence upon the laborious condition of mankind, 1 Georg. line 120 to 145.

some authors, " why are we made of such poor ma-
" terials, that we are often oppressed with pain during
" life; often tormented by our own passions, and by
" the injuries of others? Our frame too at last de-
" cays, and we yield our places with great pain to our
" successors of the same species. Why are we of such
" frail materials? why this succession of generations?
" why are our minds so imperfect either as to know-
" ledge or virtue? might we not have had too greater
" strength of understanding, and a better proportion
" among our affections?"

In answer to these arduous questions let us consider, what is highly probable, that the best possible
constitution of an immense system of perceptive beings may necessarily require a diversity of orders, some
higher in perfection and happiness, and some lower.
There may be abundant enjoyments to some orders
of beings without social action. But this we are sure
of from experience, that there are orders of beings
pretty high in the scale, whose supreme enjoyments
consist in kind affections, and in exerting their powers
in good offices from these affections. Nay 'tis impos-
sible for us to conceive an higher sort of enjoyment.
The consciousness of good-will to others tho' inactive,
is highly delightful; but there is still a superior joy in
exerting this disposition in beneficent actions. What
if this be the supreme enjoyment in nature, as our
minds seem to feel it is? This must be excluded out
of nature in a great measure, unless there be imperfection, indigence, pain, and even moral evil in nature.

Different orders necessary in the best system.

BOOK I. There may be a social congratulation and esteem a-
mong well-disposed happy beings, in a state of inactive joy, without any difficulties. But there can be no
place for action where there is no evil.

Experience of   Not to mention, what is obvious among men, that
evil gives an our sense of many high enjoyments, both natural and
higher sense of moral, is exceedingly heightened by our having obser-
good, and exer- ved or experienced many of the contrary evils. The
cises virtue.
whole life of virtue among men, which we shewed to
be the chief enjoyment, is a combat with evils natural
or moral. No place can be for liberality where there is
no indigence; or for fortitude where there is no danger;
or for temperance where there are not lower appetites
and passions; or for mercy and forgiveness, or friendly
admonitions and counsels, and long-suffering, and re-
quital of evil with good, where a species is incapable
of moral evil. Such lovely offices, the remembrance of
which must be eternally delightful, must be excluded;
or some moral evils must exist. Nay what patience,
resignation, and trust in God can be exercised in a system where misery cannot exist? If then the highest enjoyments we can conceive are fit to be introduced into the universe, some evils must come along with
them. Nay what shall we conceive the life of the
highest orders, if there were none inferior to them; no
good to be done, no kind offices, no evils to be war-
ded off, or good formerly wanting to be commu-
nicated? Can we conceive any thing more blessed,
or delightful to the *Deity*, than communicating of
good to indigent creatures in different orders? And

muſt not the higheſt goodneſs move him to furniſh to the ſeveral higher orders opportunities for ſuch divine exerciſes and enjoyments, by creating alſo orders inferior to them, and granting different degrees of abilities and perfection to the ſeveral individuals of the ſame ſpecies, that thus they may exerciſe their good affections in beneficent offices?

If thus the moſt perfect goodneſs would determine the Author of Nature to create different orders of beings, and ſome of them ſubject to many evils and imperfections; the ſame goodneſs muſt require that this plan of creation be continued down to the loweſt ſpecies in which a ſuperiority of good to the evils in its lot can be preſerved, while the creation of ſuch inferior ſpecies obſtructs not the exiſtence of as many of the ſuperior, as the moſt perfect univerſe can admit. The lot therefore of great imperfection muſt fall ſomewhere : mankind can no more juſtly complain that they were not in an higher order, than the brutes that they were not made men.

Perfect goodneſs muſt make all orders in which good is ſuperior.

Don't we ſee this confirmed in experience? We have no ground to believe that this earth could nouriſh an higher order than mankind. A globe of this kind may be neceſſary in the ſyſtem : it muſt have ſuch inhabitants or be deſolate. Beſides all the men it could maintain, there yet is room for other lower orders ſubordinate and ſubſervient to their ſubſiſtence. We find all places peopled with ſuch orders of life and ſenſe as they can ſupport; the inferior occupying what is not fit for the ſuperior, or what is neglected by them. In

This confirmed by experience.

like manner, let us afcend to higher orders: there may be as many fuch as the beft fyftem of the univerfe admits; and yet in this great *houfe of our father there are many manfions* unfit for the higher orders, but too good to be defolate; and they are occupied by men, and lower animals. This was their place, or they muft not have exifted in the fyftem. This earth perhaps could not furnifh bodies uncapable of decay, and as this decay comes on, we lofe our keen appetites and fenfes of the goods of life. The fcene cloys; we quit it, and give place to new fpectators, whofe livelier fenfes and appetites and more vigorous powers make it a greater bleffing to them.

Strict laws of fenfation neceffary. VII. But men will make further complaints. "Why " thefe harfh laws of fenfation, fubjecting us to fuch " acute pains, to fuch fympathetick forrows, and re- " morfe? why fuch furious paffions?" and cannot an " *omniprefent infinite Power* interpofe, beyond the " common courfe of nature, in behalf of the inno- " cent, the virtuous? no variety of bufinefs can fatigue " or diftract the *Deity*."

But in reply to all this: 'Tis abfolutely neceffary for the prefervation of life that deftructive impreffions from without, and indifpofitions from within, fhould occafion pain to animals. Were it not fo, how few would in any keen purfuits guard againft precipices, wounds, burning, bruifes, or hurtful abftinence from food. How could we be apprized of diforders, or guard againft what might increafe them? This law is abfolutely neceffary to men of maturity and know-

ledge; and how much more fo to the young and imprudent? Nor can we complain of the law as conftituting too acute fenfations, fince they do not univerfally obtain their end. The experience of the gout,
and ftone, and fevers, and racking fores, does not reftrain all men from the vices which expofed them to
thefe torments.*

Can we more juftly repine at other laws fubjecting us *So are all focial and moral feelings.*
to compaffion and remorfe? are they not the kind ad-
monitions and exhortations of the *Univerfal Parent*,
delivered with fome aufterity, to reftrain us from what
may hurt us or our brethren, and excite us to affift
them; or natural chaftifements when we have been deficient in our duty to any part of this family.

VIII. As to the ftopping of thefe laws in favour of *The laws fhould not be ftopped.*
the innocent who by means of them are now expofed
to many calamities, as by ftorms, fires, fhipwrecks,
the ruins of buildings, which make no diftinctions; let
us confider that the conftant ftopping or fufpending
the general laws when they would occafion any evil
not fubfervient immediately to fome prefent and fuperior good; or the governing the world by a variety
of diffimilar wills, and not by uniform rules or laws;

---

* One would think this common reafoning abundantly clear and certain; but
Θερσιτης δ' ετι μνος αμετροεπης εκολψα. Mr.
Bayle in his *Reponfe a un Provincial*
ch. 77. tells us, " That we might have
" had an ordinary fenfation of pleafure
" when all was well; and that a fenfible
" abatement of this pleafure might have
" fufficiently intimated to us our dan-
" gers: " Whereas we find that much
ftronger intimations and motives from the
acuteft pains, do not always deter from
luxury and intemperance; or give fufficient caution even to the aged. And what
will deter the rafh and young? This abatement he talks of might indeed be fufficient
if men were fuch triflers as to mind nothing but that fenfation he fuppofes.

BOOK I. would immediately fuperfede all contrivance or fore-thought of men, and all prudent action. There could be no room for projecting any kind offices to others, or concerting any fchemes for our own intereft, fince we could find no conftant or natural means for executing them.* Nay all fuch folicitudes would be ufelefs and vain, as there neither would be any proper means, nor any need of action; fince we fhould find that all evil was prevented, and good obtained, without our activity. Thus all active virtue muft be excluded.

They cannot be fufpended when evils enfue, and obtain when 'tis otherways.   Or fhall the laws obtain whenever the effect is innocent or ufeful, but always be fufpended when it is pernicious? This would make all human activity vain. No good man would be faint or weary with fafting, or labour; or be cold when he was naked. No occafion for any affiftance or good-offices to a good man. Nay our very pleafures would lofe a great deal of their relifh, which partly arifes from experience of pain. Reft is only grateful after wearinefs; and food has the beft favour after hunger. And all active virtues muft be fuperfeded as entirely fuperfluous.

All fuch fuf-penfion hurtful to virtue.   Or fhall the laws only then be fufpended when God forefees that no good fhall arife from thefe evils which

* To make this more obvious. Were there no fixed laws, no man would attempt to move. Motion would not follow his will, or not in that way he intended; or it would fail in as many inftances as it fucceeded. We could not depend on the promifes of others, nor hope for the fuccefs of any labours. Food would often ceafe to nourifh; nor would the want of it occafion pain or death. Bodies would not perfift in their ftates of reft, or motion; nor their parts cohere. None would build, plant, fow, or provide rayment. If the world remained, yet we could difcern no order in it. Poifons would nourifh; and wounds fometimes give us pleafure.

enfue upon them, but take place when good is to a-
rife from them? This may be fo in fact, tho' we do
not difcern the good that may arife from fuch evils.
But do they want that the laws fhould be ftopped
when fome prefent vifible fuperior good does not arife
from the evils they occafion? that ficknefs or pain
befalling infants or other innocents fhould be prevented, whenever God forefees that none will, or none
can, by any virtuous office relieve them? " Many e-
" vils, fay they, occafion no exercifes of virtue either
" by the fufferer, or by others. Many injuries do not
" exercife the virtues of patience, refignation, or for-
" givenefs, but draw after them bitter refentments,
" and a long train of mifchiefs. The laws of nature
" might in thefe cafes be fufpended, and take place
" in others."

But again, if the courfe of nature were ftill obferved to alter in favour of fuch whom none affifted, all
fuccour would be fuperfluous. Men would continue in
thefe fins of omiffion, that *this grace might abound.*
The good would ever be expofed to injuries and fufferings; for to fuch they would give occafion for exercifing patience, refignation, and forgivenefs; but the
obftinate, the haughty, and the proud muft remain
fecure. And why fhould men ftudy to govern their
paffions, when the worft of them, they would fee, could
do no harm.

Or fhall the courfe of nature take its full effect in
bringing evils on the wicked, but always alter in favour
of the good? Even fo, all care about the good would

be foolifh, and the moft delightful virtues would be fuperfluous. Again, the happinefs of the virtuous is often much connected with that of others. Muft all their families, friends, and countries be protected? At this rate what fhall we call the order of nature, the knowledge of which can direct our actions? The deviation muft be as common as the ordinary courfe. And then there would remain no exercife for the patience of the virtuous, their refignation, fortitude, facrificing their interefts to *God*, and the *Publick*, when they were thus made impaffible, and inacceffible to the ftrokes of fortune.

In fine, if it was worthy of a *good God* to create an order of beings whofe chief enjoyments fhould confift in the vigour and activity of kind affections, and moral pleafures, there muft be different orders of beings; the world muft be governed by general laws univerfally obtaining; and many particular evils, natural and moral, muft be permitted.

The Manichean fcheme without foundation.   IX. Now as the fole foundation of the moft plaufible fcheme of two independent principles, the one *evil* and *malicious*, and the other *good*, is the mixture we obferve of evil and good in this world; fince we have abundantly proved that there muft be fuch a mixture intended by the moft perfect Goodnefs, that fuppofition muft be without any rational foundation. Did we obferve fome beings perfectly good, and others perfectly evil, there might be fome prefumption for two oppofite principles; or did we difcover any laws plainly deftined for mifcief alone, and others deftined

for good; this too would be another prefumption. But CHAP. 9.
that *two Minds,* with oppofite intentions, fhould always unite and confpire in a mixed fyftem is inconceivable. Now the whole of natural knowledge fhews
us the contrary of thefe prefumptions: no fpecies is
conftituted abfolutely evil: no law obtains which is
not defigned for fuperior good. For this we muft refer to all the antient and modern obfervations on the
conftitution of nature.

Oppofite intentions in *two caufes* of equal art and *No effect from two oppofite principles.*
power could have no effect. They could have no mo-
tive to unite in forming a world: fince each would
know that the art and power of the other would introduce as much of what was offenfive to him, as his
own art or power could effect of what was agreeable.

Upon this fuppofition fhould we not plainly obferve
malicious mechanifm in the works of nature, as frequently as we obferve what is kind and ufeful. But
nothing of this fort occurs. No malice, original, fedate, and unprovoked appears in the works of nature;
but on many occafions we fee kindnefs gratuitous and
unmerited, in the tender relations of life, in the efteem
of virtuous characters by which we have not been profited, and in compaffion toward the unknown. No
original or natural joy in mifery, it never pleafes without fome previous notion of great moral evil in the
fufferer, or of fome oppofition to our intereft. No
moral faculty is obferved approving what is hurtful to
the publick; but in all rational agents we find a contrary one, which immediately approves all kindnefs,

Book I. and humanity, and beneficence. Sure the art of a malicious principle muſt have exerted itſelf in ſome original mechaniſm deſtined for miſchief.

Good ſuperior in life.   X. But granting the mechaniſm to be univerſally good; yet if there appeared a prepollency of miſery in this world, as ſome good men in their melancholy declamations have alledged, it would ſtill leave ſome uneaſy ſuſpicions in the mind. This preſent ſtate is the only fund of our evidence, independent of revelation, from which we conclude about other worlds, or future ſtates. If miſery is ſuperior here, 'tis true that even in that caſe, the *Deity* might be perfectly good, as this miſery of a part might be neceſſary for ſome ſuperior good in the univerſe: but then we ſhould not have full evidence for his goodneſs from the effects of it. The caſe however is otherways. Happineſs is far ſuperior to miſery, even in this preſent world; and this compleats all the evidence we could expect, or require.

Natural good ſuperior in the whole.   Firſt as to natural good: How frequent are the pleaſures of ſenſe, and the gratifications of appetite; and *Pleaſures of ſenſe.* how rare the acute ſenſations of pain? ſeldom do they employ many months in a life of ſeventy or eighty years: the weaker bodies who have a larger ſhare of it, are not the hundredth part of mankind. If bodily pleaſure is of a low tranſitory nature, ſo is bodily pain: when the ſenſation is paſt, and we apprehend no returns of it, all the evil is gone; and it begins to yield pleaſant reflections. Conſider the frequent returns of our pleaſures, and their duration will appear incom-

parably greater; and they are pretty near as intenfe in
their kind, as any pain we are commonly expofed to.
Such as are well experienced in both are not terrified
from fome high fenfual enjoyments by the danger of
pain enfuing.   To ballance the acuter pains, which
are rare, let us confider the frequent recurrence of very high pleafures. If many perifh early in life, the pain
they feel is probably neither fo intenfe, or lafting, as
that felt by men in full ftrength; nor is it increafed by
fears and anxiety.

The pleafures of the imagination, and of know- *Of imagination and fympathy.*
ledge, are pretty much a clear ftock of good, with
fmall deductions, * as there is fcarce any pain properly oppofite to them: and the pains of fympathy are
over-ballanced, by the more lafting joys upon the relief of the diftreffed, and upon the profperity of fuch
as we love: not to mention the joyful approbation of
the temper itfelf; the joyful hopes, under a good providence, for all worthy objects of our affection: and
this pain we fee plainly is a neceffary precaution in
providence, to engage us to promote the happinefs
of others, and defend them from evil.

The difficulty feems greater as to moral evil.   But *The difficulty as to moral good and evil.*
a perfon wholly devoid of all virtue is as rare as one
free from all vice. For the very kindeft purpofes, God
has indeed planted a very high ftandard of virtue in
our hearts. We expect univerfal innocence, and a long
courfe of good-offices, to denote a character as good:
but two or three remarkably vicious actions make it

* See above ch. vii. § 14.

odious. Fraud, theft, violence, ingratitude, lewdneſs, in a few inſtances, ruin a character almoſt irreparably; tho' the reſt of life be innocent, and tho' theſe actions were committed under great temptations, or flowed from no evil intention, but from ſome ſelfiſh paſſion or eager appetite, or from even ſome lovely partial tenderneſs, ſuch as that to a family. There are few in whoſe lives we will not find an hundred actions not only innocent, but flowing from ſome lovely affection, for one flowing from any ill-natured intention. Parental love, friendſhips, gratitude, zeal for parties and countries, along with the natural appetites, and deſires of the means of ſelf-preſervation, are the common ſprings of human action. And ſeldom do their vices proceed from any thing elſe than theſe principles grown perhaps too ſtrong to be reſtrained by ſome nobler or more extenſive affections, or by a regard to the rules which are requiſite for the good of ſociety. We have indeed a ſtandard of virtue ſet up in our hearts, which we cannot keep up to: and thus are all conſcious of guilt in the ſight of God. And yet the lower virtues are ſo frequent, that human life is generally not only a ſafe ſtate, but very agreeáble.

This circumſtance in our conſtitution, that the ſtandard of moral good is ſet ſo high, tho' it is apt to give the mind an unfavourable impreſſion of our ſpecies as very corrupt, is yet very neceſſary and uſeful, as it is a ſtrong reſtraint from every thing injurious or vicious, and a powerful ſpur to a continual advancement in perfection. Indeed without ſuch a ſtandard we could not have any idea of perfection, nor could Chap. 9. there be any formed intention in the human mind to make progrefs in virtue. But when we fee fo few on whom it has its full effect, even of thofe who live to mature age, it feems to carry no faint intimation, that either we once were in a higher ftate of perfection, or that fuch a ftate is ftill before us. Unlefs we be deftined for fuch a ftate, the planting fuch a ftandard muft have the fame unaccountable appearance, as the laying up of great magazines, and trains of artillery, where no military operations were intended.

XI. To confirm this prevalence of good in life, let *An appeal to men's hearts.* us confider, that men can certainly tell what they would defire upon any poffible fuppofition, as well as in matters which actually befall them. Imagine a medicine difcovered, which without pain would caft both foul and body into an everlafting fleep, or ftop all thought or exiftence for ever. In old age perhaps, or under fome fore difeafes, fome few might chufe to ufe this medicine, to efcape from all evil by the lofs of all good; but not one in a thoufand: and the few who would, have enjoyed many years during which life was eligible, for the months in which they would chufe annihilation. Many of them have had their fhare of life; they fhould be ready to leave it, as a fatisfied gueft leaves a plentiful table. What altho' at laft death fhould for a few months become eligible to every one, after an agreeable life for many years? If the judgments of the young, while all the fenfes, appetites and paffions are vigorous, and joyful hopes inflame the ima-

BOOK I. gination, may overvalue the good of life; the judgments of the aged may be equally partial on the other fide, when all the powers are become languid, and the memory of pleafures almoft effaced. Men in the middle of life, who fee the condition of it, who remember the joys of youth, feel their prefent ftate, and obferve in others the condition of old age, are certainly the beft judges. Not one in a thoufand would quit all he enjoys, to avoid all he fears. 'Tis high ingratitude in men to pique themfelves upon depreciating all the gifts of God, and aggravating all the evils of our lot. Should Mercury come at their requefts, when they have fretfully thrown down their burthens, as in the old fable, they would foon intreat him, not to take down their fouls to Lethe, but to help them to take up their loads again.

The caufes of mistake here. In thefe debates fome recite all the wickednefs and mifery they have feen, read, or heard related: wars, murders, piracies, affaffinations, facking of cities, ravaging of countries, military executions, maffacres, crufado's, acts of faith in the holy inquifition: all the frauds and villanies detected in courts of juftice: all the corruption, falfhood, diffimulation, ingratitude, treacherous undermining, and calumny, and lewdnefs, in palaces; as if thefe were the common employments of mankind; or as if a large portion of mankind were concerned in fuch things by their ftations. Prifons, and hofpitals, the abodes of the criminal and difeafed, were never fo populous as the cities where they ftand: they fcarce ever contained the thoufandth part of a-

ny ftate. Milton's defcription of the infirmary, in his CHAP. 9.
vifion, muft move the hardeft heart: but who will eftimate the health of a people from an infirmary. A monftrous plant or animal is long expofed to view in the
repofitories of the curious: the rarity makes the view
entertain us, and makes us fond to talk about it. But
millions of regular compleat forms exift for one mon-
fter; they are fo common that they raife no attention or admiration. We retain a lively remembrance of
any grievous ficknefs or danger we efcaped, of any
horrid calamity, or villany: our fouls are pierced with
wars, flaughter, maffacres, plagues; forgetting the
vaftly fuperior numbers which efcape all thefe evils,
and enjoy the common peaceful condition of life. The
fufferers in thefe calamities feldom endure more pain
than what attends a natural death; and they make not
a fortieth part of mankind. Scarce five hundred
thoufand of our countrymen have perifhed by thefe
calamities, in any century of the Britifh hiftory: and
forty times that number, in the worft of times, have
efcaped them.

'Tis that lovely natural compaffion which makes us *Compaffion the cauſe of our mif-*
fo deeply feel thefe great calamities and remember *taken reaſonings.*
them. We wifh well to all, and defire an happy ftate
of the univerfe, from a yet finer principle; and
deeply regret every contrary appearance, even when
we have no fears about ourfelves. Thefe lovely principles in our conftitution fhould plead more ftrongly
in our hearts for the goodnefs of the *all-ruling Mind*,
than thofe appearances of evil, were they as great as a

melancholy eloquence often paints them, could plead for the contrary.

Hiſtories give us a view only of a ſmall part of life. While hiſtories relate wars, ſeditions, maſſacres, and the corruptions and intrigues of courts, they are ſilent about thoſe vaſtly ſuperior numbers who in ſafe obſcurity, are virtuouſly or innocently employed in the natural buſineſs and enjoyments of mankind. We read the actions of the great, of men expoſed to all the temptations of avarice and ambition, raiſed above the common lot of honeſt labour and induſtry, with minds often corrupted from their infancy by the elevation of their fortunes, and all their paſſions inflamed by flattery and luxury The ſocial joyful innocent employments of the bulk of mankind are no ſubjects of hiſtory; nor even the ordinary regular adminiſtration of a ſtate in the protection of a people and the execution of juſtice. Hiſtories dwell upon the critical times, the ſickneſſes of ſtates, the parties, and factions, and their contentions; revolutions, and foreign wars, and their cauſes. Theſe dangers, their cauſes, and the remedies applied, muſt be recorded for the uſe of future ages; and their rarity, in compariſon of the natural buſineſs of ſocial life, makes them more entertaining. Thus authors in medicine relate not the agreeable enjoyments and exerciſes of health. The cauſes, ſymptoms, and prognoſticks of diſorders, their critical turns, and the effects of different medicines applied, are the proper ſubjects of their diſſertations.

Lower conditions as happy as the higher. Men placed in the higher conditions of life, enured to eaſe and ſoftneſs, may imagine the laborious ſtate

of the lower, to be a miſerable ſlavery, becauſe it CHAP. 9.
would be ſo to them were they reduced to it with their
preſent habits of ſoul and body. But in the lower conditions, ſtrength of body, keen appetites, ſweet intervals of reſt, moderate deſires, and plain fare, make up
all their wants in point of ſenſual pleaſure. And the
kind affections, mutual love, ſocial joys, friendſhips,
parental and filial duties, moral enjoyments, and even
ſome honour, in a narrower circle, have place in the
lower conditions as well as the higher; and all theſe
affections generally more ſincere.

XII. How ſhall a being too imperfect to compre- *How men of*
hend the whole adminiſtration of this univerſe in all *imperfect views*
                                                      can judge of the
its parts, and all its duration, with all the connexions *whole.*
of the ſeveral parts, judge concerning the preſiding
Mind, and his intentions? We ſee particular evils
ſometimes neceſſary to ſuperior good, and therefore
benignly ordered to exiſt. We ſee alſo ſome pleaſures
and advantages occaſioning ſuperior evils. There may
therefore be other like connexions and tendencies on
both ſides unknown to us. We cannot therefore pronounce of any event that it is either abſolutely good,
or abſolutely evil, in the whole. How does a wiſe and
dutiful child judge of its parent's affections? Or how
does one in mature years judge of the intention of his
phyſician when he is a ſtranger to his art? The child
is ſometimes reſtrained in its pleaſures, chaſtiſed, confined to laborious exerciſes or ſtudies; the patient receives nauſeous potions, and feels painful operations.
But the child finds the general tenor to be kind; ma-

ny pleafures and conveniences fupplied; and a con-ftant protection and fupport afforded; it has found the advantages arifing on fome occafions from re-ftraint and difcipline; it finds its powers, its know-ledge, and its temper improved. The patient has found health fometimes the effect of naufeous medicines. 'Tis juft thus in nature. Order, peace, health, joy, pleafure, are ftill prevalent in this great family, fupe-rior to all the evils we obferve. Human life is univer-fally eligible, tho' it is an unmixed ftate to none: we can have no fuch prefumptions of any intereft of the Supreme Mind oppofite to that of his creatures, as may lye againft the intentions of the beft of men. Should we not then ufe that equity in our conclufi-ons about the *Deity*, that is due to our fellows, not-withftanding a few oppofite appearances.

If God be good be is perfectly good.

XIII. Since then the whole contrivance of nature, directly intended for good, and the prevalence of hap-pinefs in confequence of it, proves the *original Mind* to be benevolent; wherever there is any real goodnefs, a greater happinefs muft be more defired than a lefs; and where there is fufficient power, the defire fhall be accomplifhed. If God be omnipotent and wife, all is well: the beft order obtains in the whole: no evil is permitted which is not neceffary for fuperior good, or the neceffary attendant and confequent upon what is ordered with the moft benign intention for the greateft perfection and happinefs of the univerfe.

Unreafonable to demand the par-ticular purpofes of all evils.

'Tis arrogant to demand a particular account how each evil is neceffary or fubfervient to fome fuperior

good. In the beſt poſſible ſcheme many things muſt CHAP. 9.
be inexplicable to imperfect knowledge. The ends
and connexions muſt be hid, as ſome ſteps in the oeconomy of the parent, or the practice of the phyſician muſt be dark to the child, or the patient. 'Tis
enough that we diſcern the natural end to be good in
all the mechaniſm of nature which we underſtand ;
that happineſs is prevalent, and our ſtate very eligible.
All new diſcoveries increaſe our evidence by ſhewing
the wiſe purpoſes of what before ſeemed an imperfection. A candid mind muſt conclude the ſame to be
the caſe of parts whoſe uſes are yet unknown. The
very anxieties of men about this grand point, help to
confirm it, as they ſhew the natural determination of
the ſoul to wiſh all well in the univerſe; one of the
cleareſt footſteps of our benevolent Creator imprin-
ted in our own hearts. This truth muſt be acceptable
to all, where vanity, affectation of ſingularity and of
eminent penetration, or an humour of contradiction,
hath not engroſſed the heart.

XIV. Add to all this, that the prevalent goodneſs *The hopes of a future ſtate uni-verſal.*
obſerved in the adminiſtration of nature leads to an
hope which at once removes all objections, that of a
future ſtate of eternal exiſtence to all minds capable
of moral ſentiments, of enquiring about the order of
the whole, of anxiety about it, of knowing its author,
or of any fore-thought about exiſtence after death.
The powers of thought and reflection, as they extend
to all times paſt and future, and to the ſtate of others
as well as our own, and are accompanied with exten-

five affections and a *moral faculty*, make all orders of being endued with them capable of incomparably greater happinefs or mifery than any of the brutal kinds. If the duration of men is to be eternal, and an happy immortality obtained by thefe very means which are moſt beatifick to us in this life; the evils of thefe few years during our mortal ſtate are not worthy of regard; they are not once to be compared with the happinefs to enfue.

No proofs of the contrary.
The ſoul ſeems diſtinĉt from matter.

The boldeſt Epicurean never attempted direĉt proof that a future ſtate is impoſſible. Many have believed it who conceived the ſoul to be material. Mankind in all ages and nations have hoped for it, without any prejudice of ſenfe in its favour. The opinion is natural to mankind, and what their Creator has defigned they fhould entertain. 'Tis confirmed not a little by arguments which fhew the fubjeĉt of thought, reafon, and affeĉtions not to be a divifible fyſtem of diſtinĉt fubſtances, as every part of matter is. The fimplicity and unity of confcioufnefs could not refult from modes difperfed and inherent in an aggregate of different bodies in diſtinĉt places.* Nor is the aĉtivity of the ſoul confiſtent with the paſſivenefs of matter. We feel our happinefs or mifery, and the dignity and perfeĉtion, or their contraries, for which we eſteem or diſlike ourfelves or others, to be qualities quite infen-

---

* This argument from our confciouf-nefs of the unity of the perceiver and a-gent, in all that multitude of fenfations, judgments, affeĉtions, defires, is well ur- | ged by Ariſtotle *de Anima.* l. i. and by Dr. Sam. Clarke. See alfo Mr. Baxter's ingenious book on this fubjeĉt.

fible, no way related to the body or its parts, or affected by any changes befalling the body.

The nature and order of our perceptions fhew this
diftinction. Firft, *external fenfations* prefent forms
quite diftinct from this *felf*, and no further related to
it than that they are perceived. Their changes to the
better or the worfe affect not nor alter the ftate of
the perceiver. A fecond fet of perceptions approaches
a little nearer, thofe of *bodily pleafure* and *pain*. The
ftate of the perceiving *felf* is affected by them, and
made eafy or uneafy. But *nature* orders in a way quite
inexplicable, that thefe perceptions are connected with
parts of the body, or the fpaces which they once occupied: and the accident is naturally conceived as affecting the body, and not altering the dignity of the
foul. Let *Anatomifts* talk of motions propagated by
nerves to the brain, or to fome gland the feat of the
foul: when the finger is cut, as fure as pain is felt
at all, tis felt in the finger, or in the fpace where the
finger was. *Nature* declares the event to be an accident to the body, not deftroying or abating the excellence of the perceiver: not even when the fenfations indicate fuch accidents as muft foon deftroy the
body altogether. Nay fome fuch fenfations of pain
increafe rather the perfonal dignity; and fome fenfations of pleafure abate it. But there is a third fort of
perceptions, when we are confcious of knowledge,
goodnefs, faith, integrity, friendlinefs, contempt of
fenfual pleafures, publick fpirit. Thefe we feel to be
the immediate qualities of this *felf*, the perfonal ex-

cellencies in which all its true dignity confifts, as its bafenefs would confift in the contrary difpofitions. We know thefe qualities, and their names, as well as we do the fenfible ones: we feel that thefe have no relation to the body, or its parts, dimenfions, fpaces, figures. * *Nature* thus intimates to us a fpirit diftinct from the body over which it prefides, in regulating its motions, as clearly as it intimates the difference of our bodies from external objects. Nay it intimates a greater difference, or difparity of fubftance; as all the qualities of the foul are quite difparate and of a different kind from thofe of matter: and 'tis only by their qualities that fubftances are known.

Direct proofs of a future ftate.   XV. *God* declares by the conftitution of nature, by the *moral faculty* he has given us, that he efpoufes the caufe of virtue and of the univerfal happinefs. Virtue in many inftances is born down and defeated in this world. In fuch events our beft difpofitions give us much forrow for others, and virtue fometimes expofes to the greateft external evils. From the goodnefs of *God* we muft hope for fome compenfation to the worthy and unfortunate; and that the injurious and oppreffive fhall find caufe to repent of their contradicting the will of a *good Deity*. There is no defect of power in *God;* no envy or ill-nature. Shall beings of fuch noble powers, fo far advanced in the perfections *God* approves, with fuch defires and hopes of immortality, be fruftrated in their moft honourable hopes? Hopes neceffary to their compleat enjoyment

* This reafoning frequently occurs in Plato. See 1 *Alcibiades.*

of virtue in this world, fince without them they could have little joy, in this uncertainty of human affairs, either from their own ftate, or from that of the deareft and worthieft objects of all their beft affections. Shall a plan of an univerfe fo admirable in other refpects want that further part which would make all compleat? What altho' *God* could not be charged with cruelty or injuftice upon this fuppofition, fince he has made virtue itfelf the chief happinefs, and vice the fupreme mifery? Shall we expect no more from the *original omnipotent Goodnefs* than what we count a poor degree of virtue in a man, the doing only that good which is neceffary to avoid the imputation of injuftice? How far is this furpaffed by the overflowing goodnefs of fome worthy men? And how unlike to the conduct of that *liberal hand* that *fatisfieth the defires of every thing that lives?*

If there are in the univerfe any rational agents capable of defection from their integrity, fpectators of human affairs, who need motives to perfeverance from the fanctions of laws: if fuch beings difcern the external profperity of the wicked, when their ftupified confciences are infenfible of remorfe, and they live in affluence of all the pleafures they relifh, and in a moment go down to the grave free from all future punifhment; how muft this encourage any imperfect fpectator in his vices? Muft not fuch impunity of tranfgreffors deftroy the authority and influence of the divine laws? The minds of a nobler relifh fee indeed that the vicious have loft the fupreme enjoyments of life; but the vicious have no taſte for them, nor re-gret for the want of them, and wallow in what they reliſh. Can ſuch unfelt puniſhments anſwer the wiſe ends of government, the correcting and reforming even of thoſe who are depraved in a great degree? How little effect can they have, if men need dread nothing further?

Should one behold a building not yet finiſhed, the ſeveral parts ſhewing exquiſite art, yet ſtill wanting a further part to make all compleat and convenient, room left for this part, and even ſome indications of this further building intended; would not a candid ſpectator conclude that this further part was alſo in the plan of the architect, tho' ſome reaſons retarded the execution of it? This is the caſe in the moral world. The ſtructure is exquiſite, but not compleat: we ſee ſpace for further building, and indications of the deſign in the deſires and hopes of all ages and na-tions, in our natural ſenſe of juſtice, and in our moſt noble and extenſive affections about the ſtate of o-thers, and of the univerſe; and ſhall we not confide and hope in the art, the goodneſs, the inexhauſtible wealth of the *great Architect.*

We have dwelt long on this head, rather pointing out the ſources of evidence than diſplaying it fully, becauſe the aſcertaining the goodneſs of *God* is the grand foundation of our happineſs and the main pillar of virtue. We ſhall briefly touch at his other attri-butes, leaſt any miſtakes about them ſhould abate that high veneration and admiration due to his excellency.

XVI. Firſt all the reaſons which prove any think-ing being to be a diſtinct ſubſtance from matter, prove that *God* is a ſpirit, and is not the great material maſs of this univerſe; as all the proofs of his exiſtence are proofs of original thought, wiſdom, conſciouſneſs, activity, affection; powers quite inconſiſtent with the nature of matter. By calling him a ſpirit we do not mean that he muſt be a ſubſtance of the ſame ſpecies or kind with the human ſoul, and only greater. Tho' all thinking beings differ in kind from all matter, yet there may be innumerable orders or kinds of ſpirits, with eſſential differences from each other, from that loweſt ſpirit of life, which is in the meaneſt animal, to the *infinite Deity.*

CHAP. 9.
The other at-tributes of God.
A ſpirit.

Again, what is *original* and *uncauſed* cannot be conceived as limited in its nature, either by its own choice, or by the will of any prior cauſe, to any particular finite degree of perfection, or to thoſe of one kind, while it wants others. No poſſible reaſon or cauſe can be aſſigned for ſome ſorts or degrees rather than others. We ſee from the effects, that the original perfections are high beyond imagination: and there was no prior will or choice of any being to confine it to one ſpecies or degree. This leads us to conceive an original boundleſs ocean of all excellency and perfection, from which all limited perfections have been derived.

Infinite

The ſame thoughts lead us to conceive the *original Being* as one, and uncompounded of diſtinct be-

And One.

ings or parts. No poſſible reaſon or cauſe for plurality, for one number of *original beings*, rather than any
other. No evidence for more, from any effects or appearances which *one original Cauſe* cannot account for.
Nay all the appearances of connexion, mutual depen-
dencies of parts, and ſimilarity of ſtructure, in thoſe
which are very remote from each other, lead us to
unity of *deſign* and *power*. This ſhews ſufficiently the
vanity of *Polytheiſm*, if any ever believed a plurality
of *original beings*. The wiſer *Heathens* had a different
Polytheiſm; and that of the vulgar aroſe from low
conceptions of the *Deities* as weak and imperfect, ſubject to diſtraction and confuſion by a multitude of
cares, or by an extenſive providence, and like men,
embaraſſed when they undertake too much. *One almighty and omniſcient Being* can preſide eaſily over all,
without toil or confuſion.

Omnipreſent.   The continual power exerted in all parts of the
univerſe, and the unlimited nature of the *original Being*, leads us to conceive him poſſeſt of ſuch *omnipre-
ſence* and *immenſity* as is requiſite to univerſal knowledge and action. And *that* which is *original* muſt be
eternal.

*God rules all
by his provi-
dence.*   XVI. From power, wiſdom, and goodneſs we infer
that *God* exerciſes an univerſal providence. To a Being endued with theſe perfections the ſtate of an univerſe of ſo many creatures capable of happineſs or miſery cannot be indifferent. Goodneſs muſt excite him
to exert his power and wiſdom in governing all for

the beſt purpoſes, the univerſal happineſs. Nor can
we conceive any exerciſe of his powers more worthy
of *God*, or more delightful to him.

What other motive to create, but a deſire to com- *Goodneſs the ſpring of creation.* municate perfection and happineſs? *God* cannot be conceived as ultimately ſtudious of glory from creatures infinitely below himſelf. And all deſire of glory
muſt preſuppoſe that ſomething is previouſly diſcern-
ed as excellent, that ſome determination of his nature, or ſome affection, is eſſentially the object of his
approbation : and what other determination can we
ſuppoſe the object of his higheſt approbation than perfect goodneſs, ever diſpoſing him to communicate
happineſs. This determination muſt move him to diſplay his own excellencies to his rational creatures by
his works, that thus he may be the ſource of the higheſt
happineſs to them, the nobleſt object of their contemplation and veneration, of their love, eſteem, hope, and
ſecure confidence, and the beſt pattern for their imitation. *God* diſplays his perfections to make his creatures happy in the knowledge and love of them; and
not to derive new happineſs to himſelf from their prai-
ſes, or admiration.

The *wiſdom* and *goodneſs* of *God* ſhew us his mo- *The holineſs of the Deity.* ral purity or holineſs. As he is independent, almighty,
and wiſe, he cannot be indigent: he can have no pri-
vate ends oppoſite to the univerſal good; nor has he
any low appetites or paſſions. Theſe are all the incite-
ments to moral evil which we can conceive. In *God*
none of them can have place, nothing contrary to

that univerſal goodneſs in which he muſt have the higheſt complacence.

His conduct toward his creatures muſt be ſuch as goodneſs and wiſdom ſuggeſt. His laws muſt be good and juſt, adapted to the intereſt and perfection of the whole. No unworthy favourites ſhall find in him a partial tenderneſs inconſiſtent with the general good or the ſacred authority of his laws: no private views ſhall ſtop the execution of their ſanctions, while the general intereſt, and the ſupporting the majeſty of theſe laws require it. 'Tis no injuſt partiality that the lot of ſome ſhould have many advantages above that of others. This, we ſhewed above, the beſt order and harmony of the whole may require. Theſe are the natural notions of juſtice in a *moral governor*. 'Tis a branch of goodneſs conjoined to wiſdom, which muſt determine the *governor* to ſuch conduct as may ſupport the authority and influence of his laws for the general good.

CHAP. X.

The AFFECTIONS, DUTY, *and* WORSHIP, *to be*
exercised toward the DEITY.

I. **I**N the confideration of the feveral enjoyments of *What affections are fuited to the Divine Perfections.* our nature we fhewed the frequent occafion men muft have for recourfe to the Divine Providence, for the fecurity of their enjoyments, and a ftable tranquillity of mind, under the adverfities of this life which may befall ourfelves, or the objects of our tendereft affections. We eftablifhed in the preceeding chapter that grand foundation of our happinefs, the exiftence, and moral perfections of *God*, and his providence. It remains to be confidered what affections and duty are incumbent on us toward the *Deity* thus abundantly made known to every attentive mind.

In this matter, as much as any, our *moral faculty* *This known by the moral fenfe.* is of the higheft ufe. It not only points out the affections fuited to thefe perfections, but facredly recommends and enjoins them as abfolutely neceffary to a good character; and as much condemns the want of them, as of any affections toward our fellow-creatures. Nay points them out as of more facred obligation. The *moral faculty* itfelf feems that peculiar part of our nature moft adapted to promote this correfpondence of every rational mind with the great Source of our being and of all perfection, as it immediately approves all moral excellence, and determines

VOL. I.   D d

the foul to the love of it, and approves this love as the greateſt excellence of mind; which too is the moſt uſeful in the ſyſtem, ſince the admiration and love of moral perfection is a natural incitement to all good offices.

Worſhip is internal, or external. The worſhip ſuited to the Divine Attributes is either internal, or external: the former in the ſentiments and affections of the foul; the later in the natural expreſſions of them.

What is due to the natural perfections. Our duty in reſpect of the natural attributes of *God* is to entertain and cultivate, by frequent meditation, the higheſt admiration of that immenſely great *original Being*, from which all others are derived; and to reſtrain all low imaginations which might diminiſh our veneration; all conceptions of the *Deity* as limited, corporeal, reſembling any brutal or human form, or confined within certain places: all which ſeem inconſiſtent with his infinite power and perfection, and his original uncauſed exiſtence.

The affections due to the moral perfections; Love, eſteem, veneration. II. Due attention to the moral attributes muſt excite the higheſt poſſible eſteem, and love, and gratitude. Extenſive ſtable goodneſs is the immediate object of approbation, love, and eſteem. Wiſdom and power joined to it, raiſe love, eſteem, and admiration to the higheſt. They muſt excite the moſt zealous ſtudy to pleaſe, the greateſt caution againſt offending, and give the higheſt ſatisfaction in the conſciouſneſs of conformity to the will of a Being poſſeſſed of ſuch excellencies. When we are conſcious of having offended him, they muſt fill our ſouls, not only with

fears of punifhment, but with inward remórfe, inge-CHAP. 10.
nuous fhame, and forrow, and defire of reformation.

Thefe divine perfections firmly believed, beget *Truſt and re-*
ſignation.
truft and refignation, and entire fubmiffion to every
thing ordered by Providence, from a firm perfuafion
that all is ordered for the beft, for the greateft univerfal intereft, and for that of every good man. Extenfive goodnefs muft defire the beft ftate of the
whole; omnifcience muft difcover the means; and omnipotence can execute them. Every thing becomes
acceptable in the place where *God* orders, or permits
it; not indeed always for itfelf, yet upon implicit truft
or faith that it is neceffary for the purpofes of infinite goodnefs and wifdom. We know that the benign intentions of the *Deity* are partly to be executed by the active virtues of good men; and that in
thefe virtues a great fhare of their fupreme perfection
and happinefs confifts. Our dependence therefore u-
pon the Divine Power and Goodnefs will retard no
kind and virtuous purpofes of ours, but rather invigorate and fupport us with joyful hopes of fuccefs. The
fame refignation and truft we exercife for ourfelves, and
our own interefts, we fhall alfo exercife for all who are
dear to us by any virtuous bonds, for every honourable
caufe in which we or others are engaged; that it fhall
be profperous in this life, or tend to the future glory
and happinefs of thofe who have efpoufed it.

III. Juft apprehenfions of the creation and provi- *Gratitude and*
humility before
dence of *God* muft raife the higheft refentments of *God, and pity to-*
gratitude, muft reprefs all vanity in his fight, all con- *ward our fel-*
lows.

tempt of others, and beget true humility. All the good we enjoy, all the pleafures of fenfe, all the delights of beauty and harmony, are fo many favours *All the good na-* conferred on us by *God.* To his power we owe our ve-*t ttral or moral* ry being, we owe thefe objects, and the fenfes by which *which we enjoy is* *due to him.* we enjoy them. If we interpofe our activity in improving the objects, or cultivating our own relifh, it was *God* who gave us all our powers, all our art or fagacity, and furnifhed us opportunities for fuch pleafant exercife, and fo agreeably rewards it. All the joys we feel in mutual love, all the advantages we receive from the aids of our fellows, are owing to *God,* who contrived that frame of foul for man, gave him fuch affections, and made him fufceptible of whatever can be the object of love in him. He gave to all animal kinds, human or brutal, their powers, fenfes, inftincts, affections. He bound together the fouls of men with thefe tender and focial bonds which are the fprings of all good offices. The external advantages we procure to each other by our active virtues, *God* could have immediately conferred by his power without any action of ours; but, fuch was his goodnefs, he chofe that we fhould enjoy fome fhare of that divine and honourable pleafure of doing good to others; and, by the exercife of our kind affections and by our *moral faculty,* we do partake of it. The joys we feel in being honoured by our fellows are alfo his gift to us; by his implanting this fenfe of moral excellence, and that natural delight we perceive in the approbation and efteem of others.

All the pleaſures of knowledge, all the effects of CHAP. 10.
art and contrivance, are owing to him, who *taught us*
more than the beaſts of the field, and made us wiſer
than the fowls of heaven; to him we owe that we can
diſcern the beauty and kind intention and wiſdom of
his works, and thus adore the footſteps of his wiſdom
and goodneſs; that we can diſcern moral beauty, the
affections and conduct which are acceptable to him,
and moſt reſemble the Divine Beauty; that we can diſcover his perfections, and imitate them; and that we
can give ſecure tranquillity to our ſouls by an entire
confidence in them, and reſignation to his providence.
By the reaſon he gave us he converſes with us, aſſures
us of his good-will, gives us the moſt friendly admonitions; and, by the affections of eſteem, love, and
gratitude he has implanted, calls us to a ſtate of friendſhip with himſelf. Thus all our happineſs and excellency is from his bounty *Not unto us, Lord, not un-*
to us, but to thy name be the praiſe.

IV. 'Tis vainly alledged, "that theſe devout affec- *The exerciſe of*
"tions are vain or uſeleſs becauſe *God* needs them *theſe affections*
"not, nor do they increaſe his happineſs." They are *neceſſary to us,*
the chief enjoyments of rational ſouls, their higheſt *not to God.*
joy in proſperity, and ſweeteſt refuge in adverſity. The
rational heart cannot approve itſelf if it wants them;
if it prefers them not to its chiefeſt joys. Without
love, friendſhip, gratitude, life is inſipid. Theſe affections, when mutual, are the more joyful the more excellent the objects are. What ſtable and tranſporting

joy muft arife from living with an habitual fenfe of the Divine Prefence, with the higheft love, admiration, and gratitude, and juftly perfuaded of being approved and beloved and protected by him who is infinitely perfect and omnipotent.

Without this confidence in *God*, what can we call fecure? Our bodies and all external things are obvioufly uncertain: fo is the profperity of our friends, of all the objects of our generous affections. Their very virtues, tho' among the moft ftable things of life, are not fecured againft change. Some accidents can difturb their reafon and their virtue. 'Tis only the foul refigned to *God*, with firm truft in his perfections, that can promife to itfelf in the whole every thing happy and honourable at laft.

In every good temper certain affections muft arife upon their natural occafions, whether they can affect the ftate of the object or not. Tho' we were fully aware of our own impotence, or want of opportunity to do good offices, or make returns, a temper muft be odious which had no love and efteem of great excellency, no gratitude for great benefits. Thus joy muft arife in a good heart upon the profperity of one beloved, tho' we cannot add to it; and forrow upon his adverfity, tho' we cannot remove or alleviate it. The want of fuch affections, where there are fuch ftrong natural caufes prefented, muft argue a depravity of foul which we cannot avoid abhorring upon reflection. Thefe affections are as it were the natural attrac-

tion of the Divinity upon our fouls, and of every excellence which refembles him in his works; and every ⌇⌇
pure foul feels its force.

Nay, without lively apprehenfions of the Divine *No ftable tran-*
Providence, and continual refignation to his will, with *quillity or hap-*
a joyful confidence in his goodnefs, which are the main *piness without*
acts of devotion, our nobleft affections muft expofe *them.*
us to grievous fympathetick forrows in this uncertain
world. But a firm perfuafion of an omnipotent, omnifcient, and moft benign univerfal parent, difpofing
of all in this fyftem for the very beft; determined to
fecure happinefs in the whole to the virtuous, whatever evils may befal them in this life; and permitting
no further évil than what the moft perfect conftitution
requires, or neceffarily brings along with it; a perfuafion of all this, with like extenfive affections in our fouls,
muft afford the ftrongeft confolation in all our tender
forrows, and bring our hearts either chearfully to embrace, or at leaft calmly to acquiefce in whatever is
ordered or permitted by fovereign wifdom and goodnefs. If our friends or favourites are at prefent unfortunate: this the very beft polity in this grand ftate
required: many more of our brethren and fellow-citizens, of as great virtue, are ftill happy. They have
their dear friends rejoicing with them; their affections
are as tender and lovely; their virtues are as valuable,
as thofe in our fet of friends. If ours are in diftrefs and
forrow, others with equal tendernefs and virtue are
rejoicing One generation paffeth, and another comes;
and the univerfe remains for ever; and ever as fruitful

in virtue, joy and felicity. Nay from the fhort period we know, we cannot conclude about the future mife-ries of fuch as are now unfortunate. We know not what the ever-during courfe of ages may bring to thofe very perfons whofe misfortunes or vices we are bewai-ling. The thoughts of a future eternity, under a good *God*, make all things appear ferene, and joyful, and glorious.

Pious affections encreafe all vir-tue and joy. A conftant regard to *God* in all our actions and enjoyments, will give a new beauty to every virtue, by making it an act of gratitude and love to him; and increafe our pleafure in every enjoyment, as it will ap-pear an evidence of his goodnefs: it will give a divi-ner purity and fimplicity of heart, to conceive all our virtuous difpofitions as implanted by *God* in our hearts, and all our beneficent offices as our proper work, and the natural duties of that ftation we hold in his uni-verfe, and the fervices we owe to this nobler country. Our minds fhall be called off from the lower views of honours, or returns from men, and from all con-tempt or pride toward our fellows who fhare not e-qually in his goodnefs: our little paffions and refent-ments fhall be fuppreffed in his prefence. Our hearts will chiefly regard his approbation, our aims fhall be obtained when we act the part affigned us faithfully and gratefully to our great Creator, let others act as they pleafe toward us. The miftakes, imperfections, provocations, calumnies, injuries, or ingratitude of others we fhall look upon as matters prefented to us by providence for the exercife of the virtues *God* has

endued us with, by which we may more approve our Chap. 10.
felves to his penetrating eye, and to the inward fenfe
of our own hearts, than by the eafier offices of virtue
where it has nothing to difcourage or oppofe it.

Thus as the calm and moft extenfive determination
of the foul toward the univerfal happinefs can have no
other center of reft and joy than the original independent omnipotent Goodnefs; fo without the knowledge
of it, and the moft ardent love and refignation to it,
the foul cannot attain to its own moft ftable and higheft perfection and excellence: nor can our *moral faculty*, naturally delighting in moral excellence, obtain
any other compleat object upon which it can be fully
exercifed, than that Being which is abfolutely perfect,
and originally poffeft of all excellence, and the fource
of all fuch excellencies in others.

IV. External worfhip is the natural expreffion of *The reafons for
external wor-
fhip.* thefe devout fentiments and affections. The obvious
reafons for it are thefe; the exercife and expreffion of
all fentiments and affections makes their impreffions
deeper, and ftrengthens them in the foul. Again ;
gratitude, love and efteem, are affections which decline concealment when they are lively; we are naturally prone to exprefs them, even tho' they give no
new happinefs to their object. 'Tis plainly our duty
to promote virtue and happinefs among others: our
worfhipping in fociety, our recounting thankfully
God's benefits, our explaining his nature and perfections, our expreffing our admiration, efteem, gratitude,
and love, prefents to the minds of others the proper

Vol. I.   E e

Book I. motives of like affections; and by a contagion, obfervable in all our paffions, naturally tends to raife them
in others. Piety thus diffufed in a fociety, is the ftrongeft reftraint from evil; and adds new force to every focial difpofition, to every engagement to good offices.

The natural ex-
preffions of devo-
tion.
The natural expreffions are, inftructing others in
the perfections of *God*, and the nature of piety and virtue, the great end of his laws; praifes, thankfgivings,
acknowledgements of his providence as the fpring of
all good by prayers, and expreffions of truft and refignation; confeffion of our fins and imperfections;
and imploring his pardon, and future aids for our a-
mendment. We may add folemn invocation of him
as the witnefs and avenger of any falfhood in our af-
fertions or promifes, wherever it may be requifite to
fettle fome important right of our fellows, or to give
them confidence in our fidelity.

All thefe requi-
red for our im-
provement in
virtue and per-
fection.
V. Our praife, admiration, or thanks, add nothing
to the Divine felicity; our confeffion gives no new information; our importunity alters not his purpofes
from what he had formerly determined as beft. Our
fwearing makes him no more attentive, or difpofed to
execute juftice, nor gives it any new right to punifh.
Thefe acts of adoration, praife, thankfgiving, confeffion, prayer, increafe our own piety, love, and gratitude, our abhorrence of moral evil, and our defires of
what is truly good, and our refignation to his will.
When we have lively difpofitions of this kind, we are
beft prepared to improve all temporal bleffings, and
may hope for them according to the gracious tenor

of Divine Providence. Invocations of *God* by oaths, in
a religious manner, and on important occasions, must
imprint the deepest sense of our obligations to fidelity,
and of the crime of falshood; and thus give the greatest security we can give, by words, to our fellow-creatures. The effect of all these acts is upon ourselves,
and not upon the *Deity*, or his purposes, which have
been originally fixed upon a thorough foresight of all
the changes which could happen in our moral dispositions; which themselves also are a part of the objects
of his eternal counsels and power.

'Tis a needless inquiry whether a society of *Atheists*   *The influence of*
religion on hu-
could subsist? or whether their state would be better or *man society.*
worse than that of men possessed with some wicked
superstition? True religion plainly increases the happiness both of individuals and of societies. Remove all
religion, and you remove some of the strongest bonds,
some of the noblest motives, to fidelity and vigour
in all social offices. 'Tis plain too that some systems
of religious tenets, where much wicked superstition
makes a part, may contain many noble precepts, rules,
and motives, which have their good effects upon the
minds of such as are not concerned in executing the
purposes of the superstition. Thus many of the best
moral precepts, and the doctrine of future rewards appointed for virtue, are retained in Popery, and excite
many to the most virtuous offices, whilst others by
the superstitious political tenets, destined for the ag-
grandising of the ecclesiasticks, and the enslaving of

the souls and bodies of the rest of mankind, are excited to the most horrid cruelties.

'Tis of no importance to determine whether such
superstitions have worse effects than *Atheism.* They
may, as to men in certain stations; tho' they hurt
not the rest considerably. The experiment of a society of *Atheists* has never yet been made. Grant
that the effects of some superstitions were worse than
those of *Atheism:* this is rather honourable to religion. The best state of religion is incomparably happier than any condition of *Atheism;* and the corruptions of the best things may be most pernicious. A
surfeit of nourishing food, may be more dangerous
than that of food less nourishing: spoiled wines are
more dangerous than bad water. 'Tis the business of
rational minds to take all the blessings of a true religion, and guard against any corruption of it, without
searching out what motives might remain to some
sorts of virtues under the joyless wretched thought
that the universe is under no providence, but left to
chance, or as blind and undesigning necessity; if religion, when depraved, does great mischief; a pure and
good religion is a powerful engine of much good.

CHAP. XI.

The CONCLUSION *of this* BOOK, *shewing the* WAY *to the* SUPREME HAPPINESS *of our* NATURE.

HAVING thus considered the several sources of *The sum of human happiness.* happiness our nature is capable of; and, upon a full comparison, found that the noblest and most lasting enjoyments are such as arise from our own affections and actions, and not the passive sensations we receive from those external things which affect the body: having also compared the several sort of affections and actions, whether exerted toward our fellows in narrower or more extended systems, or toward the *Deity*, whose nature and grand intention in the administration of the universe we have also endeavoured to discover: and having found that, as our *moral faculty* plainly approves in an higher degree, all the more extensive affections toward our fellows than it approves the more confined affections or passions; that these extensive affections are also more noble sources of enjoyment; and that our love of moral excellence; our knowledge, veneration, and love of the Deity, conceived as perfectly good and wise and powerful, and the fountain of all good; and an entire resignation to his will and providence is the source of our sublimest happiness, the grand foundation of all our tranquillity or security as to any other object of the most honourable desires: 'tis plain our supreme and compleat

BOOK I. happiness, according to the univerſal doɛtrine of the wiſeſt men in all ages,†muſt conſiſt in the compleat exerciſe of theſe nobler virtues, eſpecially that entire love and reſignation to *God*, and of all the inferior virtues which do not interfere with the ſuperior: and in the enjoyment of ſuch external proſperity as we can, conſiſtently with virtue, obtain.

The moral ſenſe and the two calm determinations, conſpire in recommending, Juſtice,

II. The courſe of life therefore, pointed out to us immediately by our *moral ſenſe*, and confirmed by all juſt conſideration of our true intereſt, muſt be the very ſame which the *generous calm determination* would recommend, a conſtant ſtudy to promote the moſt univerſal happineſs in our power, by doing all good offices as we have opportunity which interfere with no more extenſive intereſt of the ſyſtem ; preferring always the more extenſive and important offices to thoſe of leſs extent and importance; and cautiouſly abſtaining from whatever may occaſion any unneceſſary miſery in this ſyſtem. This is the cardinal virtue of *juſtice* which the antients make the ſupreme one, to which the reſt are all ſubſervient. It may include even our duties toward *God*.

and temperance,

As ſenſual enjoyments are the meaneſt and moſt tranſitory, the deſires of which, by the impetuous force of ſome of our brutal paſſions, frequently ſeduce men from the courſe of virtue, it muſt be of high importance to be fully convinced of their meanneſs, and to acquire an habit of ſelf-command, a power over theſe lower appetites in the manner we explained when we

† This is Ariſtotle's definition, Ενέργεια κατ᾽ ἀρετὴν ἀρίσην ἐν βίῳ τελείῳ.

confidered the nature of thefe enjoyments. 'Tis e-
qually neceffary by clofe reflection to make a juft eftimate of other more elegant enjoyments of the imagination, that, as they are far inferior to moral and focial enjoyments, they may yield to them in our choice
where they interfere. This is the virtue of *temperance.*

A juft eftimation of the value of this life, and of *and fortitude.*
the feveral forts of evil we are expofed to, muft be
equally neceffary. If moral evils, and fome fympathetick fufferings are worfe than any external ones, and
can make life fhameful and miferable amidft all affluence of other things, as we fhewed above; if at beft,
life is but an uncertain poffeffion we muft foon lofe;
we fhall fee fomething that is more to be dreaded
than death, and many juft reafons why it may on certain occafions be our intereft to incur the danger of
it. Were death an entire end of all thought it would
indeed put an end to all good, but furely no evil could
enfue.

———— *num trifte videtur*
Quicquam? nonne omni fomno fecurior extat.

But if we are to exift after death under a good Providence, what a glorious foundation is this for *fortitude* in every honourable caufe? what ftrength of mind
muft that hope give to every good man upon apprehenfions of death, or any of the evils which lead to it?
This is the third cardinal virtue.

Prudence is that habit of attention to the nature *Prudence pre-*
of the feveral objects which may follicit our defires, en- *requifite to vir-*
tue of all forts.
gaging us to a thorough inquiry into their impor-

BOOK I. tance, in themfelves and their confequences, either to the greateft private happinefs of the individual, or to that of the fyftem. This virtue is fome way prerequifite to the proper exercife of the other three, and is generally firft mentioned in order; tho' *juftice* is the fupreme one to which all the reft are fubfervient. We leave it to more practical treatifes to dilate upon thefe things. The proper confiderations, and the means of acquiring thefe four habits of virtue muft be evident from what is faid above concerning the comparative values of the feveral forts of good and evil, and concerning the fupreme enjoyments of our nature.

Miftakes.　　III. Many are difcouraged from a vigorous culture of their minds for the reception of all virtues by a rafh prejudice. We are dazzled with the confpicuous glories of fome great fuccefsful actions in higher ftations; we can allow fuch virtues to be the nobleft enjoyments; but they are placed fo high that few have accefs to them. Nay perfons in higher ftations often defpair when their power is not abfolute. The humours, follies, or corrupt views of others obftruct all their good intentions. They are freted with fuch difappointments, and quit the purfuits of virtue, defponding of any valuable enjoyment attending it.

To arm the foul againft this prejudice, we fhould remember that the reality and perfection of virtue, and the inward fatisfaction of it too, to a calm mind, depends not on external fuccefs, but upon the inward temper of foul. Perfifting under thefe doubts about the fuccefs or glory, in the publick offices of virtue;

or if we are excluded from them, in all the lower private offices; in a conſtant ſweetneſs of deportment in obſcurity, and a conſtant reſignation to the *ſupreme Mind;* embracing chearfully the lot appointed for us, repreſſing every envious motion, and every repining thought againſt providence, reſolving to go ſtedfaſtly on in the path pointed out to us by *God* and nature, till our mortal part fall down to that earth from whence it ſprung; muſt appear rather more noble and heroick to the *All-ſearching Eye,* and to the judgment of every wiſe man, than the more glittering virtues of a proſperous fortune. In theſe there is leſs purity and ſimplicity diſcovered, ſince the alluring views of glory and worldly intereſts may have had a large ſhare in the affections, or been the principal motives to the agent.

When we deſpair of glory, and even of executing all the good we intend, 'tis a ſublime exerciſe to the ſoul to perſiſt in acting the rational and ſocial part as it can; diſcharging its duty well, and committing the reſt to *God.* Who can tell what greater good might be attainable if all good men thus exerted their powers even under great uncertainties of ſucceſs, and great dangers of miſrepreſentations and obloquy? Or how much worſe ſhould all matters proceed, if all good men deſponded and grew remiſs under ſuch apprehenſions? If virtue appears more glorious by ſurmounting external dangers and obſtacles, is not its glory equally increaſed by ſurmounting theſe inward diſcouragements, and perſiſting without the aids of glory or

VOL. I.   F f

BOOK I. applauſe, conquering even the ingratitude of thoſe it ſerves, ſatisfied with the ſilent teſtimony of our hearts, and the hopes of Divine approbation. Thus the moſt heroick excellence, and its conſequent happineſs and inward joy, may be attained under the worſt circum-ſtances of fortune: nor is any ſtation of life excluded from the enjoyment of the ſupreme good.

THE END OF THE FIRST BOOK.

BOOK II.

Containing a Deduction of the more special LAWS *of* NATURE, *and Duties of Life, previous to Civil Government, and other adventitious States.*

CHAP. I.

The Circumstances which increase or diminish the MORAL GOOD, *or* EVIL *of Actions.*

HAVING shewed, in the former book, that the course of life which GOD and NATURE recommends to us as most lovely and most conducive to the true happiness of the agent, is that which is intended for the general good of mankind in the wisest manner that our reason and observation can suggest; we proceed, in this book, to enquire more particularly into the proper means of promoting the happiness of mankind by our actions, which is the same thing with inquiring into the more special laws of nature. And this we shall endeavour to do first abstracting from those adventitious states or relations which human institutions or actions have constituted, considering only that relation which *nature* hath constituted among all. But it may be necessary here to premise some account of many complex notions of moral qualities, the understanding of which seems prerequisite to the doctrine of the particular laws of nature. This shall be the subject of this and the two following chapters.

Book II.   I. The ground of all imputation * of actions as virtuous or vitious is, " that they flow from some af-

The ground of " fection in the agent, and thus are evidences of his
imputation, that
actions flow from " temper and affections." Virtue, as it was proved in
and discover the
affections. the former book, consists primarily in the affections. The highest kind of it is the calm and fixed principle of good-will to the greatest system; and love, esteem, gratitude, and resignation to *God,* upon a full persuasion of his moral perfections, and a constant prevalent desire of making still further progress toward that moral perfection of which we perceive ourselves to be capable. The lower kinds, are the particular kind affections and passions pursuing the good of particular societies, or individuals, consistently with the general good. This, one would think, could scarce be matter of debate among Christians, after the sum of the law delivered to us, † viz. *Loving God* and *our neighbour.* If virtue be not placed in the affections, but in some other faculty different from the will, as *reason* or *intellect,* then love is to be called an act of the understanding, contrary to all language.

Qualities and
circumstances ne-   II. From this description 'tis easy to find what cir-
cessary to the mo-
rality of actions. cumstances affect the morality of actions, or omissions, increasing or diminishing the moral good, or evil, in them; or making actions good, which otherways had been evil; or evil, which otherways had been good.

Liberty.   First. 'Tis manifest that whatever action, or rather event, happened not in consequence of one's will, ei-

---

* *Imputation* is one of the *voces mediae,* tho' more commonly used in charging men with guilt.   † Matth. xii. 30, 31.

ther at prefent, or in fome prior time, cannot be imputed as either good, or evil. Nor can any omiffion
or abftaining from action be imputed as good, or evil,
to him who could not have performed it by any efforts, and knew this impoffibility. Such events or o-
miffions can evidence no affection, either good, or bad.
Events, however, are then only called *neceffary* with
refpect to an agent, which he could not prevent tho'
he ferioufly defired it; not fuch as, through his ftrong
averfions or habits, he cannot avoid defiring. Thofe
only are called *impoffible*, which no efforts of his can
accomplifh by any means. We call any thing poffible, which one who heartily defires it, can get accomplifhed, whether by his own power, or by any aid
of others which he can obtain.*

Thefe alone are the neceffary and wholly unimpu- *Neceffary e-*
table events † which neither any prefent defire or ac- *vents, not moral.*
tion of ours can prevent, nor could they have been
prevented by any prior diligence or care which we
ought to have had about fuch matters. Such events,
as prior fore-thought and care could have prevented,
tho' they be now unavoidable, are in fome meafure voluntary ‡ and imputable; whether they happen from
free agency, or from natural inanimate caufes. Thus
if one by negligence in his office fuffers banks or
mounds to decay, when a ftorm comes he cannot prevent the inundation; and yet it is juftly counted voluntary and imputable to him.

* This explains the common maxim, *Impoffibilium et neceffariorum nulla eft imputa-*
tia. † *Involuntaria et in fe, et in fua caufa.* ‡ *Involuntaria in fe, fed non in fua caufa.*

nor the omiſſion of impoſſibilities.

So the omiſſions of actions now impoſſible are juſtly imputed, when they might have been poſſible, had that previous diligence been exerted which becomes a good man. A ſlothful profuſe man cannot now diſcharge his debts, yet as a prior courſe of prudent oeconomy would have prevented this injury to his creditors, the non-payment is imputable. In theſe caſes, indeed, the unavoidable event or omiſſion, contrary to preſent ſtrong inclination, ſhews no preſent evil affection. But the former negligence, which made one incapable of doing juſtice, argues a prior culpable defect of good diſpoſitions. And 'tis here that the guilt properly lyes. Two perſons may be equally criminal in the ſight of God, and their own conſciences, when the events of their conduct are very different. Suppoſe equal negligence in both, and that both become inſolvent, but one by an unexpected inheritance diſcharges his debts; the other, tho' equally inclined, remains incapable of it. They are equally criminal, tho' one by accident does no wrong in the event to his creditors.

What effects and conſequents imputable.

III. No diſtant effects or conſequents of actions or omiſſions, affect their morality, if they could not have been foreſeen by that diligence and caution we expect from good men; for then they are no indications of the temper of the agent. For the ſame reaſon any proſperous effects which were not intended, do not increaſe the moral goodneſs of an action; but an evil action is made worſe by all the evil conſequents, which would have appeared to a man of ſuch caution as good

affections would naturally raife, tho' the agent did not
actually forefee them. They do not indeed prove any
direct evil intention; but there are other forms of moral evil. The very want of a proper degree of good
affections is morally evil. One ftudious of the publick
good will be cautious and inquifitive about the effects
of his actions; the inquifitive will difcover fuch effects
as are difcoverable by their fagacity. He then who is
ignorant of fuch effects, tho' he had no direct evil intention, betrays a culpable weaknefs of the good affections.

In judging of the moral characters of fuch as have
not had any confiderable reformation made in their
affections, 'tis not of confequence whether the guilt
be evidenced by fome prefent action, or omiffion; or
by fome preceeding one equally criminal. That apho-
rifm therefore is juft, that " an action can be made
" virtuous only by fuch good confequents as are actu-
" ally intended for themfelves: but may be made vi-
" cious by any evil confequences which a good and
" honeft mind could have forefeen as probably en-
" fuing."

But good confequents intended then only prove an
action to be good, when the fum of them over-ballance
all the evil ones which could have been forefeen, and
when the good confequents could not be obtained
without thefe evils. If the cafe is otherways, they may
extenuate the guilt, but do not juftify the action. On
the other hand, evil confequents forefeen, but not defired for themfelves, do not always make an action

Book II. evil. 'Tis only in such cases where they over-ballance all the good effects to which this action is subservient, and for which it was intended; and where this over-ballance might have been foreseen, or when the good effect could have been obtained without these evils.

By consequents of an action we understand not only the direct and natural effects, or what the agent is the proper cause of; but all these events too which ensue upon it, and had not happened had the action been omitted. A good man regards whatever he foresees may ensue through the mistakes, follies, or vices of others; and avoids what he foresees will occasion vicious actions, or unreasonable offences, in others, * tho' otherways it might have been innocent: unless the good effects, not otherways to be obtained, over-ballance these particular evils.†

Ignorance and error, vincible, or invincible, affect actions in certain degrees.   IV. Ignorance of the tendency or effects of actions, affects their morality differently, according to the different causes of the ignorance or error, and the difficulty, greater or less, of coming to the knowledge of the truth. If the ignorance or error be absolutely invincible by any present, or any prior diligence, evil consequents thus unknown cannot be imputed, as they can shew no evil affection, nor any defect in good affections. If that degree of caution which we expect in like affairs from the best men could not surmount the ignorance tho' the utmost possible caution might, we still count it morally invincible, and wholly excusing from guilt, except in cases where all men know that

---

* Rom. xiv. 21.   † Matth. x. 34, 35.

the utmoſt caution is incumbent on them. But where
the ordinary caution of a good mind would have foreſeen ſuch conſequents, then the ignorance argues a
defect of good affections, is vincible, and tho' it may
alleviate the guilt, it does not wholly take it away.

Ignorance and error may be at preſent invincible
and involuntary, and yet prior diligence might have
prevented them; or it may be invincible and involuntary every way.* The latter only takes away all imputation: the former, ſhews that there is no direct evil
intention at preſent, but it may evidence a prior want
of good affections, and thus be juſtly culpable.

But as direct evil intention, or inſenſibility of the
evil we plainly ſee we are doing to others, are much
more odious tempers than mere inadvertence, or the
want of ſuch warm affections as would raiſe accurate
attention; all ignorance not directly affected or deſired is ſome alleviation of guilt; and that in different
degrees, according as the effects were more or leſs obvious. The eaſier the diſcovery was, the leſs does the
ignorance alleviate the guilt.

Ignorance may either be about the effects of *Ignorance of*
the action, or the true intent and meaning of laws. *the law or the*
The ſame maxims hold about both. Only, ſince wiſe *fact.*
legiſlators take care ſo to publiſh their laws that the
ſubjects may always know them by proper diligence,
ignorance of the law cannot be deemed abſolutely
invincible. If any laws are abſolutely undiſcoverable

* *Involuntaria in ſe, ſed non in ſua cauſa.* or, *Involuntaria et in ſe, et in ſua
cauſa.*

Book II. by the fubjects, they are not laws given to them; their not obeying them cannot be culpable.*

Confcience what. V. The queftions about vincible ignorance, and confciences erroneous, or doubtful, are only difficult through ambiguity of words. Confcience fometimes denotes the *moral faculty* itfelf: fometimes " the judg- " ment of the underftanding concerning the fprings " and effects of actions upon which the *moral fenfe* " approves, or condemns them." And when we have got certain maxims and rules concerning the conduct which is virtuous, or vicious, and conceive them to be, as they truly are, the laws given to us by *God* the author of nature and of all our powers; or when we are perfuaded that other divine laws are revealed to us in a different manner, then confcience may be de- fined to be " Our judgment concerning actions com- " pared with the *law.*"

How an erro- neous confcience excufes, or exte- nuates. Now firft, " A perfon purpofing to act virtuouf- " ly, and yet by miftake imagining that action to have " a good tendency, and to be conformable to the law, " which is of a contrary nature in reality, will certain- " ly during his error follow his confcience: fince no " man in an error knows that he errs." The obfervers only can make the queftion, whether 'tis better for him to follow his confcience, or counteract it? And this cannot in all cafes be anfwered the fame way.

2. " He who follows the erroneous judgment of " his mind in doing what he believes to be good, at " prefent evidences a good difpofition: and acting a-

---

* *Ignorantia juris, ignorantia facti.*

" gainſt his judgment, during his error, muſt evidence
" ſome vicious diſpoſition; ſuch as neglect of more ex-
" tenſive good, or of the lawgiver." This holds in general true as to all men who are firmly perſuaded of
the goodneſs of *God* and his laws.   As we all cenſure
a man who from any narrower affection of a lovely
ſort ſhould counteract the views of the more extenſive
affections; the ſame way we muſt cenſure the counteracting ſuch commands of God, as we believe are calculated for the moſt extenſive happineſs, tho' the a-
gent has been excited to it by ſome humane and lovely affections of the narrower ſort; which, however, in
all caſes alleviate the guilt.

But when there is no ſuch ſettled apprehenſion of
God, or his laws, as perfectly benevolent; and only a
notion of high private intereſt in obedience, and great
private danger to ourſelves from diſobedience, with a
confuſed notion of duty or obligation to obey; if ſome
very tender humane diſpoſitions of heart ſhould lead
one to diſobey ſome ſevere and cruel orders imagined
to come from the *Deity ;* whatever convulſions he
might feel in his own heart by the ſtruggles between
two ſuch oppoſite principles, a judicious ſpectator
could ſcarce condemn the counteracting ſuch a conſcience from principles of humanity: for example, if
one who believed it his duty to perſecute hereticks to
death, yet were reſtrained by compaſſion to his fellow-creatures.

3. " The falling into ſuch vincible errors, ſo oppoſite   *All errors are*
" to the humane diſpoſitions of the ſoul, in matters ſo   *not innocent.*

G g 2

Book II. " deeply affecting the interests of our fellows as that of
" persecution, and some others, must argue great prior
" guilt and deficiency of good affections." And therefore, during the error, whether one follows his conscience, or not, we have some evidence of a bad temper. If he follows it, his prior negligence is very culpable: if he does not, and yet believes the command
to have been given by a good God for the general interest, his prior negligence is culpable as in the other
case, and now he superadds the guilt of omitting his
duty to *God*, and the general interest. But where one
has no notions of the Divine Goodness, and the benign tendency of his laws, counteracting the imagined
law may be less odious, if it be from a lovely humane
disposition.

4. When the conscience is doubtful, the safest way
is to defer acting till further inquiry be made, unless
some general potent reason urges to a speedy determination. Cases happen in which 'tis plainly better to
do either of the two actions, about the preference of
which we are doubting, than to omit both; and there
may be no time for delays. In such cases we must fix
upon one or t'other, according to superior probability
of its importance. If these probabilities are equal, we
must do what first occurs.

The duty of such as err. What is the duty then of one in an error? or what
conduct will be entirely approved? 'Tis plain the er-
ror already has evidenced a prior culpable negligence.
The only conduct which now shall gain entire approbation again is correcting the error by a new unpreju-

diced inquiry. The erroneous, during their error, do not fee this to be their duty; but 'tis the only way to fet all right again. And this ſhews the great advantage of modeſty and diffidence as to our own underſtand- ings; and the danger of ſelf-confidence and bigotry.

The degree of diligence requiſite in a good man, cannot be preciſely determined. We naturally expect very different degrees from different capacities, ſtati- ons, opportunities. Ariſtotle * well obſerves, that "ma- " ny points in *morals*, when applied to individual ca- " ſes, cannot be exactly determined; but good men " know them by a ſort of ſenſation: the good experi- " enced man is thus the laſt meaſure of all things." This holds in general: " the greater the diligence and " caution about our duty is, the character is ſo much " the better; and the leſs the diligence and caution " is, ſo much the worſe is the character, when other " circumſtances are equal."

* *Nicom.* l. iii. c. 4. and l. ii. c. ult. and l. vi. c. 11, and often in the *Magna Mo-* *ralia,* particularly l. ii. c. 10. Hence the *arbitrium viri probi*, with the *Civilians*.

CHAP. II.

General Rules of judging about the Morality *of* Actions, *from the Affections exciting to them, or opposing them.*

ALtho' men cannot accurately judge about the degrees of virtue, or vice, in the actions of others, becaufe their inward fprings are unknown : yet fome general rules may be abundantly certain and ufeful in our judging about ourfelves. And we have no great occafion to make application of them to others, which muft be extremely uncertain.

General rules about the importance of actions.

1. Where kind affections alone are the fprings of action, the good effected by any agent is as the ftrength of thefe affections and his ability jointly. The ftrength of affection therefore is directly as the good effected, and inverfely as the abilities ; or, in plainer terms, when the good done by two perfons is equal, while their abilities are unequal, he fhews the better heart, whofe abilities were fmaller.

How views of private intereft affect the morality of actions.

2. Where men are alfo excited by views of private intereft, the effect of thefe felfifh defires is to be deducted, and the remainder fhews the effect of the virtuous difpofition. Where motives of private intereft diffuaded from fome good action performed, the virtue appears the higher by furmounting thefe motives.

3. In like manner we compute the moral turpitude of unkind or bafely felfifh affections leading us to injury. The ftrength of them is directly as the evil effected, and inverfely as the abilities. That is, where

equal mischiefs are done by two, who had it in their power to do more, in gratification of their evil affecti- ons, he shews the worse temper, who had the smaller power but exerted it further.

4. When private interests excite to hurtful actions, the effect of the selfish desires is not the same way to *The same circumstances affect evil actions.* be deducted to find the pure effect of some inclination wholly vicious. We seldom can have any such inclinations. The moral evils of men generally flow from the immoderate degrees of some selfish affections, which in a moderate degree would be innocent; and the very want of high degrees of some good affections is vicious. This deduction can only be made where the exciting selfish motive was the avoiding some great sufferings terrible even to very good minds; and such temptations much extenuate the guilt. Where great interests known to the agent dissuaded from the evil action, indeed the guilt is exceedingly aggravated, as the depravity of temper surmounts these interests, as well as all sense of duty and generous affection.

II. But in comparing actions and characters we *The kind of the affections to be regarded.* not only regard the strength of the exciting affection, but the kind of it, since, as we observed above, our *moral sense*, by the wise constitution of *God*, more approves such affections as are most useful and efficacious for the publick interest. It immediately approves the calm sedate good-will either to particular societies, or individuals, more than the turbulent passions of the generous sort; and of the calm affections most approves the most extensive. And thus tho' the effects

BOOK II. of two actions were equal, that one is more approved which flowed from a calm settled principle of kindness, than another from some turbulent passion. The superior excellency of these calm dispositions is allowed on all hands; and shews men what temper nature recommends to their culture, by all the power we have over our affections; and what restraints should be laid upon the less extensive affections, whether calm or passionate, that they may never defeat the purposes of the most extensive and excellent dispositions of the soul. Here we see also the reason why no great virtue is imagined in our kindness to our offspring, kindred, or even benefactors. Strong particular passions naturally arise toward persons so related to us, whether we have any of the more extensive affections lively in our breasts or not: and few characters are so depraved as to be void of these natural affections. The want of them indeed, for reasons presently to be mentioned, would argue a temper depraved in the most odious degree.

Hard to fix precise degrees of obligation.   III. When promoting the publick good is opposite to the agent's worldly interest, 'tis hard to fix a precise degree of good affection requisite merely to avoid a bad character, or obtain that of bare innocence. One may be called in one sense innocent who never hurts others in pursuit of his own interest. But notwithstanding this he may be a bad man, if he contributes little to a publick interest. God has set in our hearts, if we would attend to it, a very high standard of necessary goodness, and we must be displeased with

ourfelves when we omit any office, how burdenfome
or hurtful foever to ourfelves, which in the whole
would increafe the publick happinefs after all its confequents are confidered. In our common eftimations
of characters and actions we do not judge fo rigidly,
nor can one eafily tell precifely how far one muft facrifice his private interefts to the publick, to avoid a
bad character. The extremes of virtue and vice are
abundantly known; but intermediate degrees are lefs
difcernible from each other when they approach very
near, as in colours fhaded into each other. The following maxims feem pretty probable, or certain;

1. That affections of equal degrees of extent or *Several gene-*
ral rules.
ftrength are not expected from perfons of unequal circumftances and opportunities, tho' originally of equal
tempers. More is demanded from fuch as have had
inftruction, leifure for meditation, and accefs to better ftations.

2. Such offices as are ufeful to others, and of no
expence or labour to the agent, are juftly expected
from all toward all who need them. They are but low
evidences of virtue, but refufing them is very hateful,
and fhews a temper void of humanity.

3. Nay we univerfally condemn the refufal of fuch
fmaller expences or trouble as can fcarce difturb the
happinefs of life, when it is neceffary for any important advantage even to a ftranger.

4. The greater the expence or trouble is one fub-
mits to for the benefit of others, it muft be to others
the greater evidence of his virtue.

5. The fmaller the advantages are for the fake of which one does what is detrimental to the publick, or declines any ufeful fervices, the worfe we muft conclude his character.

How narrower affections fhould yield to more extenfive. The fame difficulties may appear in determining precifely how far the narrower affections in particular cafes fhould yield to the more extenfive; or how far the interefts of families, kindred, benefactors, friends our party, or country, fhould be facrificed to more extenfive interefts, to avoid a bad character or the charge of guilt. A calm mind, folicitous about its own conduct, will blame every defect of that moft perfect moral order, which requires facrificing all narrower interefts to the more extenfive. But there is fomething fo beautiful and fo engaging in many narrower affections of the foul, that we judge lefs rigidly of the conduct of men who from fuch lovely principles neglect the higheft perfection. And as it is but a fmall degree of attention and difcernment, which can be reafonably expected from men of lower ftations and capacities, much encumbered by procuring to themfelves and their immediate dependents the neceffaries of life, nature is far from leading us to pronounce the character bad, which does not in all cafes adhere to the moft exact rules of perfection. But withal the attentive reflecting mind cannot but fee the faireft mark fet up by *God* in his heart, a clear idea of perfection. The nearer he can come to it, fo much the better and more excellent he is. Nor was it the Divine intention that we fhould fatisfy ourfelves by merely avoiding fuch conduct as is matter of infamy. Two general maxims CHAP. 2. are abundantly obvious in these cases.

1. First, that to maintain the calm and most extenſive affection toward the univerſal happineſs the ſtrongeſt principle of the ſoul, able to controll all narrower affections when there is any oppoſition; and the ſacrificing all narrower intereſts to the moſt extenſive, while yet every tender affection in the ſeveral relations of life is preſerved in as great ſtrength as the juſt ſubordination of it to the ſuperior will admit; is the higheſt perfection of human virtue.

2. And yet when ſome of theſe narrower kind affections exceed their proportion, and overcome the more extenſive, the moral deformity is alleviated in proportion to the moral beauty of that narrower affection by which the more extenſive is overpowered. Thus 'tis more excuſable if we do what is hurtful to the moſt general intereſt, from zeal for our country, for a whole people; than if the ſame had been done for aggrandizing a party, a cabal, or a family. And any of thoſe tender affections extenuate the guilt more than any merely ſelfiſh principle could have done, ſuch as avarice, ambition, ſenſuality.

IV. The greater part of mankind, by the neceſſary avocations of life, are incapable of very extenſive deſigns, and want opportunities and abilities for ſuch ſervices. But we have this juſt preſumption, that by ſerving innocently any valuable part of a ſyſtem, we do good to the whole. The lives therefore of many of the moſt virtuous are juſtly employed in ſerving

The ordinary virtues from the narrower cauſes of love.

Book II. such particular persons, or smaller societies, who are more peculiarly recommended to them by the very order of nature. *Nature* constitutes many particular attachments and proper causes of loving some more than others. Some of these causes are of a generous kind, but in different degrees. Such as the *conjugal* and *parental relations,* and the other *tyes* of *blood ;* *benefits conferred,* which excite a generous gratitude, tho' we expect no more; *eminent virtues* observed; and the very relation of *countrymen.* Of the selfish sort are, a *profitable intercourse of offices, dependence for future preferment, or other favours.* All these are natural causes not only of keener passions, but of a stronger calm good-will in most of men. On the other hand, tho', to a man of just reflection, there can be no natural cause of any calm ultimate ill-will, yet to the greater part of mankind there are natural causes of the unkind passions, anger, indignation, envy, and aversion; some wholly selfish, such as *private injuries* received, *opposition* to our interest; others of a generous kind, such as *moral evil* observed, *injuries done to the publick, or to friends,* unreasonable *promotion,* to the exclusion of more worthy men.

General rules of computing.   Now a temper is certainly so much the better, the more susceptible it is of all sweet affections upon smaller causes, especially those of the generous kind, provided it entertains proportionally warmer·affections where greater causes appear; and the less susceptible it is of unkind passions upon any causes, especially the selfish. The temper must be very good which retains good-will, where many occurrences would readily ba- nifh it from the heart: and that temper muft be very bad, where love cannot be kindled by the natural caufes.

In general, the ftronger the merit or the natural caufes of love there are in any perfon, our want of love to him muft evidence the greater depravation: and any low degree below the proportion of the merit, muft evidence the fmaller virtue. A temper where any thing virtuous remains muft be warmed by eminent virtues, or by great benefits conferred. And fince there muft appear in the *Deity* all the higheft caufes of love, when one with tolerable attention contemplates him as the author of all good natural and moral, as the fupreme moral excellence, as the great benefactor of all; the want of the higheft love to him muft evidence the greateft moral deformity in any rational mind to whom his perfections are difcovered.

V. Thefe principles lead to fome more fpecial con- *More fpecial* clufions. 1. Defect of power, of opportunities, of the *conclufions.* means of external good offices, without any fault of ours, will not exclude us from the moft heroick virtue.* This maxim is the moft joyful to a good heart.

2. No difappointment of any wife and good attempt, by external force, or accidents which one could not forefee, can diminifh the virtue: nor do unexpected or unintended good confequents increafe it, † or diminifh the guilt of a bad action. In human affairs men muft follow probabilities. If the probable good

---

* See conclufion of book i. † B. ii. c. 1.

Book II. effects intended, which could not be obtained in a safer way, surpass all the ill effects we could foresee, the action is good, altho' superior evil consequents ensue beyond probability.

3. Prospects of private advantage then only abate the moral beauty of an action, when 'tis known by the agent, or justly presumed by others, that without this selfish motive the agent would not have done so much good.

4. Motives of private interest diminish the guilt of an evil action undertaken from them, only in proportion as they would in such cases affect a virtuous mind. The passions raised by the greatest natural evils impending or threatened, more occupy and ingross the mind than any desires of positive good to be obtained. And hence it is that when a person through fear of death, tortures, or slavery, threatened to himself, or those who are dear to him, or from some high provocation to anger, does what brings superior detriment to society, the guilt is much more extenuated, than if he had been induced to the same conduct by the highest bribes. And resisting the former temptation would show a nobler strength of virtue than resisting the latter, or any inducements of sensuality.* In general, the greater the vice is in any action we are tempted to by motives of interest, the less is the virtue evidenced by our abstaining from it: and the smaller the vice is to which we have such strong

---

* See Aristot. Ethic. Nicom. l. iii. c. ult, and Antonin. l. ii. c. 10.

temptations, the virtue of refifting them is the * greater, provided we have proportionally firmer refolutions
againft the greater vices. Some crimes are fo very odious that few amongft the moft corrupt order of men
can be brought to commit them.

5. The temper is the more depraved the greater
the motives to goodnefs are which it counteracts. He
who fins againft a known law fhews a worfe mind, by
furmounting the ftrong motives to obedience from
the fanctions, and other circumftances to be mentioned hereafter, than one who does the fame action
without any knowledge of the law.

6. Offices of no trouble or expence do not prove
an high virtue in the agent, tho' declining them fhews
great depravity, as there are no motives of intereft
againft them.

7. Common offices done to perfons of great merit in whom there are high caufes of love, are no evidences of great virtue in the agent. He has little virtue who fhews no more zeal for a friend, a benefactor,
a man of eminent virtue, than another will do from
fmaller bonds of affection. And yet the neglecting any
friendly fervices due to fuch high virtues or merit, is
more vicious than omitting offices of general humanity where there were no fuch high claims.

8. When one cannot at once do offices of both
forts, and other circumftances are equal, we fhould
follow the ftronger tyes of nature and the higher caufes of love. Thus we fhould rather do fervices to a

---

* Thus 'tis a good rule of perfection, to *abftain from the very appearance of evil.*

Book II. parent, a benefactor, a kinsman, a man of eminent virtue, than to a stranger. As *God* constituted these special bonds for the wisest purposes, 'tis for the general good that, when other circumstances are equal, these stronger bonds should engage our services rather than the weaker. The omission of the other offices, now inconsistent with the more sacred ones, is altogether innocent.

9. When only equal good is done by persons of equal abilities, from whom more might reasonably have been expected, one acting from mere humanity, the other from additional motives of divine laws and promises proposed by revelation; we have better evidence of a good temper in the former. Our good actions should rise in proportion to the stronger motives proposed, * to shew an equally good temper.

10. Yet as the true aim of virtue is to promote the publick good, and not the pleasing one's self with high notions of his own virtue; every good man must desire to present to his mind all these motives which can further prompt him to good offices, and make him steady and resolute against all difficulties. He must desire the firmest persuasion that virtue is his truest interest; that *God* will espouse his cause by making the virtuous happy either in this life, or the next. Settling these points firmly in our minds, and frequently reflecting on them to obtain constancy and vigour in a course of virtue, superior to all temptations of secular interest, shews the truest benevolence:

* Matth. v. 20. Luke vi. 32,——35.

and the rejecting such considerations would shew a CHAP. 2.
wrong temper, negligent of the natural means of for-
tifying all kind dispositions, and of removing all im-
pediments out of their way. Such will be most constant
and vigorous in all good offices, who have the strongest
motives to them, and have removed all opinions of any
opposite valuable interests. Now such are they only
who believe and often reflect upon the Divine Providence as protecting the virtuous, and ensuring their
happiness; who raise an habitual love, esteem, and gratitude to *God*, which strongly co-operate with all our
generous affections to our fellows. A like effect, in a
lower degree, arises from a just observation on human
affairs, that a course of virtue is the most probable
way of obtaining outward peace and prosperity, as it
never fails to create inward peace and joy. But all
this is no proof that one's own happiness of any kind
is the only thing he ultimately intends in his virtuous
offices.

VI. But as the affections of men are sometimes *How the action*
discovered by the actions of others to which they con- *of others are im-*
tributed, 'tis plain any good office of another, to which *puted.*
we have designedly contributed from any good affection, may be imputed in some degree to our honour.
And where we have contributed to any bad action of
another by acting or omitting contrary to our duty,
it may be imputed also as our fault; but in very different degrees, as circumstances may be very different.

1. As they who exhort, advise, or direct others in virtue *This in various*
shew a good disposition, and share in the honourable *degrees.*

VOL. I.   I i

Book II. imputation; fo the advifers of wickednefs are alike guilty whether their advice has been followed or not. But bad advice may in many inftances abate the guilt of the perfon who perpetrates the wickednefs. Human courts indeed feldom punifh for mere advice, where there was no power or authority in the advifer; and where no fhare of the profit by any injury came to him, he is not made lyable to compenfation of the damage. 'Tis hard to find what effect fuch general advices may have had on the agent, who without them might have acted the very fame part.

2. In many cafes the advifing, exhorting, or congratulating another in any wicked defign may not fhew fuch depravation as the execution of it, as many things occur in the execution to diffuade the undertaker, and make him relent, which do not occur to the advifer or congratulator; fuch as ftronger feelings of compaffion and remorfe, and views of punifhment, and even prefent danger. The furmounting all thefe motives which affect men more deeply in the execution, may fhew a greater depravity in the executer. On the other hand, when the advifer or applauder has no fuch motives of intereft, or of efcaping from fome great danger, no fuch violent paffions moving him, and yet advifes or applauds others in mifchief; the executer who performs it from thefe ftrong motives may not be fo entirely debafed, fo void of moral feelings, as the advifer and applauder.

3. He who of his own pure motion commits a crime, fhews a worfe difpofition than one who under com-

mand of a fuperior, and threatened with fevere punifhment if he declines obedience, executes a like action with inward reluctance. Where the hurt to others
from his obeying the command is much lefs than the
evil he had incurred had he difobeyed, his obedience
may be perfectly innocent, efpecially if he is ready to
compenfate the damage done to others for his own
fafety; and the only guilt will be chargeable on the
commander. In general, the perfons vefted with authority or power, are the principal caufes of what is
executed by their command: the fubject is often innocent; and where he cannot be wholly juftified, the
guilt is extenuated by the temptation. Nay the ftrong
importunities of friends are fome extenuation.

4. But whatever is done in confequence of the command of our will or of our choice, which affects the
happinefs or mifery of others, whatever were our motives, is ftill a moral and imputable action, as it is
fome indication of our affections. The fear of great
evil threatened may, as other pleas of neceffity, make
that innocent, in fome cafes, which without that neceffity had been criminal; fuch as delivering money or arms
to robbers that our lives may be preferved; throwing
our own or other men's goods over-board in a ftorm,
are imputed as innocent actions, nay matters of duty.
And even where the publick detriment enfuing is greater than that we efcape from by the action, the guilt,
tho' not quite removed, is much extenuated. Still
fuch actions are moral, and imputable as morally good
or evil.

CHAP. III.

The general Notions of Rights, *and* Laws, *explained; with their Divisions.*

Right and wrong in action. 1. FROM the conſtitution of our *moral faculty* above-explained, we have our notions of * *right*, and *wrong*, as characters of affections and actions. The affections approved as right, are either univerſal good-will and love of moral excellence, or ſuch particular kind affections as are conſiſtent with theſe. The actions approved as *right*, are ſuch as are wiſely intended either for the general good, or ſuch good of ſome particular ſociety or individual as is conſiſtent with it. The contrary affections and actions are *wrong*.

Goodneſs material, and formal. An action is called *materially good* when in fact it tends to the intereſt of the ſyſtem, as far as we can judge of its tendency; or to the good of ſome part conſiſtent with that of the ſyſtem, whatever were the affections of the agent. An action is *formally good*, when it flowed from good affections in a juſt proportion. A good man deliberating † which of ſeveral actions propoſed he ſhall chuſe, regards and compares the *material goodneſs* of them, and then is determined by his moral ſenſe invariably preferring that which appears moſt conducive to the happineſs and virtue of mankind. But in judging of his ‡ paſt actions he con-

---

* This is the *rectum*, as diſtinct from the *jus*, of which preſently : the *jus* enſues upon the *rectum*. † *Conſcientia antecedens*. ‡ *Conſcientia ſubſequens*.

fiders chiefly the affections they flowed from abftracting from their effects. Actions materially good may
flow from motives void of all virtue. And actions truly
virtuous or formally good may by accident, in the
event, turn to the publick detriment.

Our notion of *right* as a moral quality competent *The notion of rights;*
to fome perfon, as when we fay one has a *right* to fuch
things, is a much more complex conception. Whatever action we would deem either as virtuous or innocent were it done by the agent in certain circumftances, we fay he has a *right* to do it. Whatever one fo
poffeffes and enjoys in certain circumftances, that we
would deem it a wrong action in any other to difturb
or interrupt his poffeffion, we fay 'tis *his right*, or he
has a *right* to enjoy and poffefs it. Whatever demand
one has upon another in fuch circumftances that we
would deem it wrong conduct in that other not to
comply with it, we fay one has a *right* to what is thus
demanded. Or we may fay more briefly, a man hath
a *right* to do, poffefs, or demand any thing, † " when
" his acting, poffeffing, or obtaining from another in
" thefe circumftances tends to the good of fociety, or
" to the intereft of the individual confiftently with
" the rights of others and the general good of fociety,
" and obftructing him would have the contrary ten-
" dency."

II. The *righteoufnefs* or goodnefs of actions is not *not always referred to a publick good.*

---

† This is the fame with the common definition, *Facultas lege conceffa ad aliquid agendum, habendum, aut ab altero confequendum;* fince the end of the law of nature is the general good.

BOOK II. indeed the fame notion with *their tendency to univer-*
fal happinefs, or flowing from the defire of it. This
latter is the higheft fpecies of the former. Our *moral*
fenfe has alfo other immediate objects of approbation,
many narrower affections, which we muft immediately approve without thinking of their tendency to the
intereft of a fyftem. In like manner we immediately
condemn many unkind paffions and actions, without
confidering their diftant effects upon fociety. When
one by innocent induftry and fome kind affections procures for himfelf and thofe he loves the means of eafe
and pleafure, every good fpectator is pleafed that he
fhould enjoy them, and muft condemn the difturbing
his poffeffion and enjoyment immediately, without
thinking of the effects of fuch injuftice upon a community. Indeed if any grand intereft of a community
requires his being deprived of fome part of his acquifitions, then we fee a fuperior moral form; a publick
intereft, which a good mind muft more regard: and
a more extenfive affection, appearing more lovely than
the narrower, juftifies the mind in controlling it. The
former approbation was equally immediate; but this
latter is of an higher kind, to which the former is
naturally * fubordinate.

Rights feem to   Nay, as in fact it is for the good of the fyftem that
attend every na- every defire and fenfe natural to us, even thofe of the
tural defire. loweft kinds, fhould be gratified as far as their gratification is confiftent with the nobler enjoyments, and
in a juft fubordination to them; there feems a natural

* See B. i. c. 4.

notion of *right* to attend them all. We think we have
a right to gratify them, as foon as we form moral notions, until we difcover fome oppofition between thefe
lower ones, and fome principle we naturally feel to be
fuperior to them. This very fenfe of right feems the
foundation of that fenfe of liberty, that claim we all
naturally infift upon to act according to our own inclination in gratifying any defire, until we fee the in-
confiftence of its gratification with fome fuperior principles. The feveral appetites no doubt operate in us
before we have any moral notions, purfuing their feveral gratifications. But after moral notions are obtained, we affume to ourfelves, and, where our paffions are not raifed, we allow a right to others to gratify any defire which is not apprehended oppofite to
fome higher natural principle: and not only look upon
it as a damage or hurt when we are hindered without
this reafon, but deem it immoral and ill-natured in
one who affumes a power to obftruct us. We condemn
the man who fhould by violence, without the juft
caufe, obftruct the enjoyments of a third perfon with
whom we are not concerned.†

But, altho' private *juftice, veracity, opennefs of mind,* *None can be va-*
lid againft the
compaffion, are immediately approved, without refe- *publick intereft.*
rence to a fyftem; yet we muft not imagine that any
of thefe principles are deftined to controll or limit

---

† This feems the intention of *Grotius* | till we examine alfo the other, which is
de J. B. et P. l. i. c. 2. § i. where he de- | the *convenientia cum natura rationali et fo-*
duces the notion of right from thefe two; | *ciali;* ufing the phrafes of the Stoicks,
firft, the *initia naturae,* or the natural de- | tho' not precifely in their meaning.
fires, which do not alone conftitute right, |

BOOK II. that regard to the moſt extenſive good which we ſhewed to be the nobleſt principle of our nature. The moſt
extenſive affection has a dignity ſufficient to juſtify
the contracting any other diſpoſition: whereas no moral agent can upon cloſe reflection approve himſelf in
adhering to any ſpecial rule, or following any other
diſpoſition of his nature, when he diſcerns, upon the
beſt evidence he can have, that doing ſo is contrary
to the univerſal intereſt or the moſt extenſive happineſs of the ſyſtem in the whole of its effects.

The cauſes of
miſtakes.
　　When ſome ingenious and good men conceive ſome
other independent or unſubordinated notion of † juſtice in puniſhing, they ſeem to have derived it from
the feelings and impulſes of a natural paſſion, a generous indignation or anger ariſing againſt groſſer
crimes. But this paſſion, however wiſely implanted,
muſt be under the controll of an higher principle.
Its ſole impulſe is to inflict evil on thoſe whoſe vices
have excited it. This paſſion, and pity too, tho both
are lovely, muſt often be reſtrained by wiſe magiſtrates,

---

† There is a miſtake in an argument
on this head in an excellent book, Biſhop
Butler's Analogy. " Ill-deſert, or merit-
" ing puniſhment, muſt be another notion
" than this that the ſufferings of ſuch tend
" to the publick good; becauſe the ſuffe-
" rings of innocent perſons may ſome-
" times tend to the publick good; and in
" ſuch caſes, 'tis juſt to ſubject them to
" ſuch ſufferings: and yet here there is no
" ill-deſert." All men grant that under
ill-deſert one other notion is involved than
the *tendency of ſufferings to the publick good,*
viz. the notion of ſome *moral evil* preceeding. But where moral evil has preceded,
what elſe can juſtify puniſhing, but ſhewing that puniſhing, in ſuch caſes, tends to
ſome publick good? One tendency to
publick good in puniſhing where guilt preceeded juſtifies the puniſhment. Another
tendency to publick good in a different
way juſtifies the ſubjecting innocent perſons to ſufferings. This rather proves that
there is no other ultimate meaſure of juſtice than ſome tendency or other to this
end; tho' anger moves us to puniſh without this conſideration.

parents, guardians. Nay were it poffible to root out Chap. 3. all thefe paffions, and fubftitute in their place a ftrong calm regard to the moft extenfive good, ever prefent to the mind, and ever awake to difcern the feveral duties of life fubfervient to this general end, fo much the better would thefe duties be performed. Superior orders of beings may want thefe paffions altogether.

III. Rights, according as they are more or lefs ne- *Rights perfed.* ceffary to be maintained and obferved in fociety, are *and imperfed :* divided into perfect, and imperfect. Every proper right is fome way conducive to the publick intereft, and is founded upon fome fuch tendency. The obferving and fulfilling every proper right of others is matter of confcience, neceffary to obtain the approbation of *God*, and our own hearts. But fome of them are of fuch a nature that the intereft of fociety requires they fhould ever be maintained and fulfilled to all who have them, and that even by methods of force, where gentler meafures prove ineffectual; thefe are called *perfect rights ;* fuch as every innocent man has to his life; to a good name; to the integrity and foundnefs of his body; to the acquifitions of his honeft induftry; to act according to his own choice within the limits of the law of nature: this right we call natural liberty, of which liberty of confcience is not only an effential but an unalienable branch. Thefe rights fhould be maintained to all men, when no more general intereft of mankind requires any abridgement of them. Society cannot fubfift unlefs thefe rights are

BOOK II. facred. No individual can be happy where fuch rights of his are promifcuoufly violated.

both create a correfponding obligation. Other rights as truly facred in the fight of *God,* and our own confciences, yet are of fuch a nature, that for fome remote reafons of publick utility, they muft not be afferted by violence or compulfion, but left to the goodnefs of other men's hearts. Thefe are the *imperfect rights.* The regarding and fulfilling them to every one who has them is of great advantage and ornament to human life, and the violating or declining to fulfil them to others, in many cafes may be as criminal in the fight of *God* as the violation of perfect rights: but as they are not of fuch abfolute neceffity to the fubfiftence of fociety among men, and there are the moft obvious reafons why they fhould be left to men's honour and confcience, they are not matter of compulfion. Such are the rights of the indigent to relief from the wealthy: the rights of all men to offices of no trouble or expence: the rights of friends and benefactors to friendly and grateful returns: the right of every good man to fuch fervices as are to him of much greater importance than any fmall trouble or lofs they occafion to men in fplendid ftations or fortunes.

Imperfect rights not matter of compulfion. To make all thefe rights of fo delicate a nature matters of compulfion, efpecially when it is fo hard to determine the feveral claims of men, and the nice degrees of them, about which there muft be great diverfity of fentiment, would furnifh matter of eternal contention and war: and were they made matters of

compulfion, there would remain no proper opportunity for good men to difcover their goodnefs to others,
and engage their efteem and gratitude. The moft artfully felfifh, for fear of compulfion, would be the
readieft to fulfil thefe rights were the meafures of them
once determined. Nothing too would be left to choice
or natural liberty.

There remains a third fpecies, but rather a fha- *External rights.*
dow of right than any thing deferving that honour-
able name, which we call an *external right*; in the ufe
of which no man can be approved by *God*, or his own
heart, upon reflection. " When doing, enjoying, or
" demanding from others is really detrimental to the
" publick, and contrary to the facred obligations of
" humanity, gratitude, friendfhip, or fuch like; and yet
" for fome remote reafons 'tis for the intereft of fociety
" not to deny men this faculty, but on the contrary
" in fome inftances to confirm it." 'Tis thus the un-
charitable mifer has this fhadow of right even to that
fhare of his poffeffions which he fhould have employed
in offices of humanity, charity, or gratitude; or to re-
cal money unfeafonably or cruelly from an induftrious
fponfable debtor; to demand performance of too fevere and unequal covenants, while no law prohibits
them. Many fuch like claims are introduced by civil
laws in the cafes of wills, fucceffions to the inteftate,
and contracts, where the equitable and humane part
may be very different from the legal claim. This external appearance of right is all that remains when
any duty of gratitude, friendfhip, or humanity re-

BOOK II. quires our receding from what otherways would have been a perfect right.

What rights may be oppofite. Now as no action, enjoyment, or demand, and its contrary, can be alike ufeful to fociety, fo nature has in no inftance conftituted proper rights oppofite the one to the other: imperfect rights of humanity may be oppofite to external rights; but as neither the former, nor the latter, entitle one to ufe force with a good confcience, war can never be really juft on both fides. Any obligation in confcience to comply with external fhadows of right which others may have, can arife only from prudence with regard to our own intereft, or from fome remote views of the detriment that may in fome cafes redound to fociety from oppofing them, and not from any fenfe of duty toward the perfon who infifts on them in oppofition to humanity.

Juftice of laws of feveral forts. There is a like divifion of the juftice of laws. Some fyftems of them are called juft, only in this fenfe, " that they require only what is of high neceffity for " every peaceful ftate, and prohibit all that is necef- " farily everfive of good order and polity, yet without " a nice regard to promote the nobler virtues, and to " prohibit all actions of a bad tendency, when they " are not abfolutely pernicious." In fuch ftates actions are legally juft which violate none of thefe neceffary laws, and men have legal rights to do whatever the laws permit, tho' often contrary not only to humanity, but to what a finer inftitution would make neceffary. Sometimes a good legiflator is conftrained to give no better laws, from the bad difpofitions of CHAP. 3. his fubjects which would bear no better.* In another meaning of the word, that fyftem of laws only would be called juft, " where every thing is decreed in the " wifeft manner for the beft order in fociety, and pro- " moting the greateft virtue and happinefs among in- " dividuals." In the former fenfe only can the Jew- ifh fyftem be called juft, while it permitted polyga- my, divorces at pleafure, and execution of juftice on murderers and all man-flayers by private perfons the neareft kinfmen of the deceafed; and contained a very burdenfome ritual inftitution of worfhip.

IV   Our rights are either *alienable,* or *unalienable.* *Rights alienable, or not.* The former are known by thefe two characters joint- ly, that the tranflation of them to others can be made effectually, and that fome intereft of fociety, or indi- viduals confiftently with it, may frequently require fuch tranflations.   Thus our right to our goods and labours is naturally alienable.   But where either the tranflation cannot be made with any effect, or where no good in human life requires it, the right is una- lienable, and cannot be juftly claimed by any other but the perfon originally poffeffing it.   Thus no man can really change his fentiments, judgments, and in- ward affections, at the pleafure of another; nor can it tend to any good to make him profefs what is con-

---

* This is probably the moft ufeful ex- plication of the diftinction of Civilians of the *jus naturale* into the *primarium* and *fecundarium:* the former unalterable, and the later variable according to the pru- dence of civilized nations.   To call the one felf-evident, and the other not, is tri- fling: a juft conclufion is as fure as the premifes. See Grot. l. c. 1, 2.

trary to his heart.   The right of private judgment is therefore unalienable.

The degrees from imperfect, to perfect, innumerable.   V. By dividing rights into the two classes of perfect, and imperfect; we do not intimate that all those of either class are of the same importance or necessity; that the guilt of violating all perfect rights, is equal; or that the violating all imperfect rights is equally criminal. There is plainly a gradation from the weakest claim of humanity, to the highest perfect right, by innumerable steps. Every worthy man, tho' not in distress, has a claim upon the great and opulent for any good office in their way for improving his condition, when none of greater merit, or greater indigence, has an interfering claim. This is among the lowest imperfect rights or claims. A good man in distress has an higher claim.   One who has done eminent publick services has an higher still: one who had done singular services of an honourable kind to men now in power has a stronger claim upon them, especially if he is fallen into distress.   All these we call imperfect rights. The greater the merit and natural causes of love there are in the person who has these claims, the nearer also they approach to perfect rights. A worthy man in distress has an imperfect claim to the necessaries of life upon all who can relieve him, but on his children his claim is almost perfect, not only for a bare support, but for such conveniencies of life suited to the parent's station as they can afford without distressing themselves. The sense of an honest man, practised in the affairs of life,

muſt determine theſe points more preciſely in particular caſes.

In general, rights are the more ſacred the greater
their importance is to the publick good, the greater
the evils are which enſue upon violating them, the leſs
the trouble or expence is of obſerving them, the greater the merit or cauſes of love are in the perſons who
have them. And the ſtronger the claim is, ſo much
the greater is the crime of oppoſing it; and the ſmaller is the degree of virtue in complying with it.

On the other hand, the leſs the detriment is which
enſues upon violating a right, the greater the trouble
or expence is of fulfilling or complying with it, the
ſmaller the merit of the perſon is, the right is ſo much
the weaker: but then the more virtue is evidenced by
regarding it, provided there be a proportionably higher regard to the higher claims of others ; and the
moral turpitude of neglecting it is ſo much the leſs.
Small virtue is ſhewn by paying a juſt debt, by abſtaining from outrages and violence, by common returns of good offices where we have been highly obliged, by common duty to a worthy parent in diſtreſs:
but the conduct contrary to ſuch ſacred claims would
be moſt deteſtable. Offices of ſingular generoſity to
a worthy man who has no ſpecial claim upon us, are
greater evidences of a good temper (if we ſhow a
proportionably higher ardour of goodneſs where there
is equal merit and peculiar claims upon us) than offices equally beneficent toward a kinſman, or great
benefactor.

Right, and obligation, relative.

VI. To each right there correfponds an *obligation*, perfect or imperfect, as the right is. The term obligation is both complex and ambiguous. We primarily fay one is obliged to an action " when he muft " find from the conftitution of human nature that he " and every attentive obferver muft difapprove the " omiffion of it as morally evil." The word is fometimes taken for " a ftrong motive of intereft confti- " tuted by the will of fome potent *fuperior* to engage " us to act as he requires." In the former meaning, obligation is founded on our moral faculty; in the later, it feems to abftract from it. But in defcribing the *fuperior* who can conftitute obligation, we not only include fufficient force or power, but alfo a juft right to govern; and this juftice or right will lead us again to our *moral faculty.* Through this ambiguity † ingenious men have contradicted each other with keennefs; fome afferting an obligation antecedent to all views of intereft, or laws; others deriving the original fource of all obligation from the law or will of an omnipotent Being. This leads us to confider the general doctrine of laws, and the foundation of the right of governing rational agents, to which correfponds their obligation to obedience.

Indications of the Divine Will.

VII. As we fhewed in the former book that we all have fufficient indications of the exiftence and providence of *God*, and that he is the author of all our natural powers and difpofitions, our reafon, our *moral faculty*, and our affections; we can by juft reflection

† See Leibnitz's cenfure on Puffendorf and Barbeyraque's defence of him.

alſo plainly diſcern what courſe of action this conſtitution of our nature recommends both to our approbation as morally excellent, and to our election in point
of intereſt. We muſt therefore ſee the intention of
the *God* of Nature in all this, and cannot but look
upon all theſe concluſions of juſt reaſoning and reflection as ſo many indications to us of the will of *God*
concerning our conduct. When we have arrived at
this perſuaſion, theſe practical concluſions receive new
enforcements upon our hearts, both from our *moral
faculty*, and from our intereſt.

As *God* is juſtly conceived a being of perfect good- *The right of the
Deity to govern
all.*
neſs and wiſdom, and the greateſt benefactor to mankind, our hearts muſt be diſpoſed by the ſtrongeſt ſentiments of gratitude to comply with all the indications of his will, and muſt feel the ſtrongeſt diſapprobation of all diſobedience. His moral excellence muſt
add ſtrength to theſe feelings of gratitude and make a
deeper ſenſe of the duty incumbent on us to obey
him, as it ſhews that what he enjoins muſt be conducive to the univerſal intereſt. Theſe practical concluſions therefore from the conſtitution of our nature
do not ſuggeſt mere matters of private intereſt, or finer taſte, which we are at liberty either to follow as
the means of more delicate enjoyment, or to counteract, if we pleaſe to content ourſelves with another ſort
of enjoyments. They are enforced as matters of ſacred obligation by the very feelings of our hearts, and
a neglect of them muſt be diſapproved in the higheſt
manner, and be matter of deep remorſe under the odi-

Book II. ous form of ingratitude, and counteracting the universal interest. Thus it is that we are sensible of our moral obligation to obey the will of *God*. The divine perfections which suggest these sentiments are his moral attributes, and the benefits he has bestowed on mankind.

founded on wisdom and goodness. For as it must tend to the universal good that a being of perfect wisdom and goodness should superintend human affairs, assuming to himself to govern their actions, and to declare his pleasure about them; so it must undoubtedly tend to the universal good that all rational creatures obey his will. This shews his right of moral government. For the ultimate notion of right is *that which tends to the universal good ;* and when one's acting in a certain manner has this tendency, he has a right thus to act.† The proper foundation of right here is infinite goodness and wisdom. The benefits conferred on us by *God*, superadd a new enforcement to our obligation by the sense of gratitude, and our natural abhorrence of ingratitude. But benefits alone, are not a proper foundation of right, as they will not prove that the power assumed tends to the universal good or is consistent with it, however they suggest an amiable motive to obedience.

confirmed by his omnipotence But as the Deity is also omnipotent, and can make us happy or miserable as he pleases, this attribute suggests to us, not a proper foundation of right, but a strong motive of interest to obey his will, and a qua-

---

† These are the *fundamenta potestatis sive imperii.* Power is rather the *conditio sine qua non.*

lity very neceffary to execute effectually the right of government affumed. The right itfelf is founded on his wifdom and goodnefs, which fhew that his affuming of power by giving laws and annexing fanctions will conduce to the greateft good. And if this good cannot be obtained when the laws have no influence on the fubjects, nor can they have influence upon minds any way depraved, if they find that the fanctions are not executed; 'tis plain from the fame perfections, that 'tis right, or the *Deity* has a right, to execute fuch fanctions as are thus neceffary; which his power always enables him to do.

But as no man can give fuch evidence as fhall fatisfy his fellows of his fuperior goodnefs and wifdom, *Human power not thus founded.* and remove fufpicions of his weaknefs and interefted views; as there is no acknowledged criterion of fuperior wifdom for governing; and multitudes at once would pretend to it; as there is no affurance can be given of good intentions, to which the worft might by hypocritical fervices pretend; and as a people cannot be happy while their interefts precarioufly depend on perfons of fufpected goodnefs or wifdom; thefe qualities cannot be, among men, the natural foundations of power; nor can it ferve the general intereft that they fhould be deemed fufficient to conftitute fuch a right of governing, or of compelling others to obedience. Some extraordinary cafes may be excepted.

VIII. As a law is " a declaration made by him who *Laws definede* "has a right to govern, what actions he requires, or for-

BOOK II. " bids, for the publick good; and what motives of in-
" tereft he has conftituted to excite to the actions re-
" quired, and deter from thofe prohibited." It contains thefe two parts, the *precept*, fhewing the actions
required, or prohibited; and the *sanction*, fhewing the
rewards to enfue upon obedience, or the evils to be inflicted upon the difobedient. The precept muft always be expreffed, but the fanction may be underftocd
as referved difcretionary to the governor.

Practical dic-
tates of reafon This notion of a law fhews how juftly the practical
are divine laws. conclufions of right reafon from the order of nature
conftituted by *God*, and laid open to our obfervation,
are called *laws of nature*, and *laws of God;* as they
are clear declarations of his will about our conduct.
And all the private advantages, internal or external,
which we can forefee as probably enfuing upon our
complyance, from the conftitution of our own nature,
or that of others, or of the world around us, are fo
many fanctions of rewards: and all the evils in like
manner to be expected from our non-obfervance of
thefe conclufions, are fanctions of punifhment, declared or promulgated by the fame means which declare
the precepts.

The fole ufe of words, or writing, in laws, is to difcover the will of the governor. In pofitive laws it muft
by fuch means be difcovered. But there is another and
primary way by which God difcovers his will concerning our conduct, and likeways propofes the moft in-
terefting motives, even by the conftitution of nature, and the powers of reafon, and moral perception,

which he has given to mankind, and thus reveals a
law with its fanctions, as effectually as by words, or writing; and in a manner more noble and divine.*

Laws natural and pofitive in two fenfes.

IX. Laws are divided into *natural,* and *pofitive.*
But thefe two terms are ufed in very different mean-
ings. Sometimes the divifion is taken from the *diffe-*
rent manners of promulgation; and then by *natural*
laws are underftood the moral determinations of the
heart and the conclufions of right reafon from thefe
determinations and other obfervations of nature; and
by *pofitive laws,* fuch as are promulgated in words or
writing, whatever the matter of them be.

Laws neceffary or not neceffary

Others take the divifion expreffed by thefe words
from the diverfity of the *matter of laws;* as fome
laws declare the natural direct and neceffary means
of fupporting the dignity of human nature and promoting the publick good; fo that either oppofite or
different laws could not be equally ufeful, nay would
be pernicious to fociety: thefe they call *natural:* fuch
are all the laws of juftice and humanity. Other laws
have indeed in intention fome good end, and with a
view to it require certain means, but thefe are not
always the fole, or the neceffary, or preferable means.
The fame good end may be obtained by different
means, and thefe equally convenient or effectual, and
yet it may be neceffary for the good of a fociety that
a certain fet of means be agreed upon for all. Nay
certain inftitutions make fome practices ufeful which
in their own nature were of no ufe. Thus fome rites

---

* On this fubject. fee Dr. Cumberland *de Leg. Nat. Prolegom.* *et* c. i

BOOK II. of religion, in their own nature of no importance, yet, by being inftituted in memory of fome great events, the frequent remembrance of which muft increafe grateful, pious, or humane difpofitions, may become very ufeful to mankind.

The wife ends of pofitive laws. The moft frequent occafions for pofitive laws are where the fame good ends may be obtained different ways, but 'tis requifite that fome one way be fixed for all in a certain diftrict. Thus neither can focial worfhip be performed, nor courts of juftice be kept, unlefs times and places are determined: and yet 'tis feldom found that any one time is fitter than another for any natural reafon. In like manner, in the exe-cution of juftice there are different forms of procefs, different penalties for crimes, different times for exe-cutions. 'Tis convenient all thefe points fhould be known and fettled for a whole fociety; and yet no one of the poffible determinations can be faid to be abfolutely beft, fo that the fmalleft variation would make it worfe.

They are ufelefs or arbitrary. Pofitive laws are quite different from what we call arbitrary or imperious, fuch as are enacted merely from oftentation of power, without fubferviency to the publick intereft.

To the obligation of a law promulgation is necef-fary; not that every fubject fhould actually know it; but that every one have it in his power, by fuch dili-gence as he is capable of, to attain to the knowledge of it. The penalties of laws may be juftly exacted, where the laws have not been actually known, when

the fubject is culpably ignorant, and might have CHAP. 3.
known them by fuch diligence as a good man in his
circumftances would have ufed. But the ignorance
of fome laws of more difficult difcovery may be very
excufable in fome men becaufe of many avocations,
and low abilities, or opportunities, which yet may be
very culpable in others placed in more advantageous
circumftances.

X. As the laws of nature comprehend not merely *How the law of.*
the original moral determinations of the mind, but *nature is perfect.*
likeways the practical conclufions made by the rea-
foning and reflection of men upon the conftitution of
nature, fhewing what conduct is worthy and tends to
publick good, there needs be little controverfy about
their perfection, as all muft own that the reafon even
of the moft ingenious and moft improved is ftill imperfect. And that it may be very poffible that a fuperior being could fee a certain rule of conduct to
be conducive to the publick good, which none of human race could ever have difcovered to be ufeful:
and as to the bulk of mankind, they may indeed eafily difcover the general and moft neceffary rules, but
they feldom can find out or even apprehend well the
reafons upon which fome of the more fpecial laws
which yet have a fubftantial foundation in nature are
built. If one by the fyftem of the laws of nature
means the very conftitutions of nature itfelf, or the
objective evidence laid before rational beings in the
whole; this no doubt is perfect: but its perfection does
not fuperfede the ufefulnefs of the revelation of laws

BOOK II. to mankind by words or writing, or of the difcoveries of the wifer human legiflators or moralifts, or of precepts pofitive as to their matter; fince fo few of mankind can attain any great knowledge of this conftitution, and none can pretend to underftand it compleatly.

Its imperfecti-
on no blemifh in
providence.
We fhould not cenfure providence on account of this imperfection, for reafons * mentioned above, any more than we cenfure it for our fmall bodily ftrength, or the fhortnefs of our lives. If we ufe our powers and opportunities well, the condition of human life in this world will be in the main an agreeable and happy ftate; and yet by divine revelation, or even by accurate reafonings of wife men, much may be difcovered for the improvement of this life; and many fine inftitutions contrived, the reafons for which neither any one in the ruder nations, nor the populace in the more civilized, fhall ever apprehend.

All laws fhould
aim at fome good.
But this holds in general, that all wife and juft laws have fome tendency to the general happinefs, or to the good of fome part of the fyftem fubfervient to and confiftent with the general good. The moral good in obedience confifts in either a direct intention of this good end propofed by the law, whether we know it fully ourfelves, or implicitly truft to the goodnefs of the legiflator; or in fome grateful affection toward the legiflator: where obedience flows only from fear of punifhment, or hope of reward, it has no moral excellency, tho' in fome cafes it may be innocent.

* B. i. c. 9. § 12.

XI. Precepts of the law of nature, or thefe practi- CHAP. 3.
cal obfervations, are deemed immutable and eternal, 〰〰
becaufe fome rules, or rather the difpofitions which *How the law of nature is immutable.*
gave origin to them, and in which they are founded,
muft always tend to the general good, and the contrary to the general detriment, in fuch a fyftem of
creatures as we are. But we muft not imagine that all
the fpecial precepts of the law of nature are thus immutable as they are commonly enunciated univerfally. If we make the precepts immutable, we muft allow many exceptions as parts of the precept, or underftand the precept as holding only generally in ordinary cafes. As the precept is indeed no more than
a conclufion from obfervation of what fort of conduct
is ordinarily ufeful to fociety ; fome fingular cafes
may happen in which departing from the ordinary rule
may be more for the general intereft than following it.
And fome wife human inftitutions may take away or
limit fome rights which formerly were facredly confirmed to each individual by the law of nature. Before civil polity each one had a right by private violence when gentler methods were ineffectual, of obtaining reparation of wrong from the author of it. But
in civil polity private individuals ceafe to have a right
to ufe thofe means. In like manner civil laws juftly
limit our ufe of our own property, and take fome
fhare of it for publick exigences, whereas previoufly
to fome political inftitution the general law of nature allowed to each one the full ufe of all his own
acquifitions, and the right of difpofing of them at

BOOK II. pleafure. Singular cafes of neceffity are alfo juftly deemed exceptions from the ordinary laws. 'Tis injurious
ordinarily to ufe the property of another without his
confent; but an innocent man when he cannot otherways fave his life in his flying from an unjuft enemy,
does no wrong by taking the horfe of another when
he cannot wait for the owner's confent.

　The two fundamental precepts of " loving God,
" and promoting the univerfal happinefs," admit of
no exceptions; nay in the latter precept are founded
all the exceptions from the fpecial laws of nature; all
the rights of receding, in cafes of fingular neceffity,
from the ordinary rules; and all the limitations of
our rights by any wife inftitutions: fince all thefe are
juftified by their tendency in certain cafes, and upon
certain fuppofitions, to a fuperior good of the fyftem
than would enfue from following the ordinary rule.

　XII. Some intricate controverfies arife among moralifts and fchoolmen, from not obferving fufficiently
the difference between thefe practical obfervations we
call laws of nature, and the laws declared in words
and writing by legiflators, divine, or human. They
may be prevented by the following remarks.

Equity what.　1. As by * equity, they underftand, a " correction
" of any defect in the law by too great or too fmall
extent of its expreffion," when it is juftly interpreted
according to the true intention of the legiflator, extended as far as the reafon of it extends, and not extended to cafes where the reafon of the law does not

* The Επιιχπα of Ariftotle and the fchoolmen.

hold; there is no room for this fort of equity as diftinct from the letter in the law of nature; as the law
is not declared to us by words, in which alone there
can be too fmall or great univerfality. Whatever right
reafon fhews to be humane and equitable in conduct,
is a part of the law of nature.

2. The whole doctrine of *difpenfations* was introduced by the *canonifts*, after many capricious, imprudent, and unneceffary laws were impofed upon the
Chriftian world, with the worft defigns, and yet it was
often found neceffary to free men from the obligation of them. By *difpenfation* is underftood " fome
" act of the legiflator exempting certain perfons from
" the obligation of laws which extended to them as
" well as others:" and always imports fome abatement
or derogation from a law.

The doctrine of Difpenfation a-rofe from the Canon Law.

3. The word *difpenfation* is very ambiguous; and
there are different kinds of it. *Difpenfation* may be
given either from the fanction, after the law is violated, or from the precept, previoufly to any violation of the law. A difpenfation from the fanction is
" exempting a perfon from the legal punifhment who
" has incurred it by violating the law; or the abating
" or altering of the punifhment." Now, as we fhall
fee hereafter, there are fome very ftrong reafons why
a power of fuch difpenfation fhould be lodged fomewhere in every ftate, when the publick intereft may
require fuch difpenfations: and, in like manner, as to
fuch punifhments as may naturally enfue, and be ordinarily neceffary for the general good upon the vio-

Difpenfation, ambiguous.

BOOK II. lation of the laws of nature, it may be perfectly wife and benign that *God*, the great ruler of the world, fhould fometimes mercifully interpofe and prevent thefe fufferings when the true end of them can be otherways obtained. But as we cannot conceive any fuch laws limiting *God* himfelf as may limit even the fupreme magiftrates of ftates, nor are any fuch particular punifhments fpecified by the laws of nature invariably as may be by human laws, there can be little occafion for debating about the divine right of difpenfing with the fanctions of the laws of nature.

Previous dif-
penfation from
juft laws muft
be evil.

4. As to previous difpenfations from the precepts of laws, if the law itfelf be wife in all its extent, the previous difpenfing with any violation of it muft appear unjuft and imprudent in any governor. And 'tis plain that no permiffion or command of any perfon can alter the moral nature of our affections fo as to make the love of God, and our neighbour, become evil; or any contrary affections become good: nor can any permiffion or command alter the moral nature of the external actions which flow from thefe affections. No man could approve any fuch permiffions or commands, nor can they ever be given by a good *God*. Some confufed notions of the divine right of dominion or fovereignty have led fome authors into fuch fentiments, as if a divine command could juftify unkind or inhumane affections, and actions confequent upon them tending to the general detriment of the fyftem. But if one would confult the feelings of his heart, and examine well the original notion of right in

action, or the right of governing, as diftinct from CHAP: 3.
mere fuperior force, he would fee fuch tenets to be
contradictory to themfelves.

5. As to external actions required, where nothing
is in words prefcribed about the affections, the certain
command of a being who we are perfuaded is poffeffed of perfect goodnefs and wifdom, may juftly make
us conclude that fuch enjoined actions, contrary to
the prefent external appearances, may truly tend to
fuperior good in the whole, and occafion no prepol-
lent evil: when the evidence for the goodnefs of the
enjoiner, and for this fact that he is the author of
this injunction, is fo great as to furpafs fufficiently
the contrary prefumption from the external appearances of a bad tendency in the actions commanded.
This cafe can fcarce be called a difpenfation from
the laws of nature, fince the agent is acting according to the law, what he believes is tending to good,
tho' his opinion about this tendency is founded upon
the teftimony of another, and not upon his own knowledge.

6. If by difpenfation be underftood only " a grant- *What difpenfa-*
" ing external impunity to actions really evil, or con- *tion may be vin-*
dicated.
" trary to thofe rules of right reafon which fhew the
" moft perfect and virtuous courfe of actions;" human lawgivers muft often grant fuch external impunity, as we fhall fee hereafter. And 'tis alledged that
many fuch permiffions are in the *Mofaick Law,* which
may be juftified from the circumftances of that people and of the neighbouring nations: fince a more ri-

Book II. gidly virtuous inftitution would have made them revolt altogether from the worfhip of the true *God*. But then fuch a grant of external impunity does not remove or abate the moral turpitude of the actions in fuch men as know their pernicious tendency, or their contrariety to the moft perfect and virtuous inftitutions. By fuch permiffions however, and the general practice enfuing, the populace may be made generally lefs attentive to any bad tendency of fuch actions, and fecure about it, fo that the guilt may be much extenuated by the ignorance prevailing, which in fome of the loweft orders of men may become almoft invincible. But fince the guilt is not entirely removed by fuch permiffions, they are not what the Schoolmen and Canonifts generally underftand by difpenfations from the law of nature, which they fuppofe makes the actions in confequence of them perfectly innocent.

Miftakes about difpenfations.   7. Nor do thefe cafes come up to the common notion of difpenfation when a fuperior acting according to the powers vefted in him by the law difpofes in an unufual manner of things committed to his difpofal; or when the goods of the fubjects, who have a right to them valid againft their fellows, but not valid by law againft their fovereign, are difpofed of by the fovereign according to the powers vefted in him by the law, and transferred from one to another. Or when the prince impowers others to do in his name what he has a right to do by what officers he pleafes, tho' it would have been criminal in any fubject without his prince's commiffion to have done fuch ac-

tions. What is commanded by any one in confequence of the powers conftituted to him by the
law, and executed accordingly, can fcarce be faid to
be done by virtue of a difpenfing from the law. A
debtor is bound by the law to make payment: but a
remiffion or releafe from the creditor frees him from
this obligation. We fhould not therefore fay that
every creditor has a power of difpenfing with the laws
of nature. The more acute Schoolmen, upon thefe
confiderations, do not allow the extraordinary commands given to Mofes and Jofhua to be difpenfations
from the laws of nature. But 'tis needlefs to debate
about words. If the law itfelf be wife and juft in all
the extent in which it is expreffed, no act of any fuperior can make the counteracting it innocent or lovely. But moft of the fpecial laws of nature are not to
be expreffed in words ftrictly univerfal, without the
exception of many cafes; particularly that of God's
exerting his rightful dominion.

Difpenfations therefore, according to the full in- *What is com-*
tention of the Canonifts, are only to be made with *monly meant by*
them.
laws either capricious or imprudent, or too univerfally
expreffed without mentioning the reafonable and juft
exceptions, which ought to have been inferted in the
very laws themfelves. In the laws of nature there
can be no place for them, fince the fame reafon and
obfervation which difcovers the ordinary general rule,
difcovers alfo all the exceptions, which are therefore
parts of the law.

Having premifed this general doctrine about the

Book II. morality of actions, rights and laws, we proceed to the more special consideration of the rights and duties of mankind, and the special laws of nature; and that first, as they are constituted by nature itself previously to adventitious states and relations introduced by human institution and contrivance, and then as they arise and are founded in some adventitious relation or institution.

CHAP. IV.

The different STATES *of* MEN. *The State of* LIBERTY *not a State of* WAR. *The Way that private* RIGHTS *are known. The Necessity of a* SOCIAL LIFE.

What is a moral state.

WHEN we speak of the different states of men, by a *state* we do not mean any transient condition a man may be in for a little time, nor any obligation he may be under to one or two transient acts, but " a permanent condition including a long series " of rights and obligations." The conditions men may be in as to sickness or health, beauty or deformity, or any other circumstances which are considered in the other arts, are foreign to our purpose. The moral states of men alway include a series of moral obligations, and rights.

The state of natural liberty not a state of war.

I. In the first state constituted by nature itself we must discern abundantly from the doctrine of the preceeding book that there are many sacred rights com-

petent to men, and many obligations incumbent on CHAP. 4.
each one toward his fellows. The whole fyftem of the
mind, efpecially our *moral faculty*, fhews that we are
under natural bonds of beneficence and humanity toward all, and under many more fpecial tyes to fome
of our fellows, binding us to many fervices of an higher kind, than what the reft can claim: nor need we
other proofs here that this firft ftate founded by nature is fo far from being that of war and enmity, that
it is a ftate where we are all obliged by the natural feelings of our hearts, and by many tender affections, to
innocence and beneficence toward all: and that war is
one of the accidental ftates arifing folely from injury, when we or fome of our fellows have counteracted
the dictates of their nature.

'Tis true that in this ftate of liberty where there
are no civil laws with a vifible power to execute their
fanctions, men will often do injurious actions contrary to the laws of their nature; and the refentments of
the fufferers will produce wars and violence. But this
proves nothing as to the true nature of that ftate,
fince all the laws and obligations of that ftate enjoin
peace and juftice and beneficence. In civil focieties
many difobey the law, by theft and violence, but we
do not thence conclude that a political ftate is a ftate
of war among men thus united.

'Tis alfo true that the natural paffions and appetites of men will frequently lead them into mutual *Frequent inju-*
ries do not prove
injuries. But then the laws of this ftate are not deri-*it.*
ved from thefe principles alone. There are fuperior

powers naturally fitted to controll them, particularly that *moral faculty* which points out the rights and obligations of this ſtate, and ſhews how far any appetite or paſſion can be indulged conſiſtently with the inward approbation of our fouls, and what indulgences muſt be matter of remorſe, ſelf-abhorrence, and ſhame. We are alſo endued with reaſon which clearly points out even our external intereſts in this matter, and ſhews that we cannot probably gratify even our ſelfiſh deſires, except by an innocent and friendly deportment toward others. Theſe powers ſuggeſt the rules or laws of this ſtate of liberty, and all ſtates are denominated from what the laws and obligations of them enjoin or require, and not from ſuch conduct as the paſſions of men may hurry them into contrary to the laws of thoſe ſtates.

Contradictions in that ſcheme. The authors of this moſt unnatural ſcheme never fail to contradict their own doctrine, by owning and arguing that that rational faculty, which they allow we are naturally endued with for the conduct of life, will ſoon ſhew that this univerſal war of all with all muſt be the moſt deſtructive imaginable; and that it is to be ſhunned by every one as ſoon as he can; and that reaſon will alſo ſhew ſome obvious rules of conduct proper to preſerve or reſtore peace to mankind with all its bleſſings. Surely then that conduct which the natural principles of mankind ſhew to be moſt neceſſary and moſt obviouſly eligible to every one, ſhould be deemed the natural conduct in this ſtate, and not what a brutal thoughtleſs appetite may hurry one in-

to while the governing principles of his nature are a-
sleep, or unexercised.

'Tis also a foolish abuse of words to call a state of absolute solitude a *natural* state to mankind, since in this condition neither could any of mankind come into being, or continue in it a few days without a miraculous interposition.

II. This state of natural liberty obtains among those *The state of liberty always subsists.* who have no common superior or magistrate, and are only subject to *God*, and the law of nature. 'Tis no fictitious state; it always existed and must exist among men, unless the whole earth should become one empire. The parental power of the first parents of mankind must soon have expired when their children came to maturity, as we shall shew hereafter, or at least when the parents died. This state of liberty probably continued a long time among the several heads of families before civil governments were constituted. And tis not improbable that it yet subsists in some ruder parts of the world. Nay it still must subsist among the several independent states with respect to each other, and among the subjects of different states who may happen to meet in the ocean, or in lands where no civil power is constituted. The laws of nature are the laws of this state, whether they be confirmed by civil power or not: and 'tis the main purpose of civil laws and their sanctions, to restrain men more effectually by visible punishments from the violation of them. The same reasons which justify the greater part of our civil laws, shew the obligations of men to observe

BOOK II. them as laws of nature abstracting from any motives from secular authority.

Rights are those of individuals of societies, or of all mankind.

III. As men are said to " have rights to do, possess, " or demand from others whatsoever the happiness of " the individual requires and the publick interest of " mankind permits that they should be allowed to do, " possess, or obtain from others;" and all rights and obligations are founded in some tendency either to the general happiness, or to that of individuals consistently with the general good, which must result from the happiness of individuals; rights may be divided, according to the subject or persons in whom they reside or to whom they belong, and for whose good they are immediately constituted, into those of individuals, those of particular societies or corporations, and those in general belonging to all mankind as a system. The first sort are constituted immediately for the behoof of individuals, by the law of nature; the second for the common interest of a corporation or state, tho' not more immediately for any one member of it than another; in the third sort of rights neither any one individual, or any one corporation, may be more concerned than another, and yet it may be for the general interest of mankind that such rights be asserted and maintained. And each of these three classes may be either perfect, or imperfect, according as they are more or less necessary to be maintained for the publick interest, and of such a nature as to admit of compulsion and violence in the defence or prosecution of them; or, on the other hand, such as must be left to each

one's confcience and fenfe of duty: this divifion we
explained above.

IV. The private rights of individuals are obvioufly intimated to us in the conftitution of our nature,
by thefe two circumftances, jointly; firft, natural defires and fenfes pointing out the gratifications we are
fitted to receive as parts of that happinefs the author
of our nature has intended for us, and fecondly, by
the powers of reafon and reflection which can difcover
how far the gratification of our natural defires is confiftent with the finer principles in our conftitution,
which, as we fhewed above, are deftined to govern and
controll all our particular defires. Thefe principles
fhew the limits to be put, not only to the felfifh defires
aiming at the private happinefs of the agent, but to
the feveral narrower generous affections, and the gratifications which they purfue; and plainly difcover that
the grand end of our being is indeed the promoting
the moft univerfal happinefs, but that our heart at the
fame time may approve our conduct not only in acts
of particular beneficence toward perfons efpecially
dear to us in fome of the nearer relations, while this
beneficence does not interfere with more extenfive interefts; but alfo in the purfuit of all private gratifications which are confiftent with thefe interefts, and do
not engrofs the mind or contract it too much within
itfelf.

The natural appetites and defires firft intimate the
matters of private right, but we can feldom juftify to
ourfelves a compliance with their intimations till we

BOOK II. have confidered whether the gratification to which we are prompted be confiftent with the defigns of the more noble parts of our conftitution, which are the grand objects of the foul's approbation, aiming at a more extenfive or the univerfal happinefs. Indeed in many of the objects of our defires, this confiftency is fo obvious, or there is fo little prefumption of any oppofition, that we are convinced of our right to them at once without much reflection on more extenfive interefts; nay in many cafes we feem to have an immediate fenfe of right along with the natural defire, and a fenfe of moral evil in any oppofition given to us by others, as we at once apprehend the neceffity of certain gratifications to our having any tolerable enjoyment of life; and we muft abhor as cruel and inhuman any oppofition given to us, or to others, in thefe gratifications, where we do not fee fuch oppofition to be neceffary for fome more extenfive intereft.

The neceffity of great caution on this fubject. But as the chief dangers to our manners arife from the vehemence of our felfifh appetites and paffions, which often break through thefe reftraints from the finer principles in our conftitution regarding a publick intereft, it may be of advantage to fatisfy the mind on every fide of the juftice of thefe reftraints, and to fhew that its own intereft of every kind confpires to recommend this fubjection of the *felfifh,* to the *generous* and *focial principles.* Our *moral faculty* above-explained fhews both the juftice and beauty of fuch fubjection; and fhews a very fublime internal intereft in the inward delight and approbation of our

hearts. Our reaſon by diſcovering to us the moral government of the *Deity*, and his perfections, preſents
further motives to preſerve this ſubordination, both
of the generous and intereſted kind: and a juſt conſideration of the circumſtances of mankind with reſpect to external things, will afford alſo new motives
of ſecular intereſt to that ſame external conduct which
theſe ſublimer principles excite us to, as we ſhall endeavour briefly to explain.

V. In the firſt place, 'tis obvious that for the ſupport of human life, to allay the painful cravings of
the appetites, and to afford any of thoſe agreeable external enjoyments which our nature is capable of, a
great many external things are requiſite; ſuch as
food, cloathing, habitations, many utenſils, and various furniture, which cannot be obtained without a
great deal of art and labour, and the friendly aids of
our fellows.

Again, 'tis plain that a man in abſolute ſolitude, *Solitude miſe-*
tho' he were of mature ſtrength, and fully inſtructed *rable and indi-*
in all our arts of life, could ſcarcely procure to himſelf *gent.*
the bare neceſſaries of life, even in the beſt ſoils or
climates; much leſs could he procure any grateful
conveniencies. One uninſtructed in the arts of life,
tho' he had full ſtrength, would be ſtill more incapable of ſubſiſting in ſolitude. and it would be abſolutely impoſſible, without a miracle, that one could ſub-
ſiſt in this condition from his infancy. And ſuppoſe
that food, raiment, ſhelter, and the means of ſenſual
pleaſure, were ſupplied by a miracle; yet a life in ſo-

Book II litude muſt be full of fears and dangers. Suppoſe
farther all theſe dangers removed; yet in ſolitude there
could be no exerciſe for many of the natural powers
and inſtincts of our ſpecies; no love, or ſocial joys, or
communication of pleaſure, or eſteem, or mirth. The
contrary diſpoſitions of ſoul muſt grow upon a man
in this unnatural ſtate, a ſullen melancholy, and diſ-
content, which muſt make life intolerable. This ſubject is abundantly explained by almoſt all authors upon the law of nature.

The mutual aids of a few in a ſmall family, may procure moſt of the neceſſaries of life, and diminiſh dangers,
and afford room for ſome ſocial joys as well as finer
pleaſures. The ſame advantages could ſtill be obtained more effectually and copiouſly by the mutual aſſiſ-
tance of a few ſuch families living in one neighbourhood, as they could execute more operoſe deſigns for
the common good of all; and would furniſh more joyful exerciſes of our ſocial diſpoſitions.

The advantages
of ſociety.
Nay 'tis well known that the produce of the labours of any given number, twenty, for inſtance, in
providing the neceſſaries or conveniences of life, ſhall
be much greater by aſſigning to one, a certain ſort of
work of one kind, in which he will ſoon acquire skill
and dexterity, and to another aſſigning work of a different kind, than if each one of the twenty were obliged to employ himſelf, by turns, in all the different
ſorts of labour requiſite for his ſubſiſtence, without
ſufficient dexterity in any In the former method each
procures a great quantity of goods of one kind, and

can exchange a part of it for fuch goods obtained by CHAP. 4.
the labours of others as he fhall ftand in need of. One
grows expert in tillage, another in pafture and breed-
ing cattle, a third in mafonry, a fourth in the chace,
a fifth in iron-works, a fixth in the arts of the loom,
and fo on throughout the reft. Thus all are fupplied by means of barter with the works of complete
artifts. In the other method fcarce any one could be
dextrous and skilful in any one fort of labour.

Again fome works of the higheft ufe to multitudes *The advantages of large focieties.*
can be effectually executed by the joint labours of
many, which the feparate labours of the fame number could never have executed. The joint force of
many can repel dangers arifing from favage beafts
or bands of robbers, which might have been fatal to many individuals were they feparately to en-
counter them. The joint labours of twenty men will
cultivate forefts, or drain marfhes, for farms to each
one, and provide houfes for habitation, and inclofures
for their flocks, much fooner than the feparate labours of the fame number. By concert, and alternate
relief, they can keep a perpetual watch, which without
concert they could not accomplifh.

Larger affociations may further enlarge our means
of enjoyment, and give more extenfive and delightful exercife to our powers of every kind. The inventions, experience, and arts of multitudes are commu-
nicated; knowledge is increafed, and focial affections
more diffufed. Larger focieties have force to execute greater defigns of more lafting and extenfive ad-

vantage.* Thefe confiderations abundantly fhew the neceffity of living in fociety, and obtaining the aid of our fellows, for our very fubfiftence; and the great convenience of larger affociations of men for the improvement of life, and the increafe of all our enjoyments.

Good offices muft be mutual, and much felf-government. But 'tis obvious that we cannot expect the friendly aids of our fellows, without, on our part, we be ready to good offices, and reftrain all the felfifh paffions which may arife upon any interfering interefts fo that they fhall not be injurious to others. Much thought and caution is requifite to find out fuch rules of conduct in fociety as fhall moft effectually fecure the general intereft, and promote peace and a mutual good underftanding. Whatever generous principles there are in our nature, yet they are not alone, there are likeways many angry paffions to which we are fubject upon apprehenfion of injury intended, or executed; and all thefe powers by which men can fo effectually give mutual aid, and do good offices, may be alfo employed, upon provocation, to the detriment of their fellows. Provoking of others by injury muft generally be imprudent conduct in point of felf-intereft, as well as matter of remorfe and felf-condemnation. No man can be tolerably affured that his force or art fhall be fuperior to that of thofe who may be roufed to oppofe him; multitudes conceive a juft indignation againft any unjuft violence, and are

* See this whole fubject beautifully explained in the fecond book of *Cicero de Officiis.*

thence prone to repel it. And they are further roufed by pity for the fufferer and juft apprehenfions that
fuch mifchiefs unreftrained may foon affect themfelves. How dangerous then muft it be to roufe fuch
indignation by any acts of injuftice toward any of our
fellows?

Nature has alfo prefented to us all a very ftrong *A ftrong mo-*
motive to abftain from injuries, and to reftrain all the *tive from the*
extravagancies of the felfifh paffions from the delica- *lence.*
cy and weaknefs of our frame. Tho' mankind have
no powers which can properly be called engines of
mifchief, fince fuch as can hurt others can alfo be
employed in kind focial offices; and as all the governing principles of nature rather excite to good offices, all our powers are juftly deemed to be naturally
deftined for promoting focial happinefs; yet 'tis plain
our efforts in hurting others, where we intend it heartily, can more probably be fuccefsful and effectual,
than our defigns to fecure the happinefs of others,
according to a common maxim, that " few have fuf-
" ficient talents to do much good, but very mean ones
" may do much mifchief." We are of a very delicate
texture; our eafe and happinefs not only requires a
right difpofition of a great many nice bodily organs
which can eafily be put out of order, but a great many external objects and conveniencies of which we
may eafily be deprived; and the eafe of our minds
requires the profperity of many other perfons who are
dear to us, whofe texture is as delicate as our own,
and expofed to be difordered by any malicious efforts

of our fellows. To our complete eafe and happinefs the profperous concurrence of a great many things is requifite : whereas we may be heartily difturbed by any thing unprofperous in one or two of thefe circumftances: and 'tis very often in the power of our fellows to create to us this difturbance, tho' they cannot fo effectually fecure our happinefs when they defire it.

This infirm uncertain condition of our external happinefs muft powerfully move us to cultivate peace and good-will in fociety, and to fhun all offence and provocation of others; fince we hazard more by incurring the hatred of others than we can probably hope to gain. Tho' the forces of men are unequal, yet art can fupply the defects of force; and an obftinate refolution can fupply the defects of both, fo as to deprive an adverfary of life and all his other enjoyments, as well as of the advantage he aimed at by the provoking injury. Thus when men are not forced into violence for their own defence, peace and juftice are ftill eligible to the powerful and artful as well as to others; fince they know not what univerfal indignation may be raifed by any thing injurious, from the *moral fenfe* of mankind, from fympathy with the fufferer, and apprehenfions of their own future dangers: and a friendly juft kind deportment, as it naturally engages the good-will, the efteem, and good offices of others, is the only probable method of obtaining fecurity, and all the external advantages and pleafures of life.

CHAP. V.

The Private Rights *of* Men; *firſt ſuch as are called*
NATURAL; *and the natural Equality of Men.*

I. PRIVATE rights of individuals according to their
different originals are either *natural* or *adven-*
titious. The *natural* are ſuch as each one has from
the conſtitution of nature itſelf without the interven-
tion of any human contrivance, inſtitution, compact,
or deed. The *adventitious* ariſe from ſome human
inſtitution, compact, or action.

The following natural rights of each individual *The natural*
ſeem of the perfect ſort. 1. A right to life, and to *rights to life,*
and ſafety.
that perfection of body which nature has given, belongs to every man as man, while no important publick intereſt requires his being expoſed to death, or
wounds. This right is violated by unjuſt aſſaults,
maiming, or murthering. The connate deſire of life
and ſelf-preſervation intimates to every one this right,
as does alſo our immediate ſenſe of moral evil in all
cruelty occaſioning unneceſſary pain, or abatement of
happineſs to any of our fellows; not to mention the
diſmal air of the human countenance occaſioned by
grievous pain, or death, the beholding of which muſt
move every human heart with pity and terror, and
abhorrence of the voluntary cauſe of ſuch unneceſſary ſufferings.

2. As nature has implanted in each man a deſire *To liberty of ac-*
of his own happineſs, and many tender affections to- *tion.*

Book II. ward others in fome nearer relations of life, and granted to each one fome underftanding and active powers,
with a natural impulfe to exercife them for the purpofes of thefe natural affections; 'tis plain each one
has a natural right to exert his powers, according to
his own judgment and inclination, for thefe purpofes,
in all fuch induftry, labour, or amufements, as are
not hurtful to others in their perfons or goods, while
no more publick interefts neceffarily requires his labours, or requires that his actions fhould be under the
direction of others. This right we call *natural liberty*.
Every man has a fenfe of this right, and a fenfe of the
evil of cruelty in interrupting this joyful liberty of
others, without neceffity for fome more general good.
Thofe who judge well about their own innocent interefts will ufe their liberty virtuoufly and honourably;
fuch as have lefs wifdom will employ it in meaner
purfuits, and perhaps in what may be juftly cenfured
as vicious. And yet while they are not injurious to
others, and while no wife human inftitution has for
the publick good fubjected them to the controll of
magiftrates or laws, the fenfe of natural liberty is fo
ftrong, and the lofs of it fo deeply refented by human
nature, that it would generally create more mifery to
deprive men of it becaufe of their imprudence, than
what is to be feared from their imprudent ufe of it.
The weakeft of mankind are not fo void of fore-
thought but that it would occafion to them exquifite
diftrefs, and fink their fouls into an abject forrow, or
kindle all the paffions of refentment, to deprive them

of their natural liberty, and fubject their actions, and
all interefts dear to them, to the pleafure of others
about whofe fuperior wifdom and good intentions they
were not thoroughly fatisfied.   Let men inftruct,
teach, and convince their fellows as far as they can a-
bout the proper ufe of their natural powers, or per-
fuade them to fubmit voluntarily to fome wife plans
of civil power where their important interefts fhall be
fecured. But till this be done, men muft enjoy their
natural liberty as long as they are not injurious, and
while no great publick intereft requires fome reftric-
tion of it.

 This right of natural liberty is not only fuggefted
by the felfifh parts of our conftitution, but by many
generous affections, and by our *moral fenfe*, which reprefents our own voluntary actions as the grand dignity and perfection of our nature.

 3. A like natural right every intelligent being has *Private judg-*
about his own opinions, fpeculative or practical, to *ment.*
judge according to the evidence that appears to him.
This right appears from the very conftitution of the
rational mind which can affent or diffent folely according to the evidence prefented, and naturally defires knowledge. The fame confiderations fhew this
right to be unalienable: it cannot be fubjected to the
will of another: tho' where there is a previous judgment formed concerning the fuperior wifdom of a-
nother, or his infallibility, the opinion of this other,
to a weak mind, may become fufficient evidence. As
to opinions about the Deity, religion, and virtue, this

Book II. right is further confirmed by all the nobleſt deſires of the ſoul: as there can be no virtue, but rather impiety in not adhering to the opinions we think juſt, and in profeſſing the contrary. Such as judge truly in theſe matters, act virtuouſly: and as for weak men, who form falſe opinions, it may do good to inſtruct and convince them of the truth if we can; but to compel them to profeſs contrary to their opinions, or to act what they believe to be vicious, or impious in religion, muſt always be unjuſt, as no intereſt of ſociety can require it, and ſuch profeſſion and action muſt be ſinful to thoſe who believe it to be ſo. If any falſe opinions of a religious or moral nature tend to diſturb the peace or ſafety of ſociety, or render men incapable of ſuch duties of ſubjects as are requiſite for the publick ſafety, it may be juſt to oblige thoſe who embrace them to give ſufficient ſecurity for their conduct, * and to defray the charge of employing others to perform their duties for them; or to remove themſelves from this ſtate with their effects, and make way for better ſubjects, where the ſtate cannot otherways be ſafe.

Right over one's own life.   4. As *God,* by the ſeveral affections and the moral faculty he has given us, has ſhewed the true ends and purpoſes of human life and all our powers; promoting the univerſal happineſs, and, as far as is conſiſtent with it, our own private happineſs, and that of ſuch as are dear to us; in conformity to his own gracious purpo-

---

* This reſembles the *actio de damno infecto,* which is no diminution of the right of property.

fes; we muſt diſcern not only a right that each one has over his own life to expoſe it to even the greateſt dangers when 'tis neceſſary for theſe purpoſes, but that it is frequently the moſt honourable and lovely thing we can do, and what we are ſacredly obliged to out of duty to *God* and our fellow-creatures. Mankind have often a right to demand this ſervice from us, tho' we had no proſpect of eſcaping. A brave man has a right to act ſuch a part, and the publick intereſt has this claim upon him, from the conſtitution of nature, previouſly to any political conſtitutions, or any com-pacts in this affair. Magiſtrates have a right to com-pel men to ſuch perilous ſervices, becauſe they were antecedently good and right: and they are the more glorious, the more voluntarily they are undertaken.

About theſe caſes where the publick intereſt may require the hazarding life, expoſing ourſelves to cer-tain death, men muſt judge, by impartially comparing probabilities, as we judge about all human affairs where abſolute certainty is ſeldom attainable. If we have no right over our lives for the publick intereſt, we cannot juſtly expoſe them to danger; what one has no moral power over, he cannot ſubject to contingen-cies. " *God* has indeed placed us in life as ſoldiers in " certain ſtations, which we are to maintain till we are " recalled," according to the fine ſentiment of Socra-tes, or Pythagoras. But we muſt diſcharge the duties of theſe ſtations at all hazards. Our ſole buſineſs is not to prolong life on any terms. As our reaſon and *moral faculty* ſhew us our ſtation and its duties, the

BOOK II. fame powers muſt ſhew us when we are recalled, what the duties of life are, when it is to be expoſed even to the greateſt dangers; when the publick intereſt requires, then it is that our *Commander* recalls us by the fame voice which intimated to us our ſtation and its duties.

A right to uſe what is common.

5. Each one has a natural right to the uſe of ſuch things as are in their nature fitted for the common uſe of all; (of which hereafter:) and has a like right, by any innocent means, to acquire property in ſuch goods as are fit for occupation and property, and have not been occupied by others. The natural deſires of mankind, both of the ſelfiſh and ſocial kind, ſhew this right. And 'tis plainly cruel and unjuſt to hinder any innocent acquiſitions of another: when indeed ſome acquiſitions would endanger the liberty, independency, or ſafety of his neighbours, they have a right either to prevent ſuch acquiſitions, or to oblige him who makes them to give ſufficient ſecurity for the ſafety of others.

Right to ſociety with others.

6. For the like reaſons every innocent perſon has a natural right to enter into an intercourſe of innocent offices or commerce with all who incline to deal with him. 'Tis injurious in any third perſon to interfere, or confine his or their choice, when he has not acquired ſome right to direct their actions.

To the character of innocence.

7. As we all have a ſtrong natural deſire of eſteem, and the greateſt averſion to infamy, every man has a natural right to the ſimple character of probity and honeſty, and of diſpoſitions fit for a ſocial life, until he has forfeited this right by an oppoſite conduct.

To marriage.

8. From the natural and ſtrong deſires of marriage

and offspring we may difcern the natural right each one Chap. 5. has to enter into the matrimonial relation with any one who confents, and is not in this matter fubjected to the controll of others, or under a prior contract. In this matter, as much as any, an opinion of happinefs and a mutual good liking is neceffary to the happinefs of the parties, and compulfion muft create mifery.

That all thefe rights are of the perfect fort, muft appear from the great mifery which would enfue from the violation of them to the perfon thus injured; and a general violation of them muft break off all friendly fociety among men.

II. *The natural equality of men* confifts chiefly in this, that thefe natural rights belong equally to all: *Natural equa- lity of men.* this is the thing intended by the natural equality, let the term be proper or improper. Every one is a part of that great fyftem, whofe greateft intereft is intended by all the laws of *God* and nature. Thefe laws prohibit the greateft or wifeft of mankind to inflict any mifery on the meaneft, or to deprive them of any of their natural rights, or innocent acquifitions, when no publick intereft requires it. Thefe laws confirm in the fame manner to all their rights natural or acquired, to the weak and fimple their fmall acquifitions, as well as their large ones to the ftrong and artful. The fame accefs to adventiti- ous rights is open, and the fame means appointed for all who can ufe them. If great occupation and much labour employed, intitles the vigorous and active to great poffeffions; the weak and indolent have an e

Book II. qually facred right to the fmall poffeffions they occupy and improve. There is *equality in right*, how dif-.
ferent foever the objects may be; that *jus aequum* in
which the Romans placed true freedom.

None naturally
flaves.
Men differ much from each other in wifdom, virtue, beauty, and ftrength; but the loweft of them,
who have the ufe of reafon, differ in this from the
brutes, that by fore-thought and reflection they are
capable of incomparably greater happinefs or mifery.
Scarce any man can be happy who fees that all his
enjoyments are precarious, and depending on the will
of others of whofe kind intentions he can have no
affurance. All men have ftrong defires of liberty and
property, have notions of right, and ftrong natural
impulfes to marriage, families, and offspring, and earneft defires of their fafety. 'Tis true the generality
may be convinced that fome few are much fuperior
to them in valuable abilities: this finer part of the
fpecies have imperfect rights to fuperior fervices from
the reft: they are pointed out by nature as the fitteft
to be intrufted with the management of the common
affairs of fociety, in fuch plans of power as fatisfy the community that its common interefts fhall be
faithfully confulted. But without this fatisfaction given, permanent power affumed by force over the fortunes of others muft generally tend to the mifery of
the whole. Mere promifes or profeffions give no fecurity. The darkeft and moft dangerous tyrants may
make the faireft fhews till they are fettled in power.
We muft therefore conclude, that no endowments,

natural or acquired, can give a perfect right to assume *Chap. 5.*
power over others, without their consent.

III. This is intended against the doctrine of Ari- *Aristotle's doc-*
stotle, and some others of the antients, " that some *trine considered.*
" men are naturally slaves, of low genius but great
" bodily strength for labour: and others by nature
" masters of finer and wiser spirits, but weaker bodies:
" that the former are by nature destined to be sub-
" ject to the later, as the work-beasts are subjected to
" men. That the inhabitants of certain countries,
" particularly Greece, are universally of finer spirits,
" and destined to command; and that the rest of the
" world are fitted for slavery. That by this subordi-
" nation of the more stupid and imprudent to the
" wise and ingenious, the universal interest of the sys-
" tem is best promoted, as that of the animal system is
" promoted by the power of the rational species over
" the irrational."

The power of education is surprizing! this author
in these justly admired books of politicks is a zealous
asserter of liberty, and has seen the finest and most humane reasons for all the more equitable plans of civil
power. He lived in that singular century, in which
Greece indeed produced more great and ingenious
men than perhaps the world ever beheld at once: but
had he lived to our times, he would have known, that
this beloved country, for sixteen centuries, hath seldom produced any thing eminent in virtue, polity,
arts, or arms; while great genii were often arising in
the nations he had adjudged to slavery and barbarity.

Is it not abundantly known by experience, that

BOOK II. such as have a less fortunate capacity for the ingenious arts, yet often surpass the ingenious in sagacity, prudence, justice, and firmness of mind, and all those abilities which fit a man for governing well. And then 'tis often found that men of less genius for arts, or policy, may have the loveliest turn of temper for all the sweet social virtues in private life, and the most delicate sense of liberty. Are such amiable characters to be less esteemed, or their interests and inward satisfaction less regarded, or subjected to the pleasure of the artful and ambitious? The natural sense of justice and humanity abhors the thought.

Had providence intended that some men should have had a perfect right to govern the rest without their consent, we should have had as visible undisputed marks distinguishing these rulers from others as clearly as the human shape distinguishes men from beasts. Some nations would be found void of care, of fore-thought, of love of liberty, of notions of right of property, or storing up for futurity, without any wisdom or opinion of their own wisdom, or desires of knowledge; and perfectly easy in drudging for others, and holding all things precariously while they had present supplies; never disputing about the wisdom of their rulers, or having any suspicions or fore-boding fears about their intentions. But where do we find any such tempers in the human shape?

Wisdom gives no right to power. Superior wisdom or penetration of understanding, were all convinced of it, cannot give a right to govern, since it may be employed by a selfish corrupt temper to the worst purposes, even the general misery of the

community.   Goodneſs muſt be aſcertained too before the ſubjects can have any ſatisfaction or happineſs
under a dominion founded in will.   Now 'tis impoſſible with reſpect to man to give aſſurance of the ſtable
goodneſs of intention.   The worſt will pretend to it
till they are ſettled in power.   Nay do not the moſt
ignorant ſometimes ſincerely judge themſelves to be
wiſer than their neighbours, and fitter for governing?
and how ſeldom would men of ſuperior abilities agree
about the perſons moſt eminent in the arts of government.   To found therefore a right of governing others
upon a ſuperiority of abilities, without any conſent of
the ſubject, muſt raiſe eternal controverſies which
force alone can decide.

IV. As to thoſe natural rights which are of the   *Imperfect na-*
imperfect ſort, almoſt all the eminent and lovely vir-   *tural rights.*
tues of life are employed in obſerving and fulfilling
them. We may preſent to men a view of their duties
by conſidering them as fulfilling ſome private rights
of the perſons to whom they are performed which
are neceſſary to their happineſs, as a right, perfect or
imperfect, correſponds to every obligation or duty.
But moſt of theſe duties are recommended by ſtill a
nobler moral ſpecies, viz. the love of virtue itſelf, and
the dignity there is naturally felt in exerciſing every
amiable tender humane diſpoſition toward our fellows; for, as was obſerved above, the fulfilling perfect
rights rather ſhews only the abſence of iniquity, whereas all the honourable virtues and duties of life rather
correſpond to the rights called imperfect; and the ſoul

BOOK II. muſt feel as ſacred a moral obligation to theſe duties on many occaſions, and as great a turpitude in omitting them, as in direct acts of injuſtice againſt the perfect rights of others.

To offices of no trouble or ex-pence.   Theſe imperfect rights are, 1. A right each man has to all thoſe uſeful offices from his fellows which coſt them no trouble or expence.† 'Tis horridly inhuman to refuſe them.

To offices of ſome expence.   2. Any man has an imperfect right to ſuch offices, even of ſome trouble or expence, as are neceſſary to relieve him from ſome great diſtreſs or calamity incomparably greater than any little trouble or expence requiſite for his relief. 'Tis often very inhuman to decline ſuch trouble or expence, and that in proportion to the greatneſs of the ſufferer's diſtreſs.

In ſeveral de-grees.   3. Men of eminent virtue have ſtill a more ſacred claim to more important good offices, and every virtuous heart is ſenſible of a deeper obligation to ſuch offices, even where one has received no previous favours from them. Such men have a right to be received into the more near attachments or friendſhip of the virtuous, and to their good offices in promoting them to the higher ſtations, where they may do more publick good by the exerciſe of their virtues. To this we are obliged by the more extenſive virtuous affections which regard the publick intereſt.

To ſocial wor-ſhip.   4. Every perſon diſpoſed to piety, and willing to improve in it, has a like right to be admitted into any religious ſociety or inſtitution, that he may improve

† *Officia innoxiae utilitatis.*

by the inftructions and devotions of the fociety; provided that he does not forfeit this right by any impious or immoral tenets or practices, which make it
opprobrious to the fociety to entertain him.

5. Perfons in diftrefs, who are not made unworthy
of the liberality of good men by their floth or vices,
fhould not be excluded from it; nor fhould the liberality of good men, who incline to exercife it toward
them, be reftrained, unlefs more worthy objects in
greater or equal diftrefs are unprovided.

V. In liberality and munificence the importance of
any gift to the receiver is in a joint proportion to the
value of the gift and his indigence; and the real lofs
to the giver is in proportion to the faid value, and
to his wealth inverfely: that is, the greater his wealth
is, the lefs will an honeft heart feel the want of what
it gives: and that fenfe of lofs which a poor covetous
wretch may have about a trifle is not to be regarded.
The virtue of any donation is, in the fame manner,
directly as the value of the gift, and inverfely as the
wealth of the giver, as far as men can difcern it by
external evidence; as thus the ftrength of fome generous affection above the felfifh is manifeftly difplayed.

The addition made to the happinefs of the indigent may be incomparably greater than the diminution of that of the donor, where the donor is wealthy:
and this fhews that perfons in fuch circumftances are
chiefly obliged to liberality. But there is no determination can be made of the precife quantity or proportion a good man fhould give. The different at-

BOOK II. tachments in life, the numbers of the indigent, and
the degrees of their diſtreſſes, make different quantities and proportions reaſonable at different times.
Laws fixing a certain quantity, or proportion to the
wealth of the giver, would be unreaſonable; and would
much abate the beauty of ſuch actions. Liberality
would then appear like paying a tax, or diſcharging
a legal debt. Spectators could conclude nothing a-
bout the honourable or generous diſpoſition of the
giver, and liberality would ceaſe to be a bond of love,
eſteem, or gratitude.

Neceſſary cauti-
ons.
Several prudent cautions and general rules are delivered about liberality. Firſt, that it be not hurtful
to the morals of the object, under a falſe ſhew of advantage, by encouraging them in ſloth, meanneſs of
temper, or any vicious diſpoſitions; and again, that it
be not ſo immoderate as to exhauſt its own fountain,
and prevent the like for the future when more worthy objects may occur; or incapacitate the donor for
other offices of life toward thoſe whom he may be
more ſacredly obliged to ſupport.

Who to be pre-
ferred.
When many claim relief or ſupport from us at
once, and we are not capable of affording it to them
all; we ſhould be determined by theſe four circumſtances chiefly, (tho' ſome more remote ones of a publick nature in ſome caſes may for the general intereſt
be preferred) " the dignity or moral worth of the
" objects; the degrees of indigence; the bonds of af-
" fection, whether from tyes of blood, or prior friend-
" ſhip; and the prior good offices we have received

" from them." The more of thefe which confpire in CHAP. 5.
any perfon, our obligation to affift him is the more
facred. Virtuous parents in diftrefs are recommended
by all thefe circumftances in the firft place. The tyes
of blood next recommend our offspring and kinfmen.
And next to them the tyes of gratitude fhould ordinarily take place, nay fometimes be preferred to the
tyes of blood. And when other circumftances are e-
qual, the more virtuous fhould be preferred to thofe
of lefs virtue*.

Tho' the duties of mere humanity to perfons under no fpecial attachment fhould give place to the
more fpecial tyes, yet when they can be difcharged,
confiftently with more facred duties, they have great
moral beauty, and are of more general importance, than
one at firft imagines. Such offices raife high gratitude,
and by the example encourage the more extenfive affections: they give amiable impreffions of a whole nation, nay of the human fpecies. Thus courtefy and
hofpitality to ftrangers, a general civility and obligingnefs of deportment, even to perfons unknown, are
juftly efteemed high evidences of fweetnefs of temper,
and are the more lovely, that they are unfufpected of
interefted views.

VI. The duties of gratitude naturally follow thofe
of liberality, and are alfo exceedingly ufeful; as the *Claims of grati-*
neglect of them is very pernicious. The prevailing *tude.*
of gratitude encourages every generous difpofition,
and gives lovely impreffions of mankind. The truly

* See *Cicero de offic. l. i. c.* 14, 15, 16, 17, 18.

Q q 2

great mind does good to others as its natural work from its own sweet difpofitions and natural impulfe to exercife them, whatever returns are made. It has its main end when it acts its part well. But the lower virtues of others are difcouraged by ingratitude: and the ungrateful are the common enemies of all the indigent, as they difcourage liberality, and as far as they can, dry up the fountain whence the indigent are to be fupplied.

No precife meafures can be fixed for returns of gratitude, more than for liberality. Equality to the benefits received would in many cafes be too much, and in many too little. A kind grateful heart with common prudence is to itfelf the true meafure, *as the liberal mind muft devife liberal things.* There is the fame reafon againft precife laws in this cafe, as in liberality.

There is a general obligation of gratitude upon us all, toward thofe who have done any generous or ufeful fervices to any valuable part of mankind, that we fhould efteem and honour them, and promote their interefts, and give them juft praife, one fweet reward to noble minds, protecting their characters againft envy and detraction. Such conduct encourages every generous difpofition, and excites men to imitate fuch as are eminently virtuous. The hopes of honour overballance thofe difadvantages and loffes which often deter men of weaker virtue from any generous defigns.

CHAP. VI.

*The adventitious-*RIGHTS, REAL *and* PERSONAL,
PROPERTY *or* DOMINION.

I. A Dventitious rights are next to be confidered,
and they are either *real*, " when the right ter-
" minates upon fome certain goods;" or *perfonal*, when
" the right terminates upon a perfon, without any
" more fpecial claim upon one part of his goods than
" another." In perfonal rights our claim is to fome
preftation, or fome value, leaving it to the perfon o-
bliged to make up this value out of any part of his
goods he pleafes.

Of real rights the chief is property conftituted in
thefe things which are of fome ufe in life. As to the
origin of it, we firft inquire into the general right which
mankind have to the ufe of things inanimate, and the
lower animals; and then into that property which one
man may have in certain things to the exclufion of
others from all ufe of them.

II. As the inferior animals are led by their appetites and inftincts, without any capacity of confidering the notions of right or wrong, to ufe fuch fruits
of the earth as their fenfes recommend and their appetites crave for their fupport, mankind would probably at firft act the like part, without confidering
the point of right, and that from the like inftincts.
When they attained to the knowledge of a wife and
good *God*, the creator of all thefe curious forms, and

Book II. to the notions of right, they would foon difcover that it was the will of *God* that they fhould ufe the inanimate products of the earth for their fupport or more comfortable fubfiftence, and that they had a right thus to ufe them, from the following obvious reafons. They would perceive their own fpecies to be the moft excellent creatures that could be fupported by them, that without this fupport they muft foon perifh in a miferable manner ; that their inftincts and fenfes were plainly deftined to lead them into the ufe of them ; that the inftincts of lower animals, who had no fuperior powers to reftrain them, plainly fhewed the inanimate things to be deftined for the fupport of animals; that thefe forms, however curious and beautiful, muft foon perifh of their own accord, and return to the common mafs of earth without anfwering any fuch valuable purpofe as fupporting animal-life and increafing its happinefs; that to things inanimate all ftates are alike, and no diminution or increafe of happinefs is occafioned by any changes which befal them, except as they are fubfervient to things animated. Thefe confiderations would clearly fhew that a great increafe of happinefs and abatement of mifery in the whole muft enfue upon animals ufing for their fupport the inanimate fruits of the earth; and that confequently it is right they fhould ufe them, and the intention of their Creator.

A new created pair indeed could fcarce fubfift even in the fineft climates, without a place cultivated for them artificially, and ftored with fruits ready for their

subsistence. Their first days must be anxious and dan- Chap. 6.
gerous, unless they were instructed about the fruits
proper for their use, the natures of animals around
them, the changes of seasons, and the arts of shelter
and storing up for the future. They would not need
a revelation to teach them their right, but would need
one to teach them how to use it.

III. The right to use inferior animals is not so ob- *The right to use the lower animals.*
vious, and here instruction would be more necessary,
if there was early any need to use them; and yet reason would pretty soon teach one the right of mankind
in this matter. A rational being, who had notions of
right and wrong, and in some distress needed the labours or other use of creatures so much inferior in dignity, being conscious of his natural power by means of
reason to make such creatures subservient to his support and happiness, would readily presume upon his
right, and a little further reflection would confirm
his presumption.

"Tis true these creatures are capable of some hap- *Men the supreme part of the system.*
piness and misery; their sufferings naturally move our
compassion; we approve relieving them in many cases,
and must condemn all unnecessary cruelty toward
them as shewing an inhuman temper. Could we subsist sufficiently happy without diminishing the ease or
pleasure of inferior animals, it would be cruel and
unjust to create to them any needless toil or suffering,
or to diminish their happiness. But the human species is capable of incomparably greater happiness or
misery: the external senses of brutes may be equally,

or more acute, but men have fuperior fenfes or powers of enjoyment or fuffering; they have fublimer plea- fures by the imagination, by knowledge, by more ex- tenfive and lafting focial affections, and fympathy, by their *moral fenfe*, and that of honour. Their reafon and reflection collect joys and forrows, glory and fhame, from events paft and future, affecting others as well as themfelves; whereas brutes are much con- fined to what at prefent affects their fenfes. Thus mankind are plainly the fupreme part in the animal fyftem of this earth.

The right to the labours of beafts. Now fuppofe an impartial governor, regarding all animals in proportion to their dignity, and aiming at the beft ftate of all: fuppofe the higheft fpecies, man- kind, multiplying fo faft that neither the natural fruits of the earth, nor thofe procured by their own labour, are fufficient for their maintenance; and that they are op- preffed with immoderate toil and anxiety, as they muft be without the affiftance of brute animals. In this cafe men could give no aid to the tamer fpecies of brutes in defending them againft favage beafts, in pro- viding clear paftures, or ftoring forage for the winter: the tamer kinds muft generally perifh. Some of thefe kinds, by their greater ftrength, could bear any given quantity of labour, or effect certain works, with far lefs pain than men; and by want of forethought and reflection would fuffer much lefs by any labour. By their affiftance men might obtain a great increafe of happinefs, and be freed from evils much fuperior to thofe labours impofed on the beafts. Men could thus have leisure, and it would become their interest, to defend and provide for their fellow-labourers, and to incourage their propagating. Here is plainly a well ordered complex system, with a proper connexion and subordination of parts for the common good of all. It tends to the good of the whole system that as great a part as possible of the severer labours useful to the whole be cast upon that part of the system to which it is a smaller evil, and which is incapable of higher offices requiring art and reason: while the higher part, relieved from such toil, gains leisure for nobler offices and enjoyments of which it alone is capable; and can give the necessary support and defence to the inferior. Thus by human dominion over the brutes, when prudently and mercifully exercised, the tameable kinds are much happier, and human life exceedingly improved. And this sufficiently shews it to be just.

But if after all this, men and other animals mul- *Beasts no rights* tiply so fast, that there is not sufficient food for their *valid against men.* sustenance; it plainly tends to the good of the whole system, that when both the nobler and the meaner kinds cannot sufficiently subsist and multiply, that the nobler should rather be increased: and perishing by violence, by want of food, or any other cause which can be foreseen, is a greater evil to the kinds endued with fore-thought, than to those who feel only the present pain. The brutes therefore can have no right or property valid against mankind, in any thing necessary for human support. Had God intended for

VOL. I.   R r

BOOK II. brutes any such right to any parts of the earth, or any goods they once possessed, so as to exclude men in their greatest indigence of such things; this would have been a right opposite to the greatest good of the system, which is absurd. He would certainly have given to brutes some sagacity to have marked out their bounds, to have made known their claims, and treated with men about them.

Brutes may have rights. And yet brutes may very justly be said to have a right that no useless pain or misery should be inflicted on them. Men have intimations of this right and of their own corresponding obligation, by their sense of pity. 'Tis plainly inhuman and immoral to create to brutes any useless torment, or to deprive them of any such natural enjoyments as do not interfere with the interests of men. 'Tis true brutes have no notion of right or of moral qualities: but infants are in the same case, and yet they have their rights, which the adult are obliged to maintain. Not to mention that frequent cruelty to brutes may produce such a bad habit of mind as may break out in like treatment of our fellows.

Rights of men to other use of animals. IV. But if mankind so increase that all their labours, even with the assistance of that of beasts, cannot procure them sufficient support; 'tis plain they can spare no labour for the defence of such tameable kinds as are unfit for labour, unless they obtained from them some other use: such kinds must be banished from all cultivated lands, and be exposed to savage beasts, and to the winter colds and famine. It must

therefore be for the intereſt of thoſe kinds that men CHAP. 6.
ſhould make any other advantage they can from them
by their milk or wool, or any other way, which might
purchaſe to them human defence and protection. By
this means theſe creatures ſhall have an happier and a
longer life, and ſhall be more encreaſed.

But if mankind ſo increaſe, that all this uſe of liv- *Right to uſe them*
ing animals is not ſufficient, men muſt·exclude from *for food.*
their care all ſuch animals as yield no ſuch uſe; unleſs ſome other uſe of them is found out to engage
and compenſate human care about them, they muſt
be left to periſh miſerably in deſarts and mountains
by ſavage beaſts, or by want of forage: ſince many of
the tameable kinds multiply beyond all neceſſity for
any uſes men can derive from them during their lives:
nature here points out another uſe ; as we ſee many
animal kinds led by their inſtincts to feed upon the
fleſh of other animals. Thoſe of the inferior ſpecies
thus deſtined for food to the ſuperior, enjoy life and
ſenſe and pleaſure for ſome time, and at laſt periſh as
eaſily as by old age, winter-cold, or famine. The
earth and animals muſt have had quite different conſtitutions, otherways theſe ſeeming evils could not have
been prevented. The ſuperior orders muſt have had
ſome food provided: 'tis better this food be animated
for ſome time, and have ſome low ſenſe and enjoyment, than be wholly infenſible, and only ſubſervient
to nouriſh animals. Theſe lower orders alſo during
their lives may do conſiderable ſervice in the world,
as naturaliſts obſerve that the ſmaller inſects, the or-

BOOK II. dinary prey of birds and fishes, by feeding on all pu-
trefaction, prevent the corruption of the air, and thus
are useful to the whole system.

It would be the interest of an animal system that
the nobler kinds should be increased, tho' it diminished the numbers of the lower. A violent death
by the hands of men may be a much less evil to
the brutes than they must otherways have endured,
and that much earlier too, had they been excluded
from human care. By this use of them for food
men are engaged to make their lives easier and to
encourage their propagation. They are defended
and fed by human art, their numbers increased, and
their deaths may be easier ; and human life made
agreeable in those countries which otherways must
have been desolate. Thus the intention of nature to
subject the brute animals to men for food is abundantly manifest, and its tendency to the general good
of the system shews that men have a right to make
this use of them.

If all these reasonings did not soon occur to men,
'tis probable they had not soon any need of the flesh
of animals. When they needed it, their own sagacity
might discover their right. And yet this right is so
opposite to the natural compassion of the human heart
that one cannot think an express grant of it by revelation was superfluous.*

---

* This point is so little debated in these
Northern nations that these reasonings
may seem needless. But 'tis well known,
that many great sects and nations, at
this day, deny this right of mankind. And
some great names among ourselves, have

V. We next confider the right of private property Chap. 6.
which one man may have exclufive of his fellow-men.

And here firft, the natural appetites and defires of
men lead each one to take fuch things as are fit for
prefent ufe, and yet lye in common, with full perfuafion of his right, if he has attained to moral notions;
as he fees that fuch things are deftined for the ufe
of men, and none of his fellows have obtained any
prior right to them, to preclude him from ufing them.
He muft eafily fee too, fhould another take from him
what he had thus occupied, that, befide obftructing
his natural and innocent defign for his own fupport,
which muft appear odious, as it is ill-natured; fuch
practice obtaining among men muft fubject them to
the greateft mifery.   What one man now occupies,
another without any preferable claim deprives him of:
a third perfon may in like manner deprive him of
what he next occupies; he may in like manner be a-
gain defeated by a fourth: and thus the whole grant
made to him by God and nature of the inferior creatures for his fupport, might be defeated by the ill-
nature and injuftice of his neighbours, without any
neceffity; fince thefe neighbours might by their own
diligence provide for themfelves, without interfering
with his acquifitions.   Thus the firft impulfes of nature toward fupporting ourfelves, or thofe who are dear
to us, point out the right of the firft occupant to fuch
things as are fit for prefent ufe.   The obftructing this

---

alledged that without rev lation, or an exprefs grant from God, we would have had
no fuch right. Their reafons indeed, if !.

they were folid, would make any grant of
it by revelation appear incredible.

Book II. innocent defign muft appear morally evil, as it is ill-natured to hinder any man to take his natural fupport from the things granted for this purpofe by God and nature, while others can otherways fupport themfelves. And reflection upon the general tendency of fuch practice further confirms this right. Thefe confiderations eftablifh the firft rule of property, that " things fit for prefent ufe the firft occupier fhould en- " joy undifturbed." The accident of firft occupation may be a trifling difference; but a trifle may determine the right to one fide, when there is no confideration to weigh againft it on the other.†

The difficulties upon this fubject arife from fome *Confufed noti-* confufed imagination that property is fome phyfical *ons on this fub-* quality or relation produced by fome action of men. *ject.* Whereas in our inquiries about the original of property, we only mean to difcover what confiderations or circumftances fhew it to be morally good or innocent that a perfon fhould enjoy the full ufe of certain things, and that it would evidence an immoral affection in another to hinder him. Now from the natural defires of men, of which we are all confcious, and from the manifeft intention of nature, it muft appear immoral, cruel, or inhumanly felfifh, to hinder any man to ufe

---

† By occupation is underftood fometimes firft difcovering by the eye, fometimes touching with the hand, fometimes fecuring by any inftrument, fuch goods as before were common. 'Tis always immoral, when we can fupport ourfelves otherways, to defeat any innocent defign of another. If without any defign of defeating the attempts of others, feveral perfons at once occupy the fame thing, one by firft difcovering, another by touching with his hand, a third by any other method, they fhould naturally be deemed joint proprietors. Where the defign of one was previoufly known, 'tis immoral and unjuft for another, without neceffity, to prevent or intercept his advantage.

any goods formerly common, which he has firſt occupied, while there remains abundance of other things
which others may occupy for their own ſupport. And
ſuch defeating of the firſt occupiers muſt give perpetual occaſion for the moſt deſtructive paſſions and
contentions.

Before mankind were much increaſed, if the regi- *Natural rea-*
ons they poſſeſſed were ſo very fruitful and mild that *ſons for proper-*
there was plenty of all conveniencies without any un- *ty of a private*
eaſy labour, there was little occaſion for any further *kind.*
rules of property. But as the world is at preſent, and
as mankind are multiplied, the product of the earth,
without great labour, is not ſufficient to maintain one
hundredth part of them. Paſtures for cattle as well
as corn are plainly owing to human labour, ſince almoſt all lands would grow into woods unfit even for
paſture, were it not for the culture of man. The
very ſubſiſtence therefore of our ſpecies, as well as all
our agreeable conveniences, require an univerſal laborious induſtry. Nature hath given to all men ſome
ingenuity and active powers, and a diſpoſition to exert them: and each man has not only ſelfiſh deſires
toward his own happineſs and the means of it, but
ſome tender generous affections in the ſeveral relations of life. We are all conſcious of ſome ſuch diſpoſitions in ourſelves, and juſtly conclude that o-
thers have the like. We know that theſe are the
ordinary ſprings of the activity of mankind in employing their labour to cultivate the earth, or procure
things uſeful in human life. We all feel a ſenſe of

Book II. liberty within us, a ftrong defire of acting according to our own inclinations, and to gratify our own affections, whether felfish, or generous: we have a deep refentment of any obftruction given to thefe natural defires and endeavours; while accompanied with a fenfe of innocence or a confcioufnefs of being void of all injurious intention, and we muft difapprove it as unkind and cruel, where no important publick intereft requires it, whether we meet with it ourfelves, or fee others thus oppofed in their innocent defigns. From thefe ftrong feelings in our hearts we difcover the right of property that each one has in the fruits of his own labour; that is, we muft approve the fecuring them to him, where no publick intereft requires the contrary; and muft condemn as cruel, unfociable, and oppreffive, all depriving men of the ufe and free difpofal of what they have thus occupied and cultivated, according to any innocent inclination of their hearts.

Reafons of com-
-mon intereft.   If we extend our views further and confider what the common intereft of fociety may require, we fhall find the right of property further confirmed. Univerfal induftry is plainly neceffary for the fupport of mankind. Tho' men are naturally active, yet their activity would rather turn toward the lighter and pleafanter exercifes, than the flow, conftant, and intenfe labours requifite to procure the neceffaries and conveniences of life, unlefs ftrong motives are prefented to engage them to thefe feverer labours. Whatever inftitution therefore fhall be found neceffary to promote univer-

fal diligence and patience, and make labour agreeable CHAP. 6.
or eligible to mankind, muft alfo tend to the publick
good; and inftitutions or practices which difcourage
induftry muft be pernicious to mankind. Now nothing can fo effectually excite men to conftant patience and diligence in all forts of ufeful induftry, as
the hopes of future wealth, eafe, and pleafure to themfelves, their offspring, and all who are dear to them,
and of fome honour too to themfelves on account of
their ingenuity, and activity, and liberality. All thefe
hopes are prefented to men by fecuring to every one
the fruits of his own labours, that he may enjoy them,
or difpofe of them as he pleafes. If they are not thus
fecured, one has no other motive to labour than the
general affection to his kind, which is commonly much
weaker than the narrower affections to our friends and
relations, not to mention the oppofition which in this
cafe would be given by moft of the felfish ones.

Nay the moft extenfive affections could fcarce engage a wife man to induftry, if no property enfued
upon it. He muft fee that univerfal diligence is neceffary. Diligence will never be univerfal, unlefs men's
own neceffities, and the love of families and friends,
excite them. Such as are capable of labour, and yet
decline it, fhould find no fupport in the labours of
others. If the goods procured, or improved by the
induftrious lye in common for the ufe of all, the worft
of men have the generous and induftrious for their
flaves. The moft benevolent temper muft decline fupporting the flothful in idlenefs, that their own necef-

Confirmed by the extenfive affections.

BOOK II. fities may force them to contribute their part for the publick good. Thus both the immediate feelings of our hearts, and the confideration of the general inte-reft, fuggeft this law of nature, " that each one fhould " have the free ufe and difpofal of what he has ac-" quired by his own labour;" and this is proper-ty, which may be defined, when it is unlimited, " a " right to the fulleft ufe of any goods, and to difpofe " of them as one pleafes."

How communi-
ty could be tele-
rable. VI. Thefe reafons for property, from the general intereft of fociety requiring univerfal diligence, would not hold if a wife political conftitution could compel all men to bear their part in labour, and then make a wifely proportioned diftribution of all that was ac-quired, according to the indigence, or merit of the citizens. But the other reafons would ftill hold from the natural fenfe of liberty, and the tender natural af-fections. Such conftant vigilance too of magiftrates, and fuch nice difcernment of merit, as could enfure both an univerfal diligence, and a juft and humane diftribution, is not to be expected. Nay, no confidence of a wife diftribution by magiftrates can ever make any given quantity of labour be endured with fuch pleafure and hearty good-will, as when each man is the diftributer of what he has acquired among thofe he loves. What magiftrate can judge of the delicate ties of friendfhip, by which a fine fpirit may be fo at-tached to another as to bear all toils for him with joy? Why fhould we exclude fo much of the lovelieft offices of life, of liberality and beneficence, and grate-

ful returns; leaving men fcarce any room for exerci- CHAP. 6.
fing them in the diftribution of their goods? And
what plan of polity will ever fatisfy men fufficiently as
to the juft treatment to be given themfelves, and all
who are peculiarly dear to them, out of the common
ftock, if all is to depend on the pleafure of magiftrates, and no private perfon allowed any exercife of
his own wifdom or difcretion in fome of the moft honourable and delightful offices of life? Muft all men
in private ftations ever be treated as children, or fools?

The inconveniencies arifing from property, which *The faults in*
Plato and Sir Thomas More endeavour to avoid by *the fchemes of*
the fchemes of community, are not fo great as thofe *community.*
which muft enfue upon community; and moft of them
may be prevented where property is allowed with all
its innocent pleafures, by a *cenforial* power, and proper laws about education, teftaments, and fucceffion.
Plato * indeed confiftently with his fcheme of community takes away all knowlege of the particular tyes of
blood as much as poffible, and all the tender affections founded on them, at leaft among thofe of the
higheft order in his ftate. He is indeed unjuftly charged
with indulging any diffolute inclinations of thofe men:
but it feems too arrogant in that fine genius to attempt an overturning the manifeft conftitution of the
Creator, and to root out what is fo deeply fixed in the
human foul; vainly prefuming to contrive fomething
better than the *God* of nature has ordered. The more
extenfive affections will never give the generality of

* See book iii. c. 1.

men such ardors, nor give them such enjoyments, without particular affections, as are plainly necessary in our constitution to diligence and happiness. Leaving a place for all the particular bonds of nature, but keeping them in due subjection to the more noble affections, will answer better all the ends of polity and morals: and such schemes as his will never be found practicable among creatures of our constitution.

C H A P. VII.

The MEANS *of acquiring* PROPERTY. *How far it extends, in what Subjects it resides.*

I. PROPERTY is either *original* or *derived.* The original is that which is acquired by first occupation and culture: the derived, is what is obtained from some former proprietor.

Occupation and culture the means. The general reasons for property are already explained, and shew the original means of acquiring it, viz. occupation, and labour employed in cultivating. But to apprehend the natural grounds of property more fully, we may observe, that men are naturally solicitous about their own future interests, and those of such as are dear to them, as well as their present interests; and may be miserable amidst present plenty, if they have no probable assurance as to futurity. Again, a great part of those things which yield the greatest and most lasting use in human life after they are improved, require a long previous course of la-

bour to make them ufeful. Now no man would employ fuch labour upon them without fome fecurity for
the future enjoyment of the advantages they afford.
Tis neceffary therefore that a continual property, beyond all poffible prefent confumption, fhould enfue
upon the culture a man has employed upon things
formerly common. Of this kind are flocks, herds,
gardens, vineyards, fruit-trees, arable grounds, or
paftures.

II. Since property thus arifes from firft occupation
of things ready for prefent ufe, and labour employed
in cultivating goods which require it; we juftly look
upon property as begun, as foon as any perfon, with a
view to acquire, undertakes any cultivation of what
was common, or any labour previoufly requifite to cul
tivation or occupation. And the property is complea-
ted when he has occupied, begun his culture, and
marked out how far he defigns to extend it by himfelf, or thofe whom he obtains to affift him. 'Tis not
always neceffary that we have arrived at or touched
the goods occupied. Every ftep taken which is of confequence to this end, † by which goods are made rea-
dier, or more fecured for human ufe than they were
formerly, gives us a right not to be prevented by o-
thers; and it is unjuft in another to intercept or prevent our enjoying the fruits of our innocent labours which we have begun and perfift in. He who
wounded or tired out any wild creature in the chace,

---

† *Propius humanis ufibus admoventur.*

fo that it becomes an eafy prey, and continues the purfuit; or has entangled it in a net, has a property begun, and is wronged by any who intercept his prey, or fruftrate his labours. One who has fitted out fhips for a defcent upon unoccupied lands, towards the occupation of which no previous labour has been employed by others, would be wronged if another hearing of the defign made greater difpatch and prevented him, and afterwards refufed to make a divifion. Nay had one without knowing the former's defign, arrived firft, he could not juftly exclude him who arrived later, from a fhare of the land thus lying in common, if it was fufficient for the purpofes of both.

How far it may be extended.

III. But as property is conftituted to encourage and reward induftry, it can never be fo extended as to prevent or fruftrate the diligence of mankind. No perfon or fociety therefore can by mere occupation acquire fuch a right in a vaft tract of land quite beyond their power to cultivate, as fhall exclude others who may want work, or fuftenance for their numerous hands, from a fhare proportioned to the colonies they can fend. Thus it would be vain for a private man with his domefticks to claim a property, upon the circumftance of his having firft difcovered or arrived at it, in a country capable of maintaining ten thoufand families, and requiring fo many to cultivate it. Equally vain would it be in a nation of eight or ten millions of fouls to claim, upon the like foundation, a property in a vaft continent capable of maintaining three times that number; as no nation can fend a third part of their people for colonies in one age. such capricious claims, beyond all possible use or conveniency of the claimants, muft not keep large tracts of the earth defolate, and exclude nations too populous from obtaining for fome of their people that ufe of the earth which *God* intended for mankind. At this rate the caprice or vain ambition of one ftate might keep half the earth defolate, and opprefs the reft of mankind.

Nay, as we fhall fhew hereafter, that fome publick *Agrarian Laws* interefts of focieties may juftify fuch Agrarian Laws *in natural liber-* *ty.* as put a ftop to the immoderate acquifitions of private citizens which may prove dangerous to the ftate, tho' they be made without any particular injury; the fame or like reafons may hold as to acquifitions made by private men in natural liberty, or by ftates and nations. If any acquifition is dangerous to the liberty and independency of a neighbourhood, or of neighbouring ftates, thefe neighbours have a right either to defeat it altogether, or compell the proprietor to give fufficient fecurity for the fafety of all around him. This would be the cafe if one had occupied a narrow pafs, with the adjacent lands; or the lands furrounding a fountain neceffary to a whole neighbourhood, or a ftrait found, fo that he could ftop all communication and trade of multitudes with each other. But of thefe lefs ordinary rights we fhall treat hereafter.

If it be inquired what is the reafonable time to be allowed to a family or a ftate for cultivating the lands they pretend to occupy, 'tis plain they may occupy.

more than the firſt ſet of hands they ſend can cultivate. Private perſons may obtain more ſervants, and a ſtate may ſend new colonies or new ſupplies of men. No preciſe anſwer can be given. To limit a ſtate to twenty or thirty years for the cultivating all they can juſtly acquire by occupation may be too great a reſtraint; and to allow them to keep lands uncultivated for ſome centuries, in proſpect of their ſending new colonies, may often be too great indulgence. The meaſure of time muſt be different according to the exigences of neighbouring ſtates. If none be overcharged with inhabitants, a larger time may be allowed. If many are overcharged, a leſs is ſufficient. Mankind muſt not for ages be excluded from the earth *God* intended they ſhould enjoy, to gratify the vain ambition of a few who would retain what they cannot uſe, while others are in inconvenient ſtraits. Neighbouring ſtates, upon offering a rateable ſhare of the charges of the firſt diſcovery and occupation, have a right to obtain ſuch lands as the firſt diſcoverers cannot cultivate. In this and all other controverſies where there is no common judge, and the parties cannot agree by amicable conferences, the natural recourſe is to unbiaſſed arbitrators; and ſuch as decline arbitration ſhould be compelled by force.

Right beyond preſent uſe.

IV. But 'tis plain that our acquiſition by labour in any one ſort of goods may extend far beyond our own preſent conſumption and that of our families; and they may be ſtored up for the future: nay it may extend beyond all preſent or future conſumption; as

we may employ the furplus as matter of beneficence, CHAP. 7.
or of barter for goods of different kinds which we
may need. Otherways each one would be obliged to
practife all forts of mechanick arts by turns, without
attaining dexterity in any; which would be a publick detriment.

The feveral rules of property as they obtain in natural liberty, like all other fpecial laws of nature, not
only admit exceptions in cafes of great neceffity, but
may juftly be altered and limited under civil polity,
as the good of the ftate requires.

V. The origin of property above explained, fhews *What things are ftill common.*
the reafon why fuch things as are inexhauftible and
anfwer the purpofes of all, and need no labour to
make them ufeful, fhould remain in common to all,
as the air, the water of rivers, and the ocean, and even
ftrait feas, which can give paffage to all fhips without
being made worfe. Where the ufe is inexhauftible,
but fome expence is requifite to fecure it, this may
be a juft reafon for obliging all who fhare in it to
contribute in an equitable manner to the neceffary
expence, fuch as that of light-houfes, or fhips of force
to fecure the feas from pyrates. But the property in
the fhores on both fides of fuch ftraits can give no
right to exclude any who are ready to make fuch e-
quitable contribution, from paffing fuch ftraits, or
carrying on any innocent commerce with the nations
who live within them.

Where indeed the ufe of any adjacent parts of the
fea or fhore allowed to foreigners, may endanger our

poffeffions, fuch as mooring of fhips of force in thofe bays which run up into the heart of a country; we may juftly refufe it, unlefs fufficient fecurity is given againft danger. We may likeways refufe to others, or exclude them from fuch ufe of things naturally common and inexhauftible, as would occafion fome uneafy fervitude upon our lands; fuch as fifhing in rivers, or drawing water from them through our ground, tho' the river were not at all appropriated by us, and the fifhing were inexhauftible.

Property in the
fea.

'Tis fcarce conceivable upon what other foundation than compact, or confent of neighbouring ftates, any one can claim any property in the fea, or any right in it fuperior to that of other nations. Each nation indeed for its own defence, feems to have a right to prevent any fhips of force of other nations to fail fo near its coaft that they could annoy any of its fubjects in their poffeffions. But this property can extend no further than a gun-fhot. Hovering indeed without neceffity upon our coafts, tho' at a greater diftance, may give juft fufpicion of fome hoftile defign, and may be a juft reafon for expoftulation and demanding fecurity, or obliging them by force to withdraw to a greater diftance.

Things left by
God in negative
community, not
pofitive.

From what is faid we fee abundantly, that this earth, and all it contains, was placed by God in that ftate the moralifts call *negative community*, and not *pofitive*. The negative is " the ftate of things not yet " in property, but lying open to the occupation of " any one." Pofitive community is the " ftate of things

" in which not any individual but a whole fociety have " an undivided property." Goods in this pofitive community neither any individual member of the fociety, nor any other, can occupy or difpofe of without confent of the whole fociety, or thofe who govern it. Now from the preceeding reafons 'tis plain, that any man could acquire property, and fee his right to acquire any thing he firft occupied, without confulting the reft of mankind; and it would be injurious in any other perfon to hinder him. Thus we need not have recourfe to any old conventions or compacts, with Grotius and Puffendorf, in explaining the original of property: nor to any decree or grant of our firft parents, with Filmer.

VI. All things fit for human ufe either yet remain *Miftakes about the* res nullius. in this negative community, or are in the property of individual men, or of focieties. *Bona univerfitatum,* or the goods of corporations are in the property of focieties; the † *res nullius* of the Civilians, viz. things *facred* as temples and their utenfils, and lands for the fupport of religious orders, and the defraying any expences of worfhip; burial-places and what things are employed in funeral-rites ; and places railed in or fecured from promifcuous ufe, fuch as the walls of cities; are all in property either of fome larger fociety, or fome family; tho' fome fuperftitious laws may reftrain the proprietors from a free and full ufe of

---

† *Nullius funt res facrae, religiofae, et fanctae. Quod enim divini juris eft, id nullius in bonis eft.* Inftit. l. ii. tit. 1. fect. 7.

&c. where thefe three forts of goods are explained according to the notions then prevailing.

BOOK II. them, or from converting them to other ufes than what they were firft deftined to. Thefe laws are often very foolifh, and founded upon fome confufed inexplicable notions. All fuch goods are truly defigned for the ufe of men alone. The old proprietors, who gave them for thefe purpofes, may have been moved by devotion toward God to make fuch donations for the ufe of certain orders employed in religious offices, or of focieties, to accommodate fuch as inclined to worfhip in thefe places; or for the burial of their dead; or for defence of focieties by fortifications. But none of thefe lands or goods can yield any ufe to God, nor can his rights receive any increafe or diminution by any deeds of men. Such donations are acceptable to him as far as they do good to his creatures, by promoting their piety, virtue, and happinefs. Devotion to God may as juftly move men to make donations for civil ufes to their country, or friends; and thefe may be as wife and acceptable to God, as any donations to ufes commonly called pious. But none thence imagine that there is fome myftical quality infufed into fuch goods that they cannot be applied upon wife occafions to other purpofes.

'Tis a natural evidence of piety in any perfon or fociety to provide whatever is requifite to accommodate men in publick worfhip, in proportion to the wealth of a country. It would evidence avarice, and want of piety, if men would not fpare from their private ufe what is requifite to make places of publick worfhip fafe, convenient, and agreeable. When they

are mean and defpicable in proportion to private buildings, the attending there may be difagreeable. 'Tis
yet worfe if thofe whofe office it is to prefide in publick worfhip, and inftruct men in the duties of life,
are not fo fupported as may enable them to attain
knowledge themfelves, and difcharge their ufeful office. But when fufficient provifion is made for all thefe
purpofes, 'tis folly and fuperftition to employ that
wealth which might do more good in trade or other
civil purpofes, either on expenfive ornaments of
churches, or on their furniture, or in fo enriching the
inftructors of the people as to give them avocations
from their bufinefs, or temptations to luxury, ambition, and avarice; or to maintain more of them than
are requifite. 'Tis ftill more foolifh to maintain men
in floth, or ufelefs ways of life.

A beautiful metonymy has been artfully abufed by *The caufes of*
fome orders commonly called religious, with the ba- *miftakes.*
feft felfifh purpofes. Donations to them have been
called *gifts to God*, as all wife liberality and charity
may juftly be called. But thefe donations alone which
are made to their orders, or where they are the tru-
ftees, are called confecrations. God is proprietor of
all things alike, and can receive no gifts from men.
Donations can be made to men only. As far as they
contribute to the general happinefs of men, fo far
they are acceptable to God, and no further. When
they are pernicious to a country in its trade, or liberty, when they corrupt the clergy, as they are called,
by opportunities and temptations to luxury, tyranny,

or avarice, they are as offensive to God as any sins of ignorance can be. 'Tis wise and just in any state, when sufficient provision is made for the purposes of religion, to restrain or make void all further donations; to resume any useless grants that have been obtained by fraud and imposture, whether from the publick, or private persons; to free the publick from the charge of supporting useless structures, or idle hands, by converting the structures to other purposes, or demolishing them; and by obliging the idle hands to pursue some useful occupation. This must be acceptable service to God.

Some wild notion of consecration or sanctity infused into stones, timber, metals, lands, has made men imagine it impious to convert these things to other uses than what they once were destined to. And yet 'tis obvious that no religion or sanctity can inhere in such materials. We formerly used them when our minds were employed in devotion: but what then? so we did our bodies, our cloaths, our organs of speech: must they never be used to other purposes? The superstitious donors perhaps ordered " that such houses " should only be used for accommodating men in " worship, and such lands for the maintenance of such " as officiated in it." But is it not folly to confine that to one purpose only, which can answer other purposes, and be no less fit for the purpose chiefly intended? The state has a just right to annul superstitious restrictions in any conveyances, and to make void all such conveyances as prove foolish or hurtful to society.

Grant that in the confused imaginations of the vulgar, the devotion in churches would be abated, if they were used for other purposes in the intervals of worship. Should this weakness be encouraged? And then it requires no more but that such edifices while they are used for worship should not in the intervals be used for other purposes. If the worshippers are as well provided with other structures or utensils, and the instructors provided with other sufficient salaries; nothing hinders the state to apply the former structures, utensils, or lands, to any other wise purposes. But in the Popish religion the mystery of consecration is so deeply inculcated that all this appears impious. In that whole institution the chief part God is introduced as acting, is that of a sharping purveyor, or agent for the religious orders, grasping at and defending whatever they have obtained by any fraud or artifice from the weakest and most superstitious of mankind, for the most foolish or pernicious purposes.

VII. Things once in property may return again into a state of community if the proprietor quits his property by throwing them away, or designedly neglecting them: and then the next occupier may acquire them. If the proprietor lost any goods unwillingly, but being again otherways provided, neglects what he lost, and puts in no claim tho' he knows who has found them; a long neglect of this kind may sufficiently declare that he quitted the property, and so preclude his future claim against the present possessor. This seems the only prescription valid against

The right of prescription.

the old proprietor, before civil laws. There are juſt reaſons why civil laws ſhould introduce other rules of preſcription, partly to engage the ſubjects to proper care about their goods and claims in due time while they can be aſcertained; partly becauſe in a long tract of undiſturbed poſſeſſion againſt ſome latent titles, goods may be transferred upon valuable conſiderations to fair purchaſers, or be for like conſiderations ſubjected to ſettlements and entails and mortgages, which cannot be ſet aſide without great injuries to innocent perſons; and partly to exclude artful and undiſcoverable frauds, which could not be prevented, if any deeds pretended to be very old, the witneſſes of which muſt be dead, ſhould be ſuſtained as valid to overturn a long undiſturbed poſſeſſion.

The civil law makes a preſumptive title, or the *bona fides*, upon which the poſſeſſor may probably have believed the goods to be his own, a neceſſary beginning to preſcription; ſo that no length of poſſeſſion, begun without a plauſible title, can give a right. But the caſe of a fair purchaſer from an old poſſeſſor, without any intimation made to the purchaſer of a latent title of another, is ſo favourable, and his plea ſo equitable, when he cannot recover his price from the ſeller, that tho' the ſeller had begun poſſeſſion without this juſt preſumption, it would be very hard to ſet aſide all claim of the fair purchaſer, at leaſt to recover the price he paid. Some of the reaſons for preſcription may hold even where the poſſeſſion was not begun upon a preſumptive title.

VIII. As to acceffions or any additional profits of goods in property, thefe rules are obvious. 1. " All " fruits, increafe, or improvements happening to the " goods in a man's property, to which neither the " goods or labours of others contributed, belong to " the proprietor, except where another by contract, " or civil law, acquires fome right in them." But, 2. " Where the goods or labours of other perfons " have contributed to any increafe or improvement, " without the fraud or culpable negligence of any " concerned, all thofe who have contributed by their " labours or goods have a joint property in the com- " pound, or in the fruits and improvements, each in " proportion to the value of what he contributed." If the goods or the fruits can admit of divifion with- out lofs upon the whole, they fhould be divided in this proportion among thofe who contributed to them. If the fubject will not admit of divifion with- out lofs upon the whole, it fhould be ufed alternately for times proportioned to the values each one contri- buted, or be ufed in common continually if it can admit of fuch ufe. If the fubject neither admits of common or alternate ufe, it fhould fall to that part- ner to whom it is of the greateft value or importance, in this manner: firft, let the proportion of each one's right to thofe of the other partners be determined, and that partner who bids moft for it fhould have it, upon making compenfation to the reft for their fhares.*

CHAP. 7.

The rights to acceffions.

---

* See cafes of this kind in *Cicero de offic.* l. ii. c. 23. and the judgment of Aratus upon them.

Book II. Thus he obtains the goods who values them moſt, and the compenſation to the reſt is the greater. * Where any debate ariſes about the values of the ſeveral ſhares contributed, there is no other remedy, previous to civil polity, but the arbitration of wiſe neighbours who underſtand the goods.

Where by the fraud or blameable negligence of one, his labours or goods are blended with the goods of others, ſo that the compound or the new form ceaſes to be deſirable to the other innocent proprietor, this proprietor has a right to full compenſation for the value of his goods now made unfit for his uſe, and for whatever clear profits he could have made by his goods had they been let alone to him. If my goods are improved for my uſe by another's goods or labour, without commiſſion from me; I am only to pay the value of the improvement to my purpoſes, and not the value it may be of to the purpoſes of the culpable intermedler with my goods. There is no reaſon that through his fault I ſhould either loſe my goods, or be obliged to pay for more expenſive improvements than were convenient for my affairs. The proper puniſhment for this fraudulent or culpable intermedling with the goods of others, is a ſubject of inquiry quite diſtinct from this of property.

What rights included in property.

IX. The right of property, when it is entire and unlimited as it is firſt acquired, contains theſe three

---

* This ſection may determine in a natural manner moſt of the queſtions of the civilians about the acceſſions, viz. the *nativitas, alluvio, ſpecificatio, com nixtio, confuſio, edificatio, &c.*

parts. 1. A right to the fulleſt uſe. 2. A right to exclude others from any uſe of the goods in property.
and 3. A right of alienating and transferring to others
either in part or in whole; abſolutely, or upon any
condition or contingency; gratuitouſly, or for valuable
conſideration. Civil laws may ſometimes juſtly limit
men in the exerciſe of theſe rights; and ſome potent
reaſons of general utility may even in natural liberty
require ſome limitations, and juſtify ſome extraordinary ſteps contrary to the rules which ordinarily oblige us.

To this right of property correſponds a general
indefinite obligation upon all not to violate this right
or obſtruct others in the enjoyment of it. The ſa-
credneſs of this obligation, we all may find by conſidering the keen reſentment we ſhould feel upon ſuch violation of our rights by others; and by the ſtrong diſapprobation we muſt have of ſuch avarice or ſelfiſhneſs as breaks through all regards to the peace and
ſafety of ſociety, and all humanity to our fellows, for
the ſake of a little private gain; in thoſe matters too
which we look upon it as honourable and the evidence
of a great ſoul to deſpiſe. This diſapprobation we
muſt feel toward ſuch acts of injuſtice as affect the
property of others, even tho' we ourſelves ſuffer nothing by it.

Uu 2

C H A P. VIII.

Concerning DERIVED PROPERTY, *and the ways of alienating or transferring it.*

Rights real and personal. I. ADventitious rights are either *real*, or *perfonal*. All *adventitious real rights* arife from a tranflation of fome of the original rights of *property* from one to another. And all *perfonal adventitious rights* are conftituted by transferring to others fome parts of our natural liberty, or of our right of acting as we pleafe, and of obliging ourfelves to certain performances in behalf of others. The *real rights* terminate on fome definite goods. The *perfonal* do not.

The neceffity and ufe of frequent contracts and tranflations of property is in a good meafure manifeft from what is faid above,* and will ftill more fully appear hereafter. The difference between real and perfonal rights muft here be explained, and the foundation too for this diftinction, previous to any civil laws.

The ground of this diftinction. One may often incline to incur an obligation to another to a certain value, and have all moral certainty and an honeft purpofe of difcharging it faithfully, while yet he is unwilling to put any one part of his goods more than another in the power of his creditor, and keeps it in his own election what part of them he will alienate for difcharging this obligation. And a creditor may often be fatisfied with fuch engagements from the debtor, if he is affured of his

* Chap. vi. and vii.

wealth and integrity, without any fpecifick goods being fubjected to the claim. Such an agreement conftitutes a perfonal, and not a real right. The creditor
no doubt in fuch a cafe has a general fecurity from all
the debtor's goods, fince upon the debtor's default,
he may in natural liberty feize any part of them for
difcharge of the debt, if no other creditor has obtained
a real right in them. But the advantage of the perfonal obligation to the debtor is this, that he is ftill
mafter of all his goods, and retains it ftill in his
own election, within the time limited, to difcharge
the claims upon him in the manner he likes beft. And
the advantage of the real right to the creditor confifts in this, that from the goods fpecially fubjected
to his claim he may be fecure, notwithftanding of any
fubfequent debts incurred to others, or even prior perfonal debts which his debtor may be incapable of difcharging.

If one has done any damage to another, he becomes indebted to the perfon who fuffered this damage in the full value of it. And yet the fufferer has
only a perfonal right, not preferable to any claims of
a third perfon, nor affecting one part of the goods
of him who did the damage, more than another. If
full compenfation is made, he cannot limit the debtor
as to the goods out of which this compenfation is to
be made.

When the lender infifts on more fecurity than the
faith of the borrower, or fufpects his ability, and gets
a pledge or a mortgage, this conftitutes a real right,

BOOK II. as certain goods are affigned and fpecially fubjected to this claim.

Real preferable to perfonal.　　A juft man no doubt will obferve and fulfil the perfonal rights of others, as well as the real, to the utmoft of his power; but the fecurity is not the fame in both, as 'tis abundantly known, where different claims occur againft a perfon who has not effects to anfwer them. The real rights muft take place of the perfonal. He who confented to accept of a lefs fecurity, muft not expect to be equally fafe with one who infifted upon and obtained a greater, nor would have contracted or lent upon other terms.

For what reafons.　　The prefervation of the neceffary faith in commerce requires this preference of real rights, to perfonal. In the full tranflation of property, and even in affigning goods as real fecurities by pledge or mortgage, there muft be fuch publick forms as will fecure the purchafer or lender againft all prior fecret contracts with others, tho' thefe private contracts gave perfonal rights. But no man would buy goods, if he could not be fecured in the poffeffion of what he purchafed againft former private contracts of fale. Nor could he be fecured if prior fecret contracts did not yield to fuch publick ones with the ufual forms inftituted for conveying real rights. Nor would men lend upon any pledge or mortgage, were there not fome publick forms appointed to transfer a real right preferable to any prior perfonal rights conftituted to others by a latent contract.

All nations agree in having fome publick formali-

ties for transferring full property or real rights, not CHAP. 7.
to be defeated by prior latent perfonal rights. Thefe
formalities fhould intimate the tranfaction publickly,
or fome way prevent the perfon who transfers to im-
pofe afterwards upon others. Delivery anfwers this
end in moveables; and fome publick fymbolical deeds
giving poffeffion, in fuch as are immoveable; or fome
publick regiftration of the conveyance. Where thefe
confirm a contract, a real right is conftituted, which
no perfonal one fhould defeat. And yet the perfon
thus defrauded of his perfonal right by means of the
fubfequent real one transferring the property, has a
juft claim upon the feller who defrauded him not only for compenfation of all the damage * he fuftains,
but for the † full value of all the profit he could have
made had he not been deceived. But without this
preference of real rights to perfonal, there could be
no commerce.

II. Derived real rights are either fome parts of the *Derived real rights parts of*
right of property transferred to another, and fepara-*property often*
ted from the reft, or compleat property derived from *feparated from*
the original proprietor. *the reft.*

The parts of property frequently transferred feparately from the reft of it are chiefly of thefe four claffes. 1. *Right of poffeffion*, thus one may have a right
to poffefs the goods he knows belong to others, until
the true proprietor fhews his title. This right is valid
againft all others, and often may be turned into compleat property. 2. The right of *fucceffion*, which one

---

* *Penfatio damni.* † *Penfare quod intereft.*

BOOK II. may have to goods, while another retains all the other parts of property except that of alienating. 3. The rights of a *mortgage* or *pledge*. 4. Rights to some small uses of the goods of others, called *servitudes*.

As to the right of possession. The possessor by fraud or unjust violence has no right: any one who inclines to recover the goods to the owner may justly dispossess him. But he who possesses without fraud or unjust violence the goods he knows belong to others, has a right valid against all except the proprietor, or such as claim under him. If none such can be found, or if the proprietor quits his claim, the possessor becomes proprietor by occupation. The possessor is always obliged to make publick intimation that he has such goods, and to use all reasonable means to make it known to the proprietor. Designed concealment of them is no better than theft. When the possessor restores, he may justly demand to be repaid all prudent expences made upon the goods, or upon giving publick intimation about them.

Rights of the presumptive possessor. III. In instances where one possesses goods belonging to others which yet he obtained upon some plausible title, such as donation, legacy, succession, or purchase, and believes them to be his own †; the following rules seem equitable. 1. If the goods have perished by any accident without any fault of the possessor, he is not obliged to any compensation. 2. If he has consumed them he is obliged to restore as far as he

---

† This is the *bonae fidei possessor* of the Civilians, not importing that all other possessors are fraudulent.

was profited by them, or in proportion to the advantage or pleasure he obtained by them, which otherways would have confumed like goods of his own: for he is fo far enriched as he fpared his own goods. But as to pleafure enjoyed and not neceffary maintenance, if the poffeffor enjoyed it only becaufe he believed thefe goods to be his own, and otherways would not have been at fuch expence in matters of pleafure, one cannot pronounce univerfally that he is obliged to compenfate the value. 'Tis the honourable part to do it whenever the proprietor is indigent, and the poffeffor wealthy; or if they are in equal circumftances; or if the compenfating would not diftrefs the poffeffor in his affairs. But if compenfating would diftrefs him, if he obtained the goods by an onerous title, fuch as by paying a price for them which he cannot now recover he would at leaft in moft cafes feem to be under no other obligation than that of humanity, which might perhaps direct to fharing the lofs, where it would be too fenfibly felt were it to fall fingly on the original poffeffor.

3. When the goods yet remain, the poffeffor is obliged to reftore them with all their acceffions after deducting all prudent expences he has made about them. If he purchafed them, he has recourfe for the price upon the feller.

4. If the feller is not to be found, or is infolvent, the cafe is more difficult. Here a certain lofs muft be fuftained either by the proprietor, or the prefumptive poffeffor: both are fuppofed alike innocent: which

of them muft bear it? The cafe of both is equally favourable, and no publick advantage requires the cafting the whole lofs on one rather than the other. If freeing the proprietor from it will make purchafers more cautious and inquifitive about the titles of thofe they deal with, and thus thefts may be detected; the fubjecting the proprietors to the lofs, will make men more vigilant to prevent thefts, and prevent their goods thus becoming a fnare to honeft purchafers. In ftrict juftice one would think the lofs fhould be divided equally among all thofe through whofe hands the goods paffed without fraud, along with the proprietor, until they can recover the whole from the author of the fraud.

A confufed imagination to be avoided in this matter. In thefe queftions our reafon is difturbed by fome confufed imagination of property as fome phyfical quality or chain between the goods, and the proprietor, conceived to found a more facred right than many other moft equitable claims. And yet it cannot be of a more facred kind than the rights arifing from contracts and fair purchafes; fince tis by contracts and purchafes that property is moft frequently acquired: and there is no reafon that an innocent man fhould fuffer becaufe of any vice of another in which he had no hand.

Abftracting from fuch imaginations; property is thus determined by the law of nature; in certain circumftances we fee at once that it would be cruel and inhuman toward an individual, to deprive him of the full ufe of certain goods; as when they were acqui-

red by his own innocent labour, or by any fair contract; and we see also that like practices generally prevailing would be detrimental to society. In these circumstances we pronounce that the man has the right
of property. When equal circumstances of particular humanity plead for two persons in opposition to
each other; we then consider any circumstance on one
side which some remote interest of society may require to be regarded; and we deem the right to go
along with that circumstance: or at least, when a law
or custom is once received on account of this remote
utility, we deem the property to be on that side, and
do not regard the weaker claim of the other: tho' a
humane man would not disregard it altogether. Other
cases happen where the pleas from remote utilities of
society are also equal: and in them, there is no other
remedy but dividing the loss among all concerned, in
some proportion or other.

One sells me an horse this hour, in discharge of an *Some Examples.*
old debt he owed me: and next hour, upon a price paid
down, sells and delivers him to another who knew
nothing of my bargain. If the seller can be found, and
is solvent, there is less difficulty: but if he is not; on
whom shall the loss be cast? The contract and price
paid, the grand foundations of the titles and pleas of
humanity, are the same on both sides. 'Tis equally
hard that either of the innocent men should suffer.
Custom and civil laws regarding a remote interest of
ascertaining commerce, and preventing frauds, make
the delivery a most important circumstance for the

later.   But were it not for this remote intereſt, the priority in time would plead for the former. Suppoſe that the horſe had alſo been delivered to the former, but the ſeller allowed to keep him ſome hours in his ſtables.   When other circumſtances are now equal, priority of time is of great importance, and is much regarded in all contracts; as there can be no ſuſpicion of fraud in the firſt purchaſer; and as a regard. to this circumſtance too is of great neceſſity to aſcertain commerce.   In our preſent queſtion about the claim of the fair purchaſer to obtain the price he paid from the proprietor, when he can have no recovery from the ſeller, all pleas, both of a private and publick nature, are pretty near equal on both ſides.   And the ſame general obſervation about the original notions of property will be of conſiderable uſe in other queſtions, particularly theſe concerning the rights by teſtament, and by ſucceſſion to the inteſtate.

The honoura-
ble part always
clear.

In this and many like caſes there are obvious reaſons of humanity and mercy to ſhew a good man what is the lovely and honourable part. If the poſſeſſor be poor, and the proprietor rich, it would be barbarous if the proprietor did not indemnify the honeſt poſſeſſor as to the price he paid. If the poſſeſſor is wealthy, and the proprietor poor, it would be inhuman in the poſſeſſor to inſiſt on the price paid, when it bore no ſuch proportion to his wealth that the want of it could diſtreſs him. If their fortunes are nearly equal they ſhould divide the loſs, whatever civil laws may determine; or ſhould bear it in proportion to their wealth, when their wealth is unequal, but neither in diſtreſs. The want of obvious reaſons for caſting all the loſs on one ſide in this and ſome other caſes, will be little regreted by any but ſuch ſelfiſh wretches as are graſping at every advantage they can obtain without incurring the infamy of direct injuſtice, and have no humanity to others.

In general, as far as ſuch poſſeſſors are enriched or profited by means of the goods of others, ſo far they are obliged to reſtore; but they are enriched only by what remains after all expences they made in preſerving, improving, or cultivating are deducted; and theſe expences the proprietor is obliged to reſtore when he obtains his goods. Goods obtained by donation, ſucceſſion, or any gratuitous title, ſhould plainly be reſtored without any other compenſation from the próprietor than that of thoſe expences for preſervation and improvement.

IV. The next claſs of real rights often ſeparated *Right of ſucceſ-* from property is that of ſucceſſions in entails. When *ſion in entails.* one who has unlimited property conveys a right of ſucceſſion to ſeveral perſons, in a certain ſeries, upon certain contingencies, theſe perſons have a right to this ſucceſſion juſt as valid as men acquire by any donation; as unlimited property includes a right of diſpoſing upon any contingency or condition, as well as abſolutely. Such entails may be made imprudently, or contrary to reaſons of humanity, and ſo may donations. When they are ſo, the preſent tenant for life who has all the other rights of property except

BOOK II. that of alienating, is not culpable in taking all methods confiftent with the peace and order of fociety,
to break the entail: as a man would not be culpable
who ufed fuch peaceful methods to prevent imprudent or inhuman donations, or to get them revoked.
But where there is nothing imprudent or inhuman in
the entail, the tenant in reverfion has as good a right
to fucceed as the prefent poffeffor has to enjoy for
life; and it would be criminal to defraud him of it.
And the peace of fociety often requires the confirmation even of imprudent and inhuman conveyances, of
which hereafter; tho' the perfon to whom they are
made cannot with a good confcience infift on them.
Civil laws however may juftly limit this power of entail as the intereft of the ftate, or the neceffity of
encouraging induftry may require.

Rights by mort-   V. The third fort of real rights feparable from the
gage or pledge.   reft of the property are thofe of the mortgagee, and
of the perfon to whom moveable goods are pledged,
and delivered for fecurity of fome debt. By either of
thefe a right is given to the creditor, in cafe the debt
is not duly difcharged, to appropriate to himfelf the
lands mortgaged, or the goods pledged *, notwithftanding any prior perfonal rights of others againft the
debtor. The affuming a property in the lands mortgaged, or the moveables pledged, upon non-payment,
has no iniquity in it if the pledger or mortgager obtain all furplus of the value of the lands or goods

---

* *Lex commifforia in pignoribus.*

above what difcharges the principal debt with all in- CHAP. 8.
tereft and expences.

VI. The fourth clafs of real rights feparable from *Servitudes.*
the reft of the property are *fervitudes,* when one has a
right to fome fmall ufe of the goods of another. All
fervitudes are real rights terminating on fome definite
lands or tenements, or goods. But fome are conftituted in favour of a perfon and only for his behoof;
and others for the advantage of fome adjacent farm
or tenement be the proprietor who he will. The former, from the fubjects of thefe rights, and not from
the object on which they terminate, are called perfonal fervitudes, expiring with the perfon; the later for
the like reafon are called real fervitudes, and may be
perpetual. Thus the ufe of an houfe or a farm granted to a friend for his life-time when the property is
in another, is a perfonal fervitude, which cannot be
conveyed by him to another : but when a farm is
fubjected to a road for the convenience of the poffeffors of an adjacent farm, or the poffeffors of one tenement in a town have a right to put in beams into
the gabels of the contiguous houfe for fupporting the
floors or roof, thefe are real fervitudes, which may be
conftituted for the convenience of lands or tenements,
and may be perpetual.† The nature of the contracts
or deeds by which fuch fervitudes are conftituted fhews
the rights, and obligations of the parties, which too
depend much upon the cuftoms of the places where
they are received.

† See Inftit. l. ii. tit. 3, 4, 5.

VII. The complete property may be transferred
either by the *voluntary deed* of the proprietor, or by
Tranflation of   the *difpofition of the law of nature,* without his con-
compleat proper- fent, for the intereft of others. By deed of the pro-
ty feveral ways. prietor it may be transferred either *during his life,* or
upon the event of his death. And by difpofition of the
law of nature, without his confent, property may be
transferred either during the proprietor's life, or on
the event of his death. Of thefe four in order.

Voluntary deed   1. By voluntary deed of the proprietor during his
during life.   life, either gratuitoufly by donation, or for a certain
price or valuable confideration; of this we treat in the
following chapter about contracts.

By teftament.   2. Property is conveyed by the voluntary act of
the proprietor upon the event of his death by laft will
or teftament. This right of devifing by will is naturally included in the property, which contains a right
of difpofing upon any condition or contingency. Take
away this right and induftry fhall be much difcouraged after men are tolerably provided with neceffaries
for themfelves and their families during life; or men
muft be forced into a pretty hazardous conduct by actually giving away during life whatever they acquire
beyond their own probable confumption in their life-
time. Not to mention that they muft give away as
foon as they acquire any furpluffes, fince the fuddennefs of death, or a delirium, may make them incapable of donations upon the approach of death. This
right therefore of devifing by will feems manifeftly
founded in the law of nature, tho' civil laws may li

mit the exercife of it in common with all other rights CHAP. 8. refpecting property, fuch as the difinheriting or paf-~~~ fing by a child without any fault of his, or the conveying almoft all a man's wealth to one of his numerous pofterity from a foolifh defire of raifing one great family. Civil laws alfo juftly oblige men to fuch forms as fhall beft prevent forgeries. By the law of nature every declaration of a man's will of which credible evidence can be given, is valid and obligatory on thofe concerned: but that all men may be engaged to ufe the moft convenient forms, civil laws may confirm no teftaments made without them.

That the law of nature and the intereft of fociety *The foundation of this right of* eftablifh this right of devifing by will is as plain as *teftaments.* that they eftablifh other rights of the proprietor. The natural defign of mankind in any acquifitions beyond their own confumption is to promote by them the happinefs of thofe they love; this happinefs one defires they may obtain not only during his life, but after his deceafe. Thefe kind affections and fuitable offices to make others happy, whether we are to live with them or not, are the natural, joyful, and honourable exercifes of the human foul while we live. And 'tis cruel and unjuft to hinder a man either from fuch good offices while he lives, or to deprive him of the joyful hope that his furviving friends fhall be profited by the fruits of his labours. 'Tis cruel to thefe friends to intercept the benefit defigned them by their friend now deceafed. There is no method fo convenient for individuals, or for the fociety, by which goods can be

BOOK II transferred to furvivors as that by teftament, or a
"declaration of the will of the proprietor revocable,
"and not to take effect till after his death."† To leave
the goods of the deceafed in common open to occupation muft occafion the moft odious contentions and
mifchiefs. To all thefe reafons we may add that a
wifely contrived will is generally in confequence of
moral obligation, and a fulfilling of the rights or
claims either of a perfect or imperfect kind which the
furvivors had upon the goods of the deceafed. All
which proves abundantly the right of devifing, and
the obligation upon all to obferve and maintain the
will of the teftator, where it is tolerably prudent, and
not contrary to fome ftrong principles of humanity
Where it is contrary, there may be no injuftice in an-
nulling it.

Tranflation by the law of nature during the life of the proprietor. VIII. The third manner of transferring property
is by the plain law of nature, without confent of the
proprietor, during his life, whenever it is requifite to
fatisfy any juft claim another had againft him which
he declines to comply with. This will be confidered
hereafter among the rights arifing from the injuries
done by others. Thus for compenfation of damage, or
difcharging a juft debt, a man's goods are juftly feized,

† Some improper ufe of metaphyficks in this fubject has raifed great controverfies to little purpofe, as if the validity of wills imported fome phyfical action done when the agent was dead; fome trifling objections are raifed too from the nature of other tranfactions. The queftion is truly this, whether it is not requifite for an innocent fatisfaction of men that their teftaments be obferved after their death? and whether the intereft of fociety does not require it? which are obvious. See Barbeyraque's notes on Puffend. *de jure nat. et gent. lib.* iv. *c.* 10. and authors there cited.

and the property of them acquired by the perfons who had fuch claims.

The fourth manner of tranflation is by the law of nature, without the deed of the proprietor, upon the event of his death, in the fucceffions to the inteftate. The grounds of it are thefe. The intention of the deceafed in .all his acquifitions beyond his own ufe, was contributing to the happinefs of fuch as were dear to him, as 'tis abundantly known to all. We fee that one's pofterity, and failing thofe his kinfmen, are dearer to men univerfally than others, tho' they may happen to have converfed more with others, in matters of bufinefs or pleafure. When men declare their wills, we fee the general inclination to improve the fortunes of their pofterity and kinfmen, and juftly prefume the fame where it is not exprefsly declared. 'Tis cruel, without fome publick intereft requiring it, to defeat this natural hope of fucceffion founded by the tyes of blood. Our children, and failing thefe our kinfmen have plainly a right where fome undutiful conduct has not forfeited it, not only to fupport from us in their indigent ftate, but to have their condition improved by any furplus of goods we have beyond our own confumption. 'Tis contrary to nature, as well as humanity, to defeat this claim when no publick intereft requires it. 'Tis plain alfo that leaving the goods of the inteftate in common to be occupied would caufe the greateft confufion.

If friends were admitted along with kindred, it

muſt be in ſome proportion to the degrees of friend-ſhip; but theſe cannot now be determined; and much leſs could they be determined if the hopes of ſucceſſion invited all flatterers. We juſtly too preſume upon the will of the inteſtate from this, that ſince the cuſtom has univerſally obtained, in all nations al-moſt, to admit only kinſmen to ſucceſſion, had the deceaſed intended that others ſhould be admitted, he would have expreſsly declared this peculiar and leſs uſual deſire.

The natural way of ſucceſſion. The natural affections of men ſhew that their po-ſterity ſhould be admitted in the firſt place, viz. chil-dren and grandchildren; grandchildren at leaſt ad-mitted to their parents ſhare among them, where a deceaſed child has left more than one: and along with poſterity parents ſhould be admitted, if they are in ſtraits. In default of both, brothers and ſiſters, and along with them the children of a brother or ſiſter de-ceaſed, at leaſt to the ſhare their parent would have got had the parent been alive. Reaſons of humanity would recommend other proportions ſometimes, but they would occaſion great controverſies. In default of ſuch relations all kindred of equal degrees ſhould generally come in equally, and exclude the more re-mote.

Unnatural cuſ-toms. The notion of having ſome one repreſentative of the perſon deceaſed, ſucceeding to all his rights, and ſubjected to all his obligations, as the Roman heir was, has no foundation in nature; nor is there any rea-

fon why a far greater part of the inheritance fhould
go univerfally to one of many children, or one of many in the fame degree; nor why feniority among children, or kinfmen of the fame degree, fhould have
fuch preference; nor why the diftinction of fex fhould
in the firft degree of children take place of all other
confiderations, and yet be quite neglected in the degree of grandchildren, or be poftponed to that of feniority of the parent, fo that an infant grand-daugh-
ter of an elder fon deceafed, fhould take before an
adult grand-fon by a fecond fon, nay before the fecond
fon himfelf. A niece by an elder brother deceafed,
nay her daughter, take place of even a younger brother himfelf, as well as the male defcendants of younger brothers. All thefe things are founded only in
civil laws. In the fucceffion to private fortunes there
is feldom any reafon for having one heir rather than
many equally related to the deceafed. Cuftoms of
many nations and their civil laws about thefe matters are very foolifh, and have fome pernicious effects
upon fociety.

IX. Perfonal rights are conftituted againft a man *Perfonal rights now acquired.*
when he has limited fome part of his natural liberty,
or his power of difpofing of his actions and goods,
and transferred it to another, who thence acquires the
perfonal right. And when this right or claim of another is fulfilled, or abolifhed, the natural liberty of
the perfon obliged becomes again in this refpect entire, or the perfonal right is confolidated with it, as

BOOK II. it was before the right subsisted. Such rights arise either from some contract, or some deed of the person obliged; and the consideration of them leads to the subject of contracts or covenants, the main engine of constituting either personal rights or real.

THE END OF THE FIRST VOLUME.

Lightning Source UK Ltd.
Milton Keynes UK
UKHW031457071118
331904UK00016B/286/P